Guilty and Proud of It!

GUILTY AND PROUD OF IT!

POPLAR'S REBEL COUNCILLORS AND GUARDIANS 1919-25

Janine Booth

MERLIN PRESS

© Janine Booth, 2009

First published 2009 by The Merlin Press Ltd.
6 Crane Street Chambers
Crane Street
Pontypool
NP4 6ND
Wales

www.merlinpress.co.uk

ISBN. 978-0-85036-694-5

British Library Cataloguing in Publication Data
is available from the British Library

Printed in the UK by Imprint Digital, Exeter

CONTENTS

A Story That Still Inspires

John McDonnell MP

In March 1985 I was the deputy leader of the Greater London Council (GLC) and found myself in Poplar with the leader of the council, Ken Livingstone, planting a tree and unveiling a plaque in honour of George Lansbury and the Poplar councillors. There is a deep sense of irony about the event because it was the day that the Labour councillors on the GLC were required in law to set the GLC's budget and comply with the Thatcher government's ratecapping legislation or risk illegality and possible multi million pound surcharges and ultimate removal from office.

This was to be the day that Labour councillors were to emulate the Poplar councillors in defying central government to protect their communities from the cuts in spending on local services demanded by a right-wing Conservative regime. The GLC was to be the first council in Labour control to take a stand in solidarity with all those other Labour councils such as Lambeth, Islington, Camden, Greenwich, Lewisham, Sheffield, Manchester and Liverpool that had agreed to this so called 'no rate' strategy. Tragically within hours of helping me plant the commemorative tree Livingstone returned to County Hall, denounced the defiance strategy he had signed up to, complied with the law and removed from office those of us that refused to back down against Thatcher.

For many of us the story of Poplarism has been the inspiration for this defiance strategy. The Poplar struggle had been largely written out of official Labour party history. From the 1960s in the eyes of Labour's leadership George Lansbury and his comrades had become embarrassing anachronisms from an age of class struggle no longer relevant to modern day corporatist Britain.

The assault on the power bases of working-class representation, the trade unions and local councils, by the Thatcher government soon changed that. Lessons had to be learnt quickly about how the Labour movement could respond to these attacks. Interest in Poplarism was quickly revived.

The Poplar campaign, with its committed socialist councillors, its examples of selfless solidarity and its creative mobilisation of a community and movement, demonstrated the potential of the Labour movement. This book describes eloquently the setting and story of this campaign. More importantly the author provides an invaluable analysis of how and why this campaign was so successful in its mobilisation and in securing its short term demands and achieving a long term influence on the leadership and policies of the ground breaking Labour government of 1945.

Today, in what is now predicted to be a long and deep economic recession, when we will be faced with large scale unemployment, significant rises in poverty and homelessness and cuts in benefits and public services, this book is a timely reminder that individuals, communities and movements can come together to challenge the received dominant economic wisdom of the day. The Poplar story shows for this generation facing its own periodic crisis of capitalism that people can mobilise and, if determined enough, they can win through. This book is not only an incisive study of past events it is a handbook for present struggles.

PREFACE

At the turn of the millennium, my local Labour council, in the east London Borough of Hackney, was making savage cuts. It removed or cut grants to 90 community organisations, cut its own employees' annual pay by up to £1,500; took free-travel Freedom Passes away from many disabled residents; closed schools and nurseries; and sold at auction playgrounds, garages, tenants' halls, green spaces and other public assets.

Labour Councillor Luke Akehurst wrote to local newspaper the *Hackney Gazette*, reassuring us that he and his colleagues were not 'actually that happy about making cuts. They are doing it because they have to ... the council hasn't got any money to spend.'[1] Did Councillor Akehurst have a point? Did Hackney council have no choice but to make these cuts?

Petitioning to save my son's nursery from closure, and joining a rally to defend council workers' wages, I considered whether a Labour council might have an alternative. Perhaps it could fight for more funding and refuse to implement cuts, refuse to pass on the effects of its lack of money to those who could least afford to bear the cost. After all, that lack of money may have been the fault of central government, or of the previous Liberal Democrat regime in Hackney council, or of the local government funding system itself - but it was not the fault of Hackney's people.

It would be easier to show that the council had a choice if I could point to an example. I knew that in the 1980s, socialist Labour councils had argued for defiance in the face of the Conservative government's rate-capping. But they had all eventually backed down. Had anyone else seen it through? I found the answer decades distant in time, but very close geographically - in another east London Borough, Poplar, in the 1920s.

Here was another Labour council which had recently taken over power from Liberals and Tories, which faced massive demands on its meagre resources, and when its finances crashed into crisis, faced the same choices. To cut services or to refuse to? To stay within a law and a funding system that penalised and deprived working-class boroughs, or to defy those rules? To protect their personal positions and comforts, or to put them on the line in defence of socialist principles?

Poplar council chose not to concede but to fight. And by fighting, it won.

Poplar's story - of defiance, of protests, of mass participation, of prison - has to be told. It deserves its place in the list of historical struggles that each generation of socialists and labour movement activists learn about, alongside the Chartists, the Suffragettes, the General Strike, Grunwick, the Miners' Strike, the Poll Tax.

This book tells the story in five sections. It begins when newly-enfranchised working-class voters elected Labour to run Poplar Borough Council in 1919. For the next two years, the council improved life for Poplar residents, coming into ever-increasing conflict with the central authorities and the local government funding system. The second section tells of the big clash in 1921, a year of economic recession and spiralling unemployment. It was the year in which Dr Marie Stopes opened the UK's first birth control clinic in Holloway, north London; police patrolled London on motorbikes for the first time; Southwark Bridge was opened; Spurs beat Wolves 1-0 to win the FA Cup; the Derby was first broadcast live on the wireless; Charlie Chaplin visited London and was greeted by thousands – and Poplar council refused to levy a portion of its rates.

Poplar's fight took its councillors to prison in September 1921, and the third section covers imprisonment, release and victory. The fourth section takes us into 1922 and beyond, when Poplar's council and Guardians of the Poor continued to battle, but increasingly isolated and up against opponents bent on halting their progress, saw setbacks begin to punctuate further victories. The final section looks at outcomes and conclusions.

Those who admire the Poplar socialists' stand see it as 'the high point of post-war London radicalism', whereas their critics, such as Herbert Morrison and his supporters, prefer to see 'Poplarism' as 'an irrational obstruction to Labour's prospects of winning the middle-class vote.'[2]

I discovered the Poplar story in the search for ammunition in a political argument. Because of its origins, this book has a polemical style. I make no apology for this, particularly as the councillors themselves wanted their actions to be remembered not just as a historical event but as a political lesson. The most well-known Poplar councillor, George Lansbury - later to become Leader of the Labour Party - hoped that future generations would 'read the story of Poplarism and recognise that in days when to be destitute and poor was almost a crime, some poor men and women refused to accept that doctrine and together proclaimed the truth that all men are not only born equal, but were also possessed of the inalienable right to share in the products of their labour.'[3]

This book aims to satisfy George's hope. Not only can we admire the Poplar councillors' stand, we can also use their story to defend ourselves against modern-day council defeatists who insist that we have to accept our lot, that there is no choice.

As I marched in Hackney, Alan Rusbridger wrote: 'If people today even knew about Poplarism in the 1920s, if they had ever heard of George, Edgar and Minnie Lansbury, the councillors might not concede so easily to political vandalism in Hackney, and the battered working class would be more confident to resist. As it is, we will have to teach and learn those lessons all over again.'[4]

SOURCES AND ACKNOWLEDGEMENTS

My starting point for learning about the Poplar rebellion was Noreen Branson's book, *Poplarism 1919-1925*, now out of print. Noreen did a great service by telling the Poplar story in book form for the first time.

Her timing was very opportune, as the Thatcher government that came to power in the same year that the book was published, 1979, set about attacking local government and impoverishing working-class communities, prompting a renewed interest in debates about how socialists could and should resist this. Several articles, pamphlets and books listed in the bibliography appeared in the 1980s as part of this debate. Also in the 1980s, other writers, such as Rose and Gillespie, produced useful research and comment about the nature of Poplar's working-class population in the 1920s and challenged simplistic assumptions about the Labour Party and its working-class constituency.

Looking into the events in Poplar in the early 1920s, the British Library's newspaper collection at Colindale was invaluable, for contemporary issues of the socialist national newspaper the *Daily Herald*, smaller-circulation socialist newspapers, Poplar's local press, and other titles listed in the bibliography. The Newspaper Library survived a closure threat during the period in which I was writing this book. Its loss would have been a disaster for those wishing to keep history alive.

Another resource which fortunately survived a closure threat was the Tower Hamlets Local History Museum and Archive, which stores much relevant material, including Poplar Borough Council's minutes and the correspondence file of the Poplar Borough Municipal Alliance. There is also useful archive material at the National Archives in Kew, the Hackney Archive and the London Metropolitan Archive.

I would like to record my appreciation for the helpful and knowledgeable staff at all the libraries and archives that I visited.

I would like to thank Sean Geoghegan of the National Union of Rail Maritime and Transport Workers (RMT) for unearthing information about the NUR members involved in the Poplar struggle. I also appreciate the support of Thompson's Solicitors, including lending me the photograph album presented to their founder by the Poplar councillors and allowing me to use many of the photographs to illustrate this book. Thanks to Robin Sivapalan and to Paul Hampton for digging out some documents for me, and to the Alliance for Workers' Liberty for hosting me talking on this issue on a number of occasions.

Professor John Shepherd deserves particular appreciation for reading a draft of this book and giving detailed and very helpful feedback. Chris Sumner – grandson of Poplar councillors Charlie Sumner and Albert Easteal – has shared his memories and knowledge with me. Tony Zurbrugg at Merlin Press has shown me where I was going wrong with my first book and pointed me in the right direction. Thanks to Clive Bradley for encouragement and my dad for reading and commenting.

Finally, I must thank my partner John and my sons Alex, Joe and Harrison, without whose tolerance and support I would not have been able to see this book through to completion.

This book is dedicated to Joan Booth, 1931-2008,
the first socialist woman I knew.

ABBREVIATIONS

ASLEF – Associated Society of Locomotive Engineers and Firemen
BSP – British Socialist Party
CP – Communist Party
GLC – Greater London Council
ILP – Independent Labour Party
JIC – Joint Industrial Council
KC – King's Counsel
LCC – London County Council
LDCU – London District Council of the Unemployed
MAB – Metropolitan Asylum Board
MCPF – Metropolitan Common Poor Fund
NUWM – National Unemployed Workers' Movement
NUR – National Union of Railwaymen
PAC – Public Assistance Committee
PBMA – Poplar Borough Municipal Alliance
PLA – Port of London Authority
SDF – Social Democratic Federation
SLP – Socialist Labour Party
UWO – Unemployed Workers' Organisation
TB – Tuberculosis
TGWU – Transport & General Workers' Union
TUC – Trades Union Congress
WSF – Workers' Socialist Federation

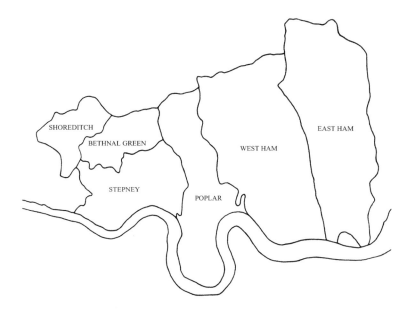

East London boroughs

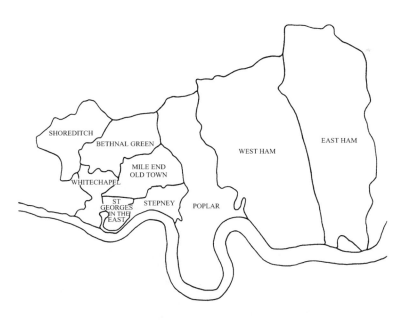

East London Poor Law Unions

1. STORM CLOUDS GATHERING

SOMETHING LIKE AN ELECTRIC SHOCK

WANTED: A New Borough Council. VOTE LABOUR. Better Homes, Cleaner Streets, Healthier Children and No Profiteering.[5]

Labour's appeal to Poplar voters in November 1919 found shocking success. The local press announced 'Great Labour Victories'.[6] On a 28 per cent turnout, Labour had won 39 of the 42 council seats.

A riverside area in East London, Poplar ranked tenth in size and population of the 28 Metropolitan London boroughs. It covered 2,327 acres, stretching from Hackney in the north to the Thames in the south; from Bethnal Green and Stepney in the west to the River Lea, and beyond that West Ham, in the east. One of its new Labour councillors, Edgar Lansbury, described it as 'a place where money is made and lives destroyed.'[7]

Edgar's father George was the best-known member of Poplar's new administration. Born in 1859, he settled in Bow, part of Poplar borough, after a brief, unsuccessful emigration to Australia in his twenties.[8] For about three centuries previously, Poplar had been shaped and scarred by the docks. The East India Dock Company was the trading bloodflow of the British Empire; it and other companies built riverside developments that transformed a collection of hamlets east of the Tower of London into a heaving industrial area, complete with overcrowding, squalor and ill-health. In the late nineteenth century, the rich moved out and Poplar became a near-exclusively working-class borough.

Many residents did not qualify to vote for their local rulers until 1918, when the Representation of the People Act enfranchised many women and dramatically cut the property qualification, giving most Poplar adults the vote and more than doubling the borough's electoral roll.[9] The very next year, Poplar's new working-class electors used their votes to unseat the right-wingers who had let their poverty continue unchallenged for years. The defeated Mayor, Reverend William Lax[10], described the result as 'something like an electric shock'. He and his Municipal Alliance associates had 'hardly expected such a washout', were reduced to 'a pitiable remnant' on the council, but were determined to prevent

Labour's victory ushering in 'out-and-out Bolshevism'.[11]

The Alliance's manifesto claimed that it was 'strictly non-political and non-sectarian, uniting all shades of opinion.'[12] In truth, the 'shades of opinion' it represented were those of business owners, who had set up the Poplar Borough Municipal Alliance (PBMA) in 1905 as an explicitly anti-socialist group. It stood local bosses in elections, and had dominated the borough council until Labour swept it aside in 1919.

Elsewhere in London, conservative 'Municipal Reform' candidates rang the alarm bells about the red upstarts who threatened their positions, warning that 'The policy of the Labour-Socialists is lavish and wasteful expenditure' and 'Many of them are avowed Bolshevists'[13]. But working-class voters rejected them. Next door to Poplar, Labour won 40 of Stepney council's 60 seats; in Bethnal Green, 24 of 28. Across London, Labour polled 39 per cent of the vote, won a majority in 12 of the 28 borough councils and was the largest party in two more. In the previous election in 1912, it had won just 46 of the 1,362 borough council seats in London; in 1919, it won 572.[14] 'Labour Knocks 'Em In The Old Kent Road' headlined the *Daily Herald*, a socialist newspaper whose editor, George Lansbury, had sat on Poplar Borough Council since 1903.

A HERALD OF THE WORKERS

The *Daily Herald* plays a starring role in our story – a newspaper that did not simply report the labour movement but campaigned as part of it. At this time, it was nearing the end of its first decade, a period described by *Herald* historian Huw Richards as 'marked by a freewheeling, independent radicalism, its dominant figure the extraordinary George Lansbury'[15].

In 1910, London printers had taken strike action for a 48-hour week and produced a bulletin, *The World*. In January 1911, the strike committee renamed it the *Daily Herald* and sold all 13,000 copies of the first issue. As the strike turned into a lockout, the *Herald* increased its paper size, broadened its coverage, got its circulation up to 27,000, and prepared to become a permanent labour daily. When the strike ended in success, the last issue of the *Daily Herald* appeared on 28 April 1911, but a committee had already formed to raise funds and make plans for its relaunch, led by dockers' leader Ben Tillett.[16] Tillett invited George Lansbury, at that time an MP, to join the committee over a cup of tea in the House of Commons.[17]

The *Daily Herald* relaunched on 15 April 1912, the day that the Titanic sank. It exposed the higher death rates among steerage passengers and railed against the conduct of the White Star Line, Titanic's owner, accusing it of putting profit and luxury fittings before safety.[18]

From October 1912, the TUC and the Labour Party supported the *Daily*

Citizen instead, believing that the *Daily Herald*'s articles and Will Dyson's cartoons were too confrontational against employers and too critical of Labour leaders. But the *Citizen* was short-lived. In 1913, the *Herald* survived one of its chronic financial crises when George Lansbury bought it from the Official Receiver for £100 and became editor. With the *Herald* newspaper came the Herald League, an activist group organising political education, fundraising, even unofficial Labour candidates.[19]

The *Herald* came out weekly during the war, when it was 'probably the most powerful and incomparably the widest-circulated 'anti-war' journal in the country',[20] and became daily again afterwards[21]. It infuriated the authorities, the Army instructing commanding officers to burn it in summer 1919[22], and supported workers' struggles. Railwaymen claimed that during their national strike that year, 'the mere appearance of the *Daily Herald* in the various districts kept heart and life in men and women who otherwise, because of the outrageous opposition of the capitalist Press, would have felt quite lost and alone'.[23]

The paper supported strikes whether official or not, championed independence struggles in India and Ireland, demanded votes for women, and saw itself as 'on the side of the downtrodden at home and abroad, and almost always in a minority'[24]. Moreover, the *Herald* offered a free platform, was 'to all intents and purposes a rank and file paper'[25], and had a policy that 'was not merely unofficial, it was avowedly anti-official'[26]. *Daily Herald* writers, claimed historian A.J.P. Taylor, 'contributed a gay, self-confident contempt for the doings of the governing class ... it broke the monopoly of establishment opinion and bore witness that the people of England were not all thinking as their rulers thought they should'.[27]

Unable to rely on advertising income and boycotted by capitalist paper suppliers, the *Herald* was in a permanent state of financial crisis. George Lansbury's book *The Miracle of Fleet Street* is full of stories of begging telegrams, stand-offs with bailiffs, even oddly-shaped issues due to using off-cuts of paper found in dark corners of the printing house.[28] Despite this, the *Herald* kept going, and by October 1920 had a circulation of around 330,000.[29]

WORKERS FIND THEIR VOICE

In 1918's 'khaki' general election, Liberal David Lloyd George had led the Tory-dominated Coalition to a landslide victory. Labour had won 20 per cent of the vote but only 57 seats. The two Poplar constituencies had re-elected their two coalition knights. Conservative Sir Reginald Blair had beaten George Lansbury in Bow and Bromley; Liberal Sir Alfred Yeo had won in South Poplar. Blair was a company chairman, a member of several private members' clubs, and a resident of Harrow Weald.[30] Yeo at least lived in Poplar, but his years of service in the borough were in support of the political and economic status quo.

Working-class people found that the land was not 'fit for heroes' as Lloyd George had promised[31]. J.B. Priestley would state early in the Second World War, 'I will tell you what we did for young men and their young wives at the end of the last war. We did nothing – except let them take their chance in a world in which every gangster and trickster and stupid insensitive fool or rogue was let loose to do his damnedest.'[32] The young Labour Party took up their grievances and attracted their support. Socialist street-corner meetings revived and multiplied.[33] Jewish workers turned to Labour as government persecution fuelled anti-semitism.[34] In March 1919, Labour stood candidates for the London County Council (LCC), declaring that 'organised Labour in London is standing alone for the welfare of all London against those types of private greed and monopoly which are out to exploit the community in the interests of the few'[35]. Labour increased its representation, but only to 15 of the 124 seats despite winning 33 per cent of the vote[36].

Established in 1899, the LCC covered what we would now call 'inner London'[37], and was the first directly-elected general local government body for London.[38] It covered 117 square miles and more than 4 million people, and was responsible for services which crossed borough borders, such as main drainage, parks and open spaces, the fire and ambulance services, education[39], street improvements, some licensing, slum clearance and housing, and tramways.[40] Of Labour's ten new seats, three were in Poplar, as trade union official Sam March, labourer Charlie Sumner and toolmaker Edward Cruse joined Susan Lawrence, Labour LCC member for South Poplar since 1913. Each of the two constituencies had two seats, and each Labour candidate polled around 3,500 votes, beating Municipal Reform candidates who promised 'Reconstruction not Revolution', and warned that Labour's policy of 'workers' control' would mean 'Anarchy and Starvation; Industry destroyed; Religion swept away; Women nationalised and enslaved'[41].

The following month, Labour won more success in the elections for boards of guardians. These were local committees covering roughly the same patches as borough councils, which administered 'relief' to the poor – meaning either toil in the workhouse ('indoor relief') or benefit payments ('outdoor relief'). Labour advocated 'the complete abolition of the whole evil system of the Poor Law'[42], which dated from the 1834 Poor Law Amendment Act[43] and set out punitive principles: no able-bodied person was to receive help from the Poor Law authorities except in the workhouse and workhouse conditions were to be very harsh as a deterrent. In the meantime, Labour argued, 'the chief business of a Guardian of the Poor is to help the poor'[44], a genuine contrast with many existing guardians! Labour won 15 of the 24 seats on the Poplar Board and 135 of the 757 seats across London[45], helped by a change in the law in 1918 allowing people who received relief to vote for those who administered it. [46] This 'pauper enfranchisement' so offended the PBMA that it called for its repeal for years to come.

Labour had condemned the PBMA's pre-war Board of Guardians regime as 'starving the poor, allowing children to be blinded ... feeding the sick on frozen meat, sacking the workmen, starving the roads, neglecting sanitation ... business administration with a vengeance ... The Alliance is the Tory Party under a new name: they want to keep things as they are, themselves on top all the time, helping the landlord and monopolist.'[47] With the borough council elections in November 1919, Labour completed its removal of the PBMA from local government power in Poplar.

The local press blamed the other parties for their defeat and Labour's success: 'The Socialistic party have been spending their money, distributing printed documents, holding meetings and in all ways spreading propaganda over the Borough; while all the other parties have been idly standing by doing next to nothing.'[48] However, as historian Julia Bush argues, Labour's strong organisation 'was no coincidence: it was a result, as well as a cause, of political strength. The war-time growth of trade unionism, and the war-time activity of socialists, had enabled the Labour Party to establish a solid base in East London in a period when the other parties relaxed their efforts.'[49] The labour movement had thrown off its deferential attitude to the established parties and insisted on direct, independent, working-class representation. The opposition understood this, a leading member of the London Municipal Society[50] writing that the borough council elections were 'a class fight, pure and simple, and anybody of any standing at all was suspect'[51].

There had been socialist candidates, and socialist groups, in the area for several decades. The Marxist Social Democratic Federation[52] (SDF), its successor the British Socialist Party[53] (BSP), and the Independent Labour Party[54] (ILP) had local branches. The Poplar Labour League had developed from union organiser Will Crooks' local election campaigns, and was part of the 'Lib-Lab' trend, standing working-class candidates in elections but tying itself politically to the Liberal Party. Crooks and others supported the Fabian Society's[55] pre-war view that the labour movement should ally itself with the Liberals in municipal politics. But others insisted that the working class must strive for independent political representation.

The Herald League backed future Poplar alderman John Scurr as an independent Labour Parliamentary candidate in Bethnal Green and in Ipswich[56], and when George Lansbury won election to the LCC in 1911, he and two others formed its first independent Labour caucus. The London Labour Party did not

even exist at this time, and would only come into being after a long struggle
by the London Trades Council.[57] From the 1890s, SDF members had won the
Trades Council in Bromley, part of Poplar borough, to the policy of independent
labour representation in politics.[58] By 1914, Poplar's Labour Representation
Committee had 43 trade union branches, with a total of over 10,000 members,
affiliated to it along with socialist groups.[59] Moreover, Poplar's socialists worked
together, Bush arguing that even before the war, 'the most striking feature' of
socialist propaganda in East London was 'its unity of purpose'.[60]

It laid the ground for Labour to contest every seat on Poplar council for the
first time in 1919.[61] Labour had hoisted its own flag, and George Lansbury
explained that 'all the muddle-headed Fabian intellectualism which caused
the old Poplar Labour League to unite itself with Liberalism masquerading as
Progressivism, has been swept away ... We are all clear class-conscious socialists
working together.'[62] November 1919 was a new dawn for working-class politics
in Poplar and elsewhere. 'The sky is brighter and we can all join in a shout of
triumph that at long last, the workers are coming into their own.'[63]

So who were these women and men who carried the hopes of the workers into
Poplar's council chamber?

POPLAR'S NEW COUNCILLORS

Labour's electoral triumph delighted London Labour Party Secretary Herbert
Morrison, but he was also worried: 'we had the responsibility of majority
administration with little or no previous experience. If we made a mess of it
we could expect to go out into the wilderness for many years ... in some of the
Labour majority boroughs there was not a single member of the council with
previous municipal experience.'[64]

Poplar was not one of those boroughs. The longest-serving Labour councillor
was Charlie Sumner, 'a short, jovial, old-style trade unionist'[65] elected in 1900[66].
By the time this large and popular man became part of a majority Labour
council, he had put in 19 years of dogged opposition where, 'well able to "hold
his end up" ... He would argue in the face of any chance of winning and move
amendments which had not the remotest likelihood of being passed.'[67] Sumner
was equally belligerent as a Poor Law guardian, one report describing how
he badgered the PBMA majority through a meeting of the Board, exposing
mistreatment of paupers and 'thus did a good night's work for the poorest
of Poplar's poor', he and his fellow socialists leaving the Alliance guardians
'squirming and wriggling'[68].

Alfred Partridge, Sam March and Joe Banks had been elected with George
Lansbury in 1903. Banks was a railwayman until sacked in 1910 for taking
leave to act as Lansbury's agent in his successful bid to become MP for Bow

and Bromley[69]. Postman Thomas Goodway had joined the council in 1912, railwayman James Jones in 1917. Among 1919's new intake were Labour people with experience on the Board of Guardians, including dock trade unionist Dave Adams and railway signaller Joseph Hammond. Thirteen Labour women and men were elected to both the council and the guardians in 1919.

Poplar's Labour councillors also had a wealth of experience beyond serving on committees. They were labour movement activists with years under their belts of organising, building a base in their local working-class community, and making the case for socialism.

Many – both men and women – had been active in the local campaign for women's suffrage which, led by Sylvia Pankhurst, had involved many more working-class women than 'Votes for Ladies' campaigns elsewhere. Sylvia's appearance on a platform with George Lansbury (and James Connolly) in support of Dublin's locked-out workers in 1913 had so disgusted her sister Christabel that she expelled Sylvia from the mainstream suffrage organisation. Before the war, future Poplar councillor Nellie Cressall had spoken out for women's votes at Blackwall Tunnel Dock Gates; Jennie Mackay had been arrested while defending Sylvia from arrest; and Julia Scurr had led an east London suffragette deputation to Liberal Prime Minister Herbert Asquith. Various Lansburys had spent time in prison for militant suffrage campaigning;

Other councillors had been prominent in the various socialist groups that had come together to form the Labour Party. The largest was the ILP, which counted George Cressall, Thomas Kelly, George Lansbury, John Scurr, Nellie Cressall and Jack Wooster amongst its activists. In 1907, George Cressall helped to form the Limehouse branch of the ILP, to which he later recruited a Stepney boys' club volunteer – future Labour Prime Minister Clement Attlee.

Even during the War, Poplar's socialists had been politically active, involving themselves in the Distress Committee, the Tribunal that dealt with appeals against conscription, and various women's organisations.[70] Their constant theme was independent labour representation – that working-class people should have their own representatives on the bodies established to deal with their wartime hardships, rather than beg for help from those representing a more privileged class. Socialists supported protests against price rises[71] and strikes for war bonuses and wage rises[72]. Julia Bush explains that, 'Labour representatives, whether 'patriots' or 'pacifists', refused to acquiesce in policies which they felt were against workers' interests, and were seldom silenced by appeals to place the 'national interest' first.'[73]

In 1919, for the first time ever, Poplar's council now looked like its electorate. It included railworkers, dockers, labourers, postmen, a road engineer, a toolmaker, a lead worker and a farrier. The Municipal Alliance found this most worrying: 'All may be estimable in the spheres which they adorn, but who would ever think of entrusting to them alone the expenditure of more than half a millions sterling annually?'[74] The women councillors were officially listed as either 'married woman' or 'spinster', defined by their relationship to a man.[75]

George Lansbury himself had been a local employer. Together with sons William and Edgar, he owned and ran a sawmill until he sold it in 1914[76], one of very few local businesses whose owners deigned to live in poverty-infested Poplar. George explained that 'I would sooner live here in the Bow Road where the unemployed can put a brick through my window when they disagree with my actions than be in some other place far away where they can only write me a letter. It's good for me and it's better for them.'[77] Lansbury's later son-in-law, biographer and political associate Raymond Postgate noted that, by 1910, 'the Lansbury family was no longer a poverty-stricken family, it is true, but it was never well-to-do. Its standard of living remained throughout his life working-class.'[78]

In contrast, the opposition councillors were a manufacturer, a solicitor and a Clerk in Holy Orders. Poplar's Labour representatives contrasted with parts of the socialist movement too, which had too often come across as outsiders, upper-class intellectuals who could not communicate with, did not live amongst, and were even faintly repelled by, working-class communities. The Webbs and their Fabian Society typified this, historian Kenneth Morgan describing how 'They wished to uplift the toiling working man, but never understood him, knew him, or sought his company'.[79] In Poplar's labour movement, it was different – not just because of the councillors' working-class credentials, but also because of their politics and their commitment to representing not themselves but a movement.

At its first meeting, Poplar's Labour council added aldermen[80] to its number, drafting in four local labour movement activists. Jewish schoolteacher Minnie Glassman had married Edgar and become Minnie Lansbury in 1914, also becoming full-time assistant secretary of Sylvia Pankhurst's East London Federation of Suffragettes[81]. Many considered her the sharpest intellect on the council.[82] *Daily Herald* writer John Scurr, a tall man in his forties, had been active in the SDF and then the Poplar Labour League. Toolmaker Robert Hopwood was secretary of the Bow branch of the Amalgamated Society of Engineers and had worked at Bryant and May matchmakers. Fourth Alderman Susan Lawrence was Poplar Labour's odd one out. From a rich family, she had attended university, then much more a preserve of the upper class even than now, and had begun political life as a Tory! The Conservatives' refusal to improve the appalling working conditions of school cleaners drove 'Our Susan' to Labour in 1912.

While no women could vote in Parliamentary elections until their qualified enfranchisement in 1918, some women had been voting, even standing, in local elections for decades previously.[83] Suffragette Emmeline Pankhurst reported that 'the leaders of the Liberal Party advised women to prove their fitness for the Parliamentary franchise by serving in municipal offices, especially the unsalaried offices'[84]. Perhaps the all-male Parliaments of the nineteenth and early twentieth centuries thought women competent for unpaid public duties that reflected their unpaid domestic work – care for the poor, education, health – but not for the 'masculine' spheres of law-making, economics and foreign policy. But so it was that Susan Lawrence had been elected to the London School Board in 1900, Minnie Lansbury had served on the War Pensions Committee, Julia Scurr had been a Poplar guardian since 1907, and Jennie Mackay served on a school care committee.

That first council meeting was packed to overflowing with triumphant Labour supporters, who cheered George Lansbury's arrival. Lansbury was, at sixty years of age, one of the most vocal and high-profile socialists in Britain. Charlie Sumner proposed him for Mayor, declaring 'there was no-one better fitted by his work in the borough and throughout the country to occupy the chair'. Even Reverend Lax, in his handover speech, admitted that, 'everyone would accept his [Lansbury's] extreme ability as a man of international renown'.[85]

George Lansbury took the Mayoral chain from Lax and hung it on a chair. He refused the scarlet robes of his predecessors. In his acceptance speech, he said he had thought that he would always be fighting forlornly in opposition, but now in power, Labour would direct its efforts 'towards lightening the load of those who had to bear it and making life sweeter and better for all'[86]. He stressed that they would have to fight for a fairer rating system, flagging up the issue that would propel the council into a dramatic collision course with the state over the next two years and beyond.

After the meeting, the councillors, five hundred supporters and an Irish band marched around Poplar. It was another display of the new-found political confidence of the workers, their 'desubordination'[87], which was also crackling in industry.

ANOTHER GREAT UNREST

Between 1910 and 1914, the 'Great Unrest' saw workers taking action on a large scale, trade union membership leaping from 2.5 million to 4 million. When the First World War ended in 1918, the Unrest resumed. Soldiers protested at the slow progress of demobilisation, and returned home determined to improve working-class life in Britain after their sufferings in foreign fields. People were angry at rapid price rises, unemployment, and the continuation of wartime shortages of food and housing. By 1919, 610,000 new homes were needed[88]; food rationing introduced in February 1918 would continue until 1921[89].

Adding insult to injury, fat-cat businessmen were ostentatiously profiteering. Government ministers joined in, as Parliament boosted Cabinet members' pay at a time when thousands of railwaymen earned less than £50 per year and the government was trying to push wages down! 179 MPs were company directors, and future Tory Prime Minister Stanley Baldwin described government benches filled with 'hard-faced men who looked as if they had done well out of the war'.[90]

Bush argues that East London trade unions came out of the war stronger than before, 'not only larger, but also more demanding'[91]. In 1918, there were 80 per cent more union members in East London than in 1914[92]; that summer, there were strikes in London by dockers, gas workers, council workers, tram, bus and Tube workers, co-op employees, clothing workers and even the police.[93] In February 1919, rope workers, rag pickers and jam makers from East London joined others at a National Federation of Women Workers' conference demanding 'the Right to Work, the Right to Life and the Right to Leisure'.[94] In 1919, an average of 100,000 workers were on strike each day. The years until 1921 saw more strikes than in any other three-year period in British history, an average 40m days per year[95]. The miners struck, and there was a general strike for a 40-hour week on the Clyde.

The uprising was winning for workers, pushing up wages, cutting hours and unemployment.[96] In March 1919, the Transport Workers' Federation won a 44-hour week for all waterside workers, cutting some men's working week by ten hours. Rank-and-file committees had grown during the Great Unrest and were now in action again. In February 1919, the River Thames Shop Stewards' Committee[97] organised a major unofficial ship-repairers' strike for a 15s (75p) per week pay rise, holding mass meetings at the Hippodrome in Poplar. Its full-time organiser was boilermakers' shop steward Harry Pollitt, later to become General Secretary of the Communist Party.

The railway industry, Poplar's other large employer, was the arena for a gladiatorial contest between workers and bosses. The companies wanted to introduce new pay scales, which would cut the wages of over 100,000 of the worst-paid railworkers. For nine days in September and October 1919, members of the National Union of Railwaymen (NUR)[98] and the smaller, driving-grades union ASLEF stopped work, stopped the country, and won.[99] Their solid action gave the lie to Lloyd George's claim that ordinary workers did not support the strike, which he called an 'anarchist conspiracy' for 'subversive ends'. Poplar's residents would face the same scaremongering against their Labour council, and in the same way, their own involvement in the struggle would ensure that they knew better than to believe it.

Britain's ruling class, fearing revolution and already suppressing rebellion in Ireland, responded with both repression and concession. It sent troops to the coalfields and to some urban areas. It also agreed a seven-hour day in the pits, a royal commission to consider nationalising the coal industry, and a Court of Inquiry into Port Labour. Lloyd George may have claimed some sympathy to the demands of labour, but he was 'more concerned to maintain social order'[100].

It was because of, and into, this storm of working-class assertion that Poplar's Labour council was elected. Discussion about what socialists can do with municipal power is empty without discussing the massive boost to that power which working-class mobilisation gives. It would be like debating how far a car can travel without petrol.

'WE HAVE COME TO MAKE A CHANGE'

Having established the principle of contesting elections independently for working-class interests, Poplar's socialists now turned their attention to governing independently in working-class interests. Now Labour had power in Poplar council, what was it to do? Make small improvements here and there? No. These councillors made a clear and bold choice: they would use all their powers to dramatically improve the lives of Poplar's working class. Councillor Charles Key, a 'dapper schoolmaster'[101], wrote: 'The Labour Movement here had to face the question that, sooner or later, nationally and locally, the whole movement will have to answer: 'You now have the power – what are you going to do with it?' ... We have come to make a change.'[102] George Lansbury asked rhetorically, 'Labour councillors must be different from those we have displaced or why displace them?'[103]

Lansbury appreciated that not only must Labour deliver to the working class, but that to do this, it must challenge capital. 'The workers must be given tangible proof that Labour administration means something different from Capitalist administration, and in a nutshell this means diverting wealth from the wealthy ratepayers to the poor. Those who pretend that a sound Labour policy can be pursued nationally or locally without making the rich poorer should find another party.'[104] Discussing 'Labour In Local Affairs' in the *Daily Herald*[105], Lansbury explained that they would have to campaign to compel changes in local government financing, and could not wait for a Labour government because in the meantime, poor working-class ratepayers would have to meet the costs of the improved services that they needed.

The councillors had a commitment that would drive their coming conflicts: it matters not just what you say, but what you do. What did this mean in practice in Poplar, a narrow, long, riverside area dominated by docks, canals, railways and acute poverty? It meant pursuing policies to meet human need rather than private profit, advancing what Karl Marx had called 'the political economy of the working class'[106]. Poplar council's policy was 'to compel the capitalist system to maintain its victims'.[107]

A quarter of the borough was so poor as to be officially recognised as such, their 24 per cent poverty rate the highest in London.[108] Poplar was a filthy pool from which fat cats, perched on its comfortable banks, fished out the fruits of sweated labour and threw back the minimum possible to sustain it. Edgar Lansbury remarked that 'people who could afford to live out of it wouldn't be seen dead in it'[109]. Poplar's 160,000 inhabitants lived in appalling conditions, not helped by either the Tory-Liberal government or by the previous Municipal Alliance borough council. Unable to rely on sparse incomes from casual and sweatshop employment, many were dependent on charity handed down 'in the name of the class that battens upon their toil'.[110] They needed more than benevolence dished out from the council chamber. They needed to take power themselves, through their elected labour movement representatives.

Twelve Poplar districts were officially slums. Riddled with damp and vermin, no-one could pretend that human beings should live in these hovels. Yet their landlords were content to let them for as long as the rent money came in and the authorities took no action. The Royal Commission on Housing in 1917 had concluded that, 'most of the troubles we have been investigating are due to the failure of private enterprise to provide and maintain the necessary houses, sufficient in quantity and quality'[111]. Defeated Mayor Lax knew that, 'Many a gentleman's stables are better' than many Poplar homes[112], but offered only Christian salvation and Municipal Alliance inaction in response. In contrast, Poplar's new Labour council surveyed unfit housing and recommended a huge acceleration of slum clearance. It appointed three new sanitary inspectors, who ordered slum landlords to make homes fit to live in. If the landlord failed to do so, the borough council did the work and sent the landlord the bill.

Poplar people squeezed into tightly overcrowded dwellings. The 1921 Census showed 10,479 homes each occupied by two families; 1,799 by three or even more. The Ministry of Health's standard for 'overcrowding' was 'more than two people per room'. Think of your own home: count the number of rooms and double it. This number of people could live in your home and it would still not be officially overcrowded. It was an appallingly mean standard, but 33,104 people lived in officially designated overcrowded homes in Poplar. Councillor Key reported that 'An average of three, four or five per room is frequently found, whilst six, seven, and eight were not uncommon.'[113] Sardines would move out of a tin that closely packed.

On 30 January 1920, new Mayor George Lansbury ceremonially cut the first turf at the site of the Chapel House Street Estate, a new council housing scheme of 120 homes on 7½ acres of undeveloped land at Millwall.[114] This was the first time that Poplar Borough Council had ever built homes, and its series of 'cottage estates' on the Isle of Dogs was the first new public housing in the borough since LCC blocks some twenty years previously.

Poverty plus poor housing equals illness. Chief disease was tuberculosis (TB), also known as consumption or 'white plague', which haunted poor communities, infecting the chest, causing weight loss, fever and often death. Poplar council took over the borough's voluntary TB Dispensary, appointed a TB officer and made plans for an open-air school for children at risk of TB.

The council expanded maternity and child welfare services, giving free milk to expectant and nursing mothers and increasing the annual attendance at its clinics from 14,000 to 40,000 over the following six years. By 1923, the council employed 17 full-time health visitors. The Baths and Wash-houses Committee decided to create a new department with increased resources; to provide slipper baths for children; and to heat the second-class swim.[115]

Before the First World War, infant mortality ran at 124 per 1,000 births: Poplar parents bore babies only to see one in eight of them die. George and Bessie Lansbury were amongst those who suffered this awful loss, burying two of their twelve children in infancy – their first son Little George at the age of five, and daughter Doreen, one of twins, aged three. In 1919, infant mortality was 83 per 1,000; by 1925, Poplar council's work would reduce it to 60.

The council also improved the recreation grounds and playgrounds; electrified the borough; planted trees; expanded the library service, doubling book-borrowing within four years; and extended leisure and entertainment.[116]

John Scurr described the lives that he and his fellow councillors tried to improve:

> Cramped together under overcrowded conditions in dark mean streets and alleys; overworked at miserable wages; never enough to eat; seldom able to buy a new dress or suit of clothes; content to purchase cast-offs in the pawnshop or on the stall in the street market; subject to disease from conditions of work and conditions of living. What chance have they or their children? They have been cast into an abyss of ignorance, and our society passes them by and abuses them for their dirt and the ignorance which our social system has thrust upon them.[117]

If this quote seems to cast the locals as victims, denouncing the political right for despising rather than pitying them, that was not in fact Poplar council's attitude. While George Lansbury's Christianity flavoured his view that the councillors 'live[d] a life of service', this came with a commitment to 'teaching the masses to think and act for themselves'.[118] There were many attempts to improve living conditions in London's East End. From Barnado to Booth[119], philanthropists, charities, religious missionaries and others wanted to alleviate misery and 'raise morals'. However, it seems that Poplar was so destitute that even philanthropists steered clear, the *Poor Law Officers' Journal*'s editors observing that, 'relief works in Poplar have been conspicuous by their absence, and the poverty of the neighbourhood is such that charitable agencies, which operate freely in more fortunate areas, scarcely exist'.[120]

Poplar Labour did not beg for charity: it organised people to fight for better conditions for themselves. Working-class self-activity was at Poplar Labour's heart. They knew that they needed to win people's trust, to deliver material improvements, so that people could imagine and demand more. This mobilisation would carry the councillors through the battles of the next few years.

The Council's first meeting appointed a profiteering committee, and voted to convene a cross-London conference to discuss the supply and price of milk and coal. Proposing, Edgar Lansbury complained that dairy companies were inflating their prices by pouring thousands of gallons of milk down the drains, and the Ministry of Food knew about it but was doing nothing. Sixty-six borough, county and district councils sent representatives to the conference on 10 December[121]. George Lansbury argued that many working-class families could not afford milk, with disastrous effects on their health. Councils wanted to supply milk, especially to expectant and nursing mothers, but could only fund this by increasing the rates. It was another case that 'the poor must keep the poor'. Poplar councillor Charles Key proposed a resolution calling for: a cut in the price of milk; the government to allow councils to run their own depots; and schools to provide free milk. The conference unanimously agreed[122], and passed a similar resolution about coal.[123]

Leading a deputation to the Prime Minister two days before Christmas[124], George Lansbury told Lloyd George that some families were going without milk and fuel, and that poorer Boroughs like Poplar were struggling to support them. Lloyd George suggested 'letting the thing be fought out in the usual way in the market'. When Bethnal Green's Mayor Joe Vaughan described the anaemic children of anaemic mothers dying 'in hundreds and thousands like rotten sheep' and insisted that, 'We in the East End of London want something done. We have not come here to be fenced', the Prime Minister warned him, 'You have come here to be civil and courteous, or you do not remain here at all.' Maybe Lloyd George expected a little more deference from workers' representatives. If so, he was in for a shock over the next few years, as they became much more 'uncivil' than simply answering back in meetings.

Nevertheless, he agreed to amend the law to meet some of the deputation's demands.[125] Working-class self-assertion was already reaping results.

IN AND OUT OF WORK

Work in Poplar meant the docks, railways, small factories, domestic service or sweatshops. In 1921, 75 per cent of Poplar residents worked in the East End – a higher percentage even than other East End boroughs – the big majority in Poplar itself. Most of the rest worked in adjacent or nearby boroughs such as West Ham, Hackney, the City, or south-of-the-river Bermondsey or Woolwich.[126]

Half of Poplar's women worked for wages: of these, over 20 per cent did so in textiles, an industry plagued by short-time working and seasonal lay-offs[127]; just under that number in personal and domestic service; 10 per cent were packers, mainly in food and drink processing factories. One-eighth of men worked in engineering, over a quarter in transport.[128]

Dock labour was casual labour: dockers left home each morning unsure if there was work for them, and went to bed each night uncertain whether there would be work the next day. Dock work fluctuated, affected by the flow of trade, rises and falls in prices, the seasonal character of some goods, even the weather: 'One week a dozen boats might arrive together, the next none at all. One week there would be work for hundreds, day and night, the next for no more than a handful.'[129] Reforms of dock working conditions since 1889's great strike had had limited effect, and although the Port of London Authority (PLA) had taken over the operations of the dock companies in 1908, it changed their employment practices little.[130] Dockers were in and out of work, but never out of poverty. A Poplar council leaflet explained: 'For the worker it means a continual struggle for irregular work. For his family it means underfeeding and constant sickness. It causes a steady deterioration, not only in the morale of the worker, but in the physique of himself and his family.'[131] Moreover, the accident rate on the docks was second only to that in the mines.[132]

Although there was a general trend towards 'de-casualisation' of work, Gillespie argues that Poplar and other East End boroughs felt the effects of this less than elsewhere.[133] Capitalists often preferred to build new factories further out from central London where land was cheaper; and what factories were built contracted out a lot of their work to small workshops and homeworkers, which therefore persisted.[134]

Poplar and the other new East End Labour councils set about accelerating de-casualisation, mechanising functions such as street-sweeping and making casual workers permanent council employees. Poplar council introduced a licensing system preventing a 'ring' extorting money from street traders.[135]

As an employer, Poplar council sought to apply its socialist principles. It introduced a £4 minimum wage for its employees in May 1920, and instituted equal pay for men and women not just in the minimum wage but across the board. Labour had adopted this as Party policy in 1918, but most Labour councils saw it as something to aspire to rather than implement. Poplar's new policy more than doubled some workers' wages, and lifted women's wages by an average 70 per cent.

The council caused a storm when it offered a pay rise to its workers dependant on their being a member of a trade union or joining one within four weeks. 'Coercion!' cried opposition councillor Walter Cowl, unsuccessfully opposing the proposal[136]. Sir Reginald Blair was so appalled that he raised the matter in Parliament. Charles Willows, the only council watchman not in a union, took legal action against the council to recover the rise he had not received between the date of the policy and his retirement, aged 74, a few months later.[137] His barrister argued that, 'although the sum involved was the nominal amount of £4, there was at stake the liberty of the subject and the right of a man to sell his labour in any market and in any form he chooses.' By his own admission, Willows wanted to avoid losing money by striking and being bound by union agreements, but still wanted the benefits won by trade unions. Today, Willows would have won. But in 1920, Judge Graham ruled for Poplar council, stating that the pay rise was simply an offer that the council was at liberty to make and Willows at liberty to accept or refuse.

Similar outrage from the PBMA greeted what one local newspaper headlined the 'Extraordinary action of Poplar guardians - all employees to be trades unionists'[138]. The Board of Guardians had written to its employees stating that 'all applications for increases in salary are to be made through the trade union' and that the war bonus would be consolidated into wages conditional on trade union membership. Challenged about the 'liberty' of those not wanting to join a union, guardian A.A.Watts replied: 'It seems a strange kind of liberty which would allow one employee to benefit by the concerted action of others from whom he stood aloof.'[139]

But not everyone in Poplar even had a job. A minority on the Board of Guardians before 1919, Labour's representatives had nonetheless improved the treatment of the poor and out-of-work. George Lansbury had first won a seat as a guardian in 1893 alongside Will Crooks, who had been in the workhouse as a boy after his father lost an arm at work.[140] They found themselves administering the notorious Poor Law system, designed to humiliate and punish, to deter workers from 'idleness' as though people became destitute because they could not be bothered to work.

Lansbury described his first visit to a workhouse thus: 'the poor dreaded and hated these places ... all these prison and bastille sort of surroundings were organised for the purpose of making self-respecting, decent people endure any suffering rather than enter ... everything possible was done to inflict mental and moral degradation.'[141] Lansbury wrote a pamphlet with the straight-to-the-point title, 'Smash Up The Workhouse', in which he wrote that, '[t]he whole paraphernalia is designed for the express purpose of bringing home to the inmate what a horrible person he must have been ever to have sunk so low as to have become a charge on the rates'.[142] Care for children was so poor that in some workhouses, 40 per cent of babies died in their first year.[143]

Lansbury and Crooks set about reforming the hellish workhouse and, to the horror of the right wing, paying support to poor people without sentencing them to the workhouse. The pillars of the Poor Law considered this 'outdoor relief' an indulgence of the undeserving poor.

In 1905, the newly-formed Poplar Borough Municipal Alliance demanded the Local Government Board inquire into the Poplar guardians' alleged extravagance and corruption, and what the PBMA demanded, the PBMA got. The Davy Report 'record[ed] charges which were unproved and ... permit[ted] questionings which were scandalous'[144], but was unable to find any evidence of corruption, so damned the Poplar guardians for being too kind to the poor. Raymond Postgate wrote that, 'No action followed the report ... The first of three conflicts had ended, as the next two were to do, in the discomfiture of the central authority.'[145] Lansbury dismissed the Davy Report as 'merely an excuse for a concerted attack upon the principle of outdoor relief and an attempt to reintroduce the old workhouse system'[146], and later wrote that, 'From the first moment I determined to fight for one policy only and that was decent treatment of the poor and hang the rates!'[147] A few years later, he would indeed hang the rates.

But before then, he sat on the Royal Commission on the Poor Laws from 1905 to 1909. The Commission's Majority Report was so plainly inadequate that the government ignored it. Lansbury joined Beatrice Webb and others in signing a Minority Report advocating the abolition of the Poor Law and the introduction of decent state support for the poor, sick and elderly. Postgate argues that the Commission was a stage in Lansbury's realisation of the importance of independent working-class representation: 'Unlike the Webbs, he had already decided that the policy of cajoling and tricking Liberal or Conservative ministers into carrying out Socialist policies had reached the end of its usefulness (if it ever had any) ... His energies and thoughts were turned wholly to independent Labour politics.'[148]

Finally winning an outright majority in 1919, Poplar's Labour guardians increased outdoor relief to 33s (£1.65) per week for a couple (the Ministry of

Health's recommended level was 25s (£1.25)). Unlike most Boards, they paid a rent allowance on top, aiming to avert evictions and to prevent overcrowding through poverty-driven sub-letting. They provided bedclothes, boots, clothes and other 'extras'. Their opponents would call this extravagance, but to the Poplar socialists, it was redirecting a little wealth to give some dignity to the poor. Within months of their election, Poplar guardians' spending had increased dramatically[149], and a Municipal Alliance councillor warned borough council electors, 'that increase should show the ratepayers what they might expect in November if the same class of men were elected as were returned for the Guardians in April'.[150] In July 1919, the guardians asked the Institution Committees to look for efficiencies, but 'efficiencies' alone could not balance the books because the funding system was unfair.

Guardians received their money from their borough council. The poorer the area, the less money the council could raise through the rates but the greater the demand on the guardians. It was a case of 'the poor keeping the poor', a label of injustice that the labour movement continually pinned on the rating system. The Metropolitan Common Poor Fund (MCPF), established in 1867, provided a little pooling of funds between rich and poor London boroughs, but was intended exclusively for indoor relief[151], and its contribution had stayed static at 5d (2p) per workhouse inmate for over 50 years while costs had risen tenfold.[152] In 1916, the Fund had frozen its payments to poor boroughs, and Poplar was now getting less money from grants than it had in 1914.

In November 1919, the government withdrew from civilians the 'unemployment donation', its contribution to financial support for the jobless introduced the year before. [153] Outraged councils, including Hackney and Poplar, passed resolutions condemning the cut and the hardship it would cause. Poplar council requested a deputation to the Prime Minister, and held public protest meetings.

The unemployed had three sources of financial support, all inadequate. Ex-servicemen received allowances from the Ministry of Pensions, but ordinary soldiers got only half the rate that officers received. National Insurance schemes were low-level and short-term. The last resort was the Poor Law. The government's dole cut forced more jobless people to turn to the guardians for help. It was a shift in responsibility for the unemployed from central government to local - the opposite direction from what was needed.

The Poplar guardians went to the borough council meeting in December and asked for road-building schemes to provide work, arguing that the cost should be borne nationally not locally. The council agreed with the guardians and decided to send a deputation to the Ministry of Health. It was another deputation whose pleas would fall on unhearing ears. Another followed, when

Poplar council petitioned the Industrial Court about transport labour, Julia Scurr arguing that, 'if proper wages were paid, there would be no need for free milk or any subsidies'[154]. But it was another constitutional lobbying effort and another brick wall.

On 26 February 1920, the council threatened to withhold from the Metropolitan Police the monies it collected on their behalf, known as 'precepts', until the Met reinstated the officers it had sacked for striking the previous year.[155] But other councils that had promised to do the same went back on their word, a deputation to the Home Secretary came to nothing, and Poplar council backed down three weeks after issuing its threat. Nevertheless, Poplar had tasted two things to come - the potential power of withholding precepts to cross-London bodies, and the importance of councils sticking together due to their weakness and isolation if they do not.

The Poplar guardians decided at their meeting on 23 July 1920 to write to the Ministry of Health, asking for steps to relieve the rate burden on poor boroughs and to consider moves to equalise rates. It was one of many attempts by Poplar's council and guardians to achieve reform by constitutional means. Not only did the government ignore their request, it actually made matters worse. It promised to update the MCPF but did not. It had earlier blocked the guardians' efforts to create work and raise money by tendering for the contract to supply uniforms for the borough council's baths department.[156]

Poplar could continue with fruitless lobbying, or it could choose more confrontational methods. Its increasingly militant stand was finding inspiration from the Russian revolution.

REVOLUTIONARY VISION

Most of the British labour movement supported the 1917 revolution, when the Bolsheviks led the Russian workers to power. In March 1918, George Lansbury chaired a meeting in the Albert Hall welcoming the revolution: 12,000 packed into the Hall, a further 5,000 could not fit.[157] Poplar Borough Council released Lansbury from his Mayoral duties to visit Russia, and he entered the country on 5 February 1920 for a nine-week tour, during which he addressed the Moscow Soviet and met Lenin.

Lansbury's biographer John Shepherd reports that, 'Though the Christian socialist and the atheist revolutionary disagreed over religion, pacifism, and politics, Lansbury was clearly impressed by Lenin's revolutionary vision and the simple lifestyle he led in the Kremlin.'[158] On Lansbury's return to England, he reported to several enthusiastic meetings and wrote a pamphlet, 'What I Saw In Russia'. In it, he described Lenin's relationship with the Russian people: 'he is their comrade, their champion in the cause of social and economic freedom.'[159]

It was a description that Lansbury himself could claim.

The government by now saw George Lansbury as an enemy of the state, and Winston Churchill instructed MI5 to gather information on him, saying that 'My object is to secure in one document the complete statement of the case against Mr. Lansbury'.[160] But although supporting the Bolshevik revolution, George did not join the British Communist Party (CP) when it formed in 1920, believing revolution was right for Russia but reform was the way forward in Britain, and writing that 'we want the same revolution accomplished here, not by bloodshed and violence, but by the use of industrial organisation and the vote'[161]. 'I am a Communist', he would write in 1925, 'my differences with the Communist Party are purely concerning organisation and method.'[162]

Several of George's Poplar comrades, though, did join the CP. A.A.Watts was on its founding Executive, and both Edgar and Minnie Lansbury also joined, Edgar going on to be elected a substitute member of the CP's central committee in 1924 - the same year that the Labour Party voted to exclude CP members. Fellow Communists Sylvia Pankhurst and Harry Pollitt were organising in the dockland area. At one public meeting in March, Sylvia called local people to action: 'There never was a body of people who needed to rise up and change things more than you down here'. Pollitt added that, 'if the women of East London were to march to Poplar and raid the docks, they would do more to bring down food prices than all the resolutions passed'.[163]

The Soviet Union and Poland were at war, with Britain and France heavily backing Poland in an attempt to crush the young workers' state. The labour movement had set up the Hands Off Russia Committee, and both the TUC and the Labour Party opposed British intervention. In Poplar, members of the Labour Party and of Sylvia Pankhurst's Workers' Socialist Federation (WSF) fly-posted Poplar's walls with 'Hands Off Russia' posters, and handed out copies of Lenin's 'Appeal to the Toiling Masses' at the dock gates.[164] On 10 May 1920, a ship called the Jolly George sat in the East India Dock waiting to be loaded with munitions for Poland. But led by Poplar councillor Dave Adams, local branch secretary of the Dock, Wharf and Riverside Workers' Union, the dockers refused to load the arms and the coal trimmers refused to coal the ship. The Jolly George sailed empty, and the government's war effort took such a blow that it officially ended three months later, after the Labour Party's and TUC's August declaration that they would call a general strike if Britain declared war on Russia.[165]

But by then, things were turning bad for the working class.

SLUMP, UNEMPLOYMENT AND RESISTANCE

The post-war boom was short-lived. 1920 was the year in which night bus services started in London, the League of Nations met for the first time, the Westminster Parliament voted to partition Ireland – and towards the end of which, prices began to fall sharply and trade decline. During 1921 – a year *The Economist* would label 'one of the worst years of depression since the industrial revolution'[166] – Britain's exports and imports fell by nearly half. The employers argued that trade could only revive if prices were made more competitive, so they must cut costs, especially wages.

In any recession, the two main classes fight over who is to carry the cost. The employers made workers pay the price, as the next three years saw the fastest fall in wages in British history. Despite employers' predictions, this did not reverse the slump. But it did have a catastrophic effect on workers and their families.

When trade collapses, the docks collapse too, so Poplar was at the front of the line of dominoes to fall. Casual workers became unemployed, permanent workers became casual, and men laid off from other industries came to the docks searching for casual work.[167] The loss of work brought fear of a return to the bad old days of dockers literally fighting each other at the gates to get a few hours' toil.

The railways were next. Over the year from August 1920, both freight and passenger use fell dramatically.[168] The government, having taken control of the railways during the war, was to hand them back to the private companies in August 1921. Management prepared for the handover by drastically cutting costs. In May 1921, they suspended the guaranteed working week, with the support of union leaders who were so scared of job losses that they accepted attacks on working conditions rather than fight both. Then the job losses came too: from March 1921 to March 1922 the employers sacked nearly 60,000 railworkers.[169]

Poplar soon had 92.5 outdoor paupers[170] per thousand people; nearby Whitechapel had 0.2. Nationally, unemployment stood at 2,171,288 (17.8 per cent) by June 1921, a more-than-threefold increase on the 691,103 of just six months earlier. Ramsey describes the harrowing result: 'Many of those out of work were ex-service-men, forced to rely on Poor Law relief for their support. Some ex-bandsmen had organised small parties of musicians to parade in the gutters of busy streets playing their instruments, with collecting boxes carried by disabled veterans; some blind, some limbless. All wore their campaign medals and some carried placards bitterly reminding passers-by of the pledge made by the Prime Minister, David Lloyd George, in his election campaign of 1918, to provide 'a fit country for heroes to live in'.[171] A.J.P. Taylor describes how that pledge now 'seemed a mockery. Lloyd George lost his last shadow of hold over the working class. He had become for them a fraud, a sham.'[172]

If the coalition government had, as Morgan claims, considered social reform a priority in 1919 and 1920, the slump brought an abrupt reversal.[173] The Tory-Liberal coalition claimed to continue the national unity forged during the war. But it was a coalition built on an anti-socialist consensus, and it now showed its true colours, fixing its sights on cost-cutting and abandoning all pretence at reform, whatever the cost to working-class people. No wonder 'Labour men everywhere viewed the Lloyd George era as a time of class war and class rhetoric'.[174]

The government made a few adjustments to regulations, but took no serious action to address unemployment. It extended unemployment insurance to most workers only in November 1920, too late for many of those already unemployed to benefit. Its small extension of unemployment benefit excluded domestic servants, cleaners and home workers, and thus millions of working-class women. Labour councils passed resolutions deploring Lloyd George's lack of interest and demanding action: peace with Russia to resume trade; grants to poor boroughs to employ the jobless in public works; and central government to fund dole payments.

Poplar council passed such a resolution in September 1920, after hearing a deputation introduced by Councillor Chris Williams. It also agreed practical measures, including opening a register of the unemployed at the Town Hall to help people find work. By December it had also opened registers at Bromley Public Hall, Bow Library and Cubitt Town Library, and was allowing unemployed people to use public baths for free. The council sent a delegation to lobby the government but, expecting this to fail, began to mobilise the local community.

The London Labour Party urged its borough councillors to demand towns' meetings in every borough to be held on the same evening.[175] On October 3, so many people attended Poplar's meeting that an overflow meeting had to be held. [176] John Scurr made the point that 'Eight millions a day was spent on the prosecution of war. Surely they could spend that amount to find work for the unemployed.' George Lansbury explained the impracticality of tackling unemployment entirely through local rates – they would have to be £25 in the pound instead of 25s (£1.25)! The meeting passed a resolution calling for public works schemes. The demand itself exposes the irrationality of the capitalist market. There was work that needed doing – building roads, improving recreation grounds, modernising housing – but the workers who could do it were forced to be idle.

The same night, another big crowd packed into the Town's Meeting in Bromley Public Hall.[177] The council had invited local MP Sir Reginald Blair, but he refused, writing 'Much as I would like to have been associated with anything that might benefit ex-Servicemen, I regret that under existing circumstances, I prefer not to be associated meantime with Mr. Lansbury', which prompted laughter from the meeting when read out. Blair went on to blame trade unions for unemployment, which Lansbury condemned as an attempt 'to divide the ex-Servicemen from the Trade Unions ... an absolute outrage on the labour movement'. This statement typified a core feature of the Poplar labour movement's politics and strategy: always to resist hostile attempts to divide the working class. They constantly stressed the common interests of workers and jobless, ex-services and civilians, poor ratepayers and poor service users.

That month, jobless activists formed the London District Council of the Unemployed (LDCU)[178]. Six months later, the LDCU called a national conference, promoted by the *Daily Herald*, which set down the foundations for the National Unemployed Workers' Movement (NUWM)[179]. Communist Party member Wal Hannington took up leading positions in both. He was one of many former shop stewards, out of work through redundancy or victimisation, who brought organisational experience and political understanding from the factories to the unemployed movement.

Labour's left and right polarised in their response to the slump and to the assertive unemployed. The left wanted to confront the government and ally with the out-of-work, while Herbert Morrison and the right opposed the 'excessive' demands of the jobless, and wanted local Labour Parties to work with them only to convince them of 'the impossibility of achieving anything of real worth by militant local action'. Morrison wanted 'thoughtful action' rather than 'mere ignorant appeals to the baser kind of mob passion'.[180]

Unwilling to assign the unemployed a passive role merely cheerleading the council while it fought on their behalf, the Poplar labour movement and the *Daily Herald* urged the jobless to 'Go To The Guardians', not only for personal financial assistance but as a political mobilisation against unemployment. The *Herald*'s 'Go To The Guardians' campaign deliberately challenged the Poor Law. It asserted the right of those out of work to claim relief outside the workhouse, an idea still anathema to the Poor Law patriarchs. It refused to acknowledge a distinction between 'deserving' and 'undeserving' poor. It removed the shame attached to claiming dole. It also targeted the Poor Law's public face: the guardians. Outside Poplar and a few similar Labour areas, boards of guardians were no friends of the poor. Instead, they ranged from the paternalistic but mean to hostile, judgemental bullies who put their efforts into refusing help to those in dire straits – people described by Emmeline Pankhurst as 'guardians, not of the poor but of the rates'.[181] Many were 'delegates of interests', representatives of slum landlords or employers; others were small tradesmen chasing contracts from the board.[182] Unemployed movements would relate to such bodies as enemies; 'Go To The Guardians' was a call not just to claim your dole, but also to collectively protest against the system and its administrators.

Facing such mobilisations, writes one of his biographers, 'Lansbury was neither afraid nor resentful. He hated poverty. He saw daily ill-nourished children and distraught parents who had parted with children they could not afford to feed and clothe. He preferred poor people to be angry rather than apathetic.'[183] When unemployed protesters occupied Poplar Town Hall one December night, the mayor welcomed them and had them use the occupied building as a campaigning base.

In contrast, when Hackney's unemployed occupied buildings and marched to their guardians' offices, their Labour mayor, Herbert Morrison, disowned their actions[184] and wrote to the Prime Minister that he had 'set his face against disorder and illegality'[185]. Morrison penned a stinging attack on the *Herald*'s 'Go To The Guardians' campaign, denouncing it as a 'stunt' which 'would play bang into the hands of Lloyd George and the Municipal "Reformers". It diverts the attack from the Government ... and places the burden on poor Boroughs controlled by Labour councils.'[186] Perhaps Morrison wanted people to vote for Labour councils but not ask them for help.

'Go To The Guardians' expressed only one side of the NUWM's demand for 'work or full maintenance'. Wal Hannington wrote in the LDCU's newspaper *Out Of Work*, 'George Lansbury's advice is to March to the Guardians. My advice is to March to the Factories.'[187] One of the LDCU's main activities was to 'raid' factories, demanding – often successfully – that the bosses raise wages and stop overtime.[188]

Sylvia Pankhurst, who was soon to part company with the Communist Party, formed the Unemployed Workers' Organisation as an alternative to the LDCU/NUWM, and believed that 'Go To The Guardians' was not just inadequate but positively regressive, a distraction from the key demand to abolish the system of wage labour. Sylvia was on a political journey away from her unmatched record of organising working-class women and men for the vote and for workers' rights, towards a position on the margin of the labour movement.

The NUWM's demand for 'work or full maintenance' was not just a demand on the poor law authorities for dole, but a challenge to the capitalist system and those in power to provide work. Poplar and other councils wanted to rise to that challenge through public works schemes, but they needed the government's financial support. Would they get it?

2. DEFYING THE SYSTEM

Councillor George and Mrs. Lansbury and the young of Poplar backing the cause.

AN UNFAIR FUNDING SYSTEM

Poplar council had prised from the LCC a small grant for road improvements earlier in 1920[189], but only after protesting against an initial refusal. After a previous, tortuous attempt to obtain funding to supply library books to schools, Sam March had commented that, 'it was difficult to get anything out of the LCC, which was a past master in the art of passing on costs to other people'.[190]

In October 1920, the government responded to labour movement pressure and announced that it would pay grants to schemes that created work in building or improving roads. Under this scheme, Bethnal Green council employed more than 2,000 men for 8-13 weeks that winter, and Shoreditch council over 1,000 men for four weeks.[191] Poplar council immediately set about organising its scheme, costing around £32,000, £18,850 of this for labour. The council submitted its plan to Minister of Labour Thomas Macnamara[192]: 'All the facts were disclosed to him, and the work was proceeded with, with his approval and promised support, no limiting conditions being suggested'.[193] The council started the work in December.

Then came the bombshell. In January 1921, the Government Unemployed Grants Committee refused the grant.[194] With the money already being spent, the government had imposed new conditions that Poplar could not and would not meet. The first was that the council must recruit its workers through Labour Exchanges. But with no Labour Exchange in Poplar, the council used its own unemployment registers, compiled in co-operation with nearby Labour Exchanges.[195] Moreover, Labour Exchanges may not have been the best way to recruit jobless men, who so distrusted them because of their association with the Poor Law and with strike-breaking that 'The unemployed skilled worker preferred to walk the streets seeking work rather than rely on the Exchange.'[196]

The second was that schemes must prioritise ex-servicemen. Poplar, however, had offered work on the basis of need not service record, prioritising those with large or young families. Nearly half of those employed on the scheme – 2,199 out of 4,444 by 23 February[197] – were ex-servicemen, but Poplar also had a large number of rail and dock workers whom the government had told not to join the armed forces because their work was vital. Now they were to be excluded from government support when their 'vital' work was no longer there and poverty weighed heavily on them and their families.

When the council discussed the refusal[198], railway signaller Joe Hammond was angry because the government wanted to exclude his unemployed workmates, and ex-soldier Chris Williams denounced the government for attempting to turn ex-servicemen and civilians against each other.

The cost of road materials had risen by over 400 per cent, and while Poplar needed both roads and jobs, its council did not have the money. The ball rolling towards conflict with the central authorities had gained weight and picked up speed. The council had to find £30,000 from the rates. That was impossible, especially under a rating system already so burdensome on poor boroughs like Poplar.

Paying poor relief from local rates dated back to 1601. It was a time before capitalism, when people generally lived in distinct areas, villages with a Lord of the Manor and a Squire ruling over and living off the serfs. In such self-contained units, there was a sense to raising money from the place in which it was spent. Come industrialisation, people moved to cities. The rich did not want to live near the filthy factories that they owned nor in the slum areas where their workers lived. So the cities distilled into rich areas and poor areas. The poorer areas had more people with greater needs, but little wealth to tax.

This inequality persists to this day, with councils in working-class London boroughs charging higher Council Tax because of their populations' greater need. In 1921, this problem was magnified by the burden on local rates to fund poor relief as well as other council services. Under the Poor Law, guardians were supposed to force all claimants into the workhouse rather than pay outdoor relief, although the Relief Regulations Order 1911 had allowed outdoor payments in exceptional cases. But when the flood of relief claimants came in 1920, Boards abandoned forced workhouse admission and the 'work test': there was not room in the workhouse, nor the labour yard – where work tests were carried out – for all the jobless.

Businesses, homeowners and landlords paid rates[199], with landlords adding them to the rent. The 'rateable value' of a district was the total value of property from which it could raise rates; the rate charged was expressed as a certain sum per pound. The five wealthy boroughs of West London[200] had a rateable value of nearly £15m, with 5,000 poor people to support. The five poor areas of East London[201] had a rateable value of just over £4m, with 86,500 poor to support. The East End carried 17 times the burden of the West End but with only a quarter of the capacity to pay. If Westminster increased its rate by 1d, it would raise £29,000; in Poplar, a 1d rise would raise just £3,200.[202] Poplar council issued a leaflet to residents denouncing a system that it called 'robbery of the poor in poor Boroughs to save the purses of the rich in the rich Boroughs'[203].

Even the mainstream press could see the problem, the *Westminster Gazette* explaining that 'Labour rules, as a whole, in the poorer districts, in which rates were always high and the yield of the penny rate low. Naturally, the increases in these boroughs are higher. It costs as much for materials and labour to repair a road in Poplar as it does in Westminster, but there is no comparison between the produce of a penny rate upon the poor property of Poplar and the rich buildings in the centre of London.'[204]

The labour movement had long campaigned for reform of the rating system, and the unemployment crisis brought vigour and urgency to the demand. Deptford was one of many borough councils to pass a resolution demanding action, specifically: equalisation of rates, meaning a far greater pooling of boroughs' contributions to poor relief; a great extension of national grants; landlords to pay rates on empty properties; and a capital levy to help fund local authority spending.[205] It was calling on the government to tax capital and capitalists to tackle the crisis that capitalism had created.

Even some local capitalists supported change. The leader of the Moderates on the West Ham Board of Guardians wrote that, 'As a landlord myself, I do not think it is the duty of the Guardians to provide the money. Hungry men, however, are dangerous ... Their upkeep should be a national charge and not forced upon the borough.'[206] This quote shows both fear of working-class revolt and tension between local and national capitalists. So by demanding reform, was Labour simply siding with one group of landlords and employers against another? No, it was demanding what was independently in the interests of the working class. The rating system as it stood both over-charged working-class people as their landlords passed on rate rises, and deprived them of the relief and services they needed.

There was one more element to the rating system in London. Through the rates, borough councils collected funds, called precepts, for the London County Council, Metropolitan Asylum Board[207], Metropolitan Water Board[208] and Metropolitan Police.

Polite requests having failed, here was Poplar council's chance to defy the system.

REFUSING TO COLLECT THE RATES

The council elected a new mayor each year; in 1921 was Sam March, a former driver of horse-drawn vehicles who was now full-time General Secretary of the National Union of Vehicle Workers. He took over at the helm of a council the demands on which were massive and growing but whose only source of income was to tax its own cash-starved residents. What was it to do? Scale down its work? Insist the guardians pay pittances for dole? Satisfy itself with minor housing repairs, the odd new street light or repaired paving stone? That is what many would have chosen, and have chosen since. The system had boxed them in, and now either they or the system must crack. George Lansbury saw this as 'the whole question of whether the Labour Movement means business. Are we going to attempt to carry out what we say on the platform, or are we to be misled and side-tracked by considerations of "statesmanship"?'[209]

Many committed socialists have entered local government determined to pursue socialist policies and win significant improvements for working-class people, knowing that this must mean challenging fundamental aspects of the system itself. But often they find themselves unable to make the impact they had hoped, and so concentrate on small local issues, or even administer policies that they do not at heart agree with. It is as though their horizons have fallen in on them. The existing system is like a cage around them: they give up trying to break out and manage the best they can within its bars.

Why were Poplar councillors able to resist this? Because of their socialist politics, and because they were part of a movement and made their choices as a movement. Poplar's labour movement convened a conference of trade union branches to thrash out its strategy. George Lansbury proposed that the council should stop paying precepts to cross-London bodies.[210] The conference discussed every aspect of the proposal in detail, ensuring that the local labour movement was well equipped to implement and defend its strategy.

By March 1921, the precepts were overdue. Poplar council owed the LCC £30,000, the Metropolitan Police £25,000 and the Metropolitan Water Board £40,000. The charges on the council had risen massively over the past year: from the Board of Guardians by 42 per cent, the LCC 25 per cent, Metropolitan Police 32 per cent and the Water Board by a whopping 54 per cent.[211] Poplar could not, and would not, pay.

The council took its decision at two meetings. The first, on 22 March, voted to delete the precepts from the Finance Committee's report. Nine days later, on the same day the government declared a state of emergency in response to a miners' strike, Poplar council set the rate for the quarter at 4s4d (22p) in the pound instead of the 6s10d (34p) it would have been with the precepts included. The Finance Committee had included the precepts in its report to the first of these two meetings, not because it wanted to levy them, but so that the whole council would vote in unity to delete the precepts and the repercussions would be borne on all their shoulders.[212]

Charles Key, Chair of the Public Health Committee, proposed the deletion of the precepts, explaining that this was 'not an adventure which they desired lightly to embark on … [but] their … duty demanded the most effective protest against the studied indifference of the Government to the serious problems of local finance … It was time the people were made aware of the hypocrisy and criminal indifference of the central powers.'[213] George Lansbury saw refusing to pay the precepts as the equivalent of striking in industrial matters or taking direct action in campaigning matters. From the Great Unrest and the suffragettes to the railway strike and the Jolly George, direct action had shown that it could win for working-class people, and Poplar council was importing it into municipal politics.

Poplar's Town Clerk, J.Buteaux Skeggs, had cautioned against this move, writing to George Lansbury before the meeting [214], 'Before the council is irrevocably pledged to levy a rate for local requirements only, I think it right to call your attention to the effects which may be expected to ensue thereon.' Skeggs feared loss of grants and loans; action by creditors; refusal of overdrafts by the bank; inability of the council to pay wages and consequent rise in unemployment; abandonment of extensions to the Electricity Undertaking; and chaos due to rent adjustments. George wrote back to the Town Clerk that he could not imagine creditors taking action and that if the bank did, then the council would 'immediately transfer the account to the Co-operative Wholesale Bank. But the Bank, like everyone else with whom we do business, has no right to take sides on this matter.'[215] Lansbury had Skeggs' letter read out to the council meeting on 22 March, but even such a stern warning from the most senior council official did not deter the councillors.

The decision passed with only one vote against – that of Reverend Kitcat, the independent elected with the support of the Municipal Alliance[216], whose own four councillors either voted for the proposal (Knightbridge and Brandy) or stayed away from the meeting (Cowl and Cohen).[217] Even Kitcat expressed sympathy with the council's cause, but said that he could not endorse breaking the law.

At the same time that it fired its starting pistol for defying the authorities financially, Poplar council launched its efforts to win popular support. At its 22 March meeting, the council voted to set up a sub-committee to draft a statement explaining the council's decision, that this statement be 'delivered to every householder and lodger in the Borough; and that Towns Meetings be held to explain the policy to the Ratepayers'. The sub-committee consisted of George Lansbury, Charlie Sumner, Charles Key, and the PBMA's Clifford Knightbridge.[218]

For the past few months, Poplar had been shrouded in despair. Now there was confidence, of the sort that the bullied child gets when he or she stops giving in to the bullies and starts standing up to them. Edgar Lansbury recalled that 'The air was electrical'.[219] The immediate consequence of the decision was a significant cut in rates and therefore rent, benefiting every working-class individual and family in the borough. The people of Poplar were ready to rally round their rebel councillors.

Throughout April the council held public meetings to explain its actions and involve local people. The response was huge enthusiasm. On Wednesday 20 April, a big crowd attended a public meeting at Poplar Town Hall, where Mayor Sam March reported on their recent deputation to the Minister for Transport, who had said that he would do his best to obtain a grant for the borough. It was a pitiful response from a Cabinet member who could have awarded such a grant at will, and it would not deflect Poplar council from its defiant course of action. George Lansbury 'declared that the capitalists were out to crush the miners and workers, and the authorities were out to injure and cripple those borough councils who had labour majorities. It was up to them to act peacefully, but at the same time firmly.'[220] One local newspaper reported that, 'during the latter part of the meeting there was considerable interruption by members of the communist party'.[221]

There was a collection on the door for the children of striking miners. More than six decades later, local councils and miners would also be in struggle at the same time against a Tory government. On both occasions, solidarity – or lack of it – would be key to their chances of success. Just five days before the public

meeting at Poplar Town Hall the miners' strike suffered the fatal blow of 'Black
Friday', as the rail and transport unions failed to support them and broke up the
hugely powerful Triple Alliance. The *Daily Herald* mourned this as 'the heaviest
defeat that has befallen the Labour Movement within the memory of man. It
is no use trying to minimise it. It is no use pretending that it is other than it
is. We on this paper have said throughout that if the organised workers stood
together they would win. They have not stood together and they have reaped
the reward.'[222]

The extent of local support for Poplar council's action was perhaps surprising
given that its key demand, 'equalise the rates', seemed unlikely to excite
hungry, overcrowded, impoverished people. Sylvia Pankhurst argued that, 'To
the unemployed, half-starved on the paltry pittances doled out to them, the
equalisation of the Rates is a rather remote question. To them the size of the
dole is necessarily more important than the question of where the relief comes
from.'[223] However unlikely, though, thousands of people did mobilise in support
of the demand. People responded to 'equalise the rates' because many of them
had taken part in making the decision, and because the councillors repeatedly
explained it to them in leaflets and at meetings. At one later meeting, 'There
were old women, mothers with babies in their arms, and spirited factory girls
with eyes aglow with enthusiasm. They sat listening intently while Councillor
Key explained municipal finance to them and demonstrated by statistics the
case for equalisation of the rates.'[224]

The councillors sought endorsement of their action; many reports of meetings
tell of a vote at the end in support of the council's latest tactical move. There were
union reps, Labour Party subs collectors, and all manner of activists spreading
the word and hearing people's views. Weekly Wednesday evening meetings of
the Poplar Labour Women's Guild regularly attracted 300 attendees.[225] The
mass meetings were 'only the most visible outcrop; beneath the surface was a
confused network of communication which hummed with life ... the people
around Lansbury were capable of tuning into the thoughts of large sections of
advanced workers.'[226] Crucially, Poplar council never allowed itself to become
an autonomous body, cut off from the labour movement. Many councillors
drift away from their constituents, their political activity revolving more around
committee meetings than around streets, workplaces and estates. But Poplar
council made sure that every step of its action involved local people.

Gillian Rose argues that Poplar Labour's commitment to participatory
politics came from the ILP and the WSF. [227] The ILP's Poplar branch was on
the left even of the ILP, with a communist faction, the Revolutionary Policy
Committee, publishing its bulletin from the Poplar ILP branch office. The ILP
also gave Poplar Labour its belief that local government should be accountable

to its electors rather than to the central state.

Poplar's Labour council now faced opposition from both government laws and local ratepayers. The Poplar Borough Municipal Alliance was in a tight spot. Its most basic aim was to keep the rates down and the socialists out. Yet the hated socialists had just achieved in one decision the very thing that the PBMA treasured: it had drastically cut the rate.

It called a public meeting, at which its secretary, prominent freemason and former Mayor of Poplar[228] Sir Alfred Warren, proclaimed that 'if the action of the council was persisted in it would reduce the district comparable with Bedlam.'[229] When the council first made its decision, he had said that 'There is a right way and a wrong way, and the Socialistic majority on the Poplar council have chosen the wrong way.'[230] Representatives of several Poplar firms attended the PBMA's public meeting, but its councillors did not. They had, after all, either voted with Labour or absented themselves from the vote. The public meeting adopted a resolution:

> That this meeting including most of the largest ratepayers of the Metropolitan Borough of Poplar, enters its strongest protest against the unconstitutional action of the present members of the borough council in definitely declining to levy a rate sufficient to meet the legitimate liabilities of the borough, therebye occasioning great difficulty and confusion, and ultimately involving the ratepayers in additional charges in respect of costs etc. And demands that the obligations for the current period be immediately levied.[231]

As advised by the PBMA meeting, several firms returned their rate bill to the council, asking for a new one with the precepts included. The council replied that it would take steps to enforce payment. The firms paid up, lacking the stomach for direct action of their Labour adversaries, or perhaps the passion to go through with their fight to pay more!

None of Poplar council's critics questioned the justice of its cause, merely the wisdom of its tactics. The *East London Observer* sympathised with the call for rates equalisation, but thought that the council's defiance was doomed. It argued that Poplar council would fail because 'Nobody supposes that this new form of strike can be successful, because no Government could possibly allow a local authority to set the ordinary law at open defiance.'[232] The paper's gloomy prediction was about to be put to the test.

On 28 May, the first instalment of the council's precept to the LCC was due - £33,944, part of the £135,778 due for the half year. As the deadline loomed, the LCC wrote to Poplar council to ask whether it intended to pay, and warning of enforcement steps if it did not. At its meeting on 26 May, Poplar Borough Council noted the letter and kept on refusing to pay. The council's bold choice had forced the central authorities also to make choices. Having neither the legal nor the material capacity to step in and collect the rates itself, the LCC took the matter to court.

BREAKING BAD LAWS

The Poplar councillors knew that their action was illegal and that they could not win in court. They understood, as Sam March put it, that 'The master class has made the laws'[233], and took the stance that if the law makes you choose between breaking it and attacking the people you represent, then you break it. George Lansbury wrote that 'All reforms come from those who are ready to break bad laws'[234].

With no faith in the legal system, Poplar's strategy in the court hearings it now faced was to use them as a platform to explain their case to an ever-wider audience. They would also use them as a focus for mobilisation, and would seek to delay the proceedings in order to build up their campaign's momentum and buy time for other councils to join in.

The signatories to the Council's reply to the complaint made to the High Court by the London County Council and the Metropolitan Asylums Board.
(Left to right) Cr. George Lansbury; Town Clerk Mr Buteux Skeggs; Ald. John Scurr; Mayor Cr. March; the Deputy Mayor Cr. Sumner.

Their solicitor was W.H.Thompson, a 'young and energetic' man,[235] who had been jailed three times for conscientious objection to the First World War,[236] and went on to found Thompson's Solicitors, now a leading legal firm for trade unions and their members. A man who 'defend[ed] seemingly lost causes [and] people attacked as subversives',[237] Thompson believed in the justice of Poplar's case and the soundness of its tactics even though they were plainly illegal! A modern law professor argues that Thompson had 'a clear and most singular identification of the needs of a very large part of the British population; people whose concerns were either being ignored or systematically under-represented in our society. That group was the working population.'[238]

On 3 June, the LCC successfully applied to court for a provisional mandamus[239] (or instruction) requiring Poplar Borough Council to pay its first instalment or else attend court on 20 June to explain itself. On 10 June, the Metropolitan Asylum Board (MAB) obtained a similar mandamus[240]. The Metropolitan Police and Water Board did not take legal action, the Police receiving advice that it would serve no purpose to do so in addition to the action by the MAB and LCC.[241] The Water Board appeared satisfied when it received Poplar's precept for the previous year[242], as it did not discuss the issue again.

The council's affidavit[243] argued to no avail that with unemployment at 15,000 and rising, 'it would be inopportune and useless to levy the ratepayers' and that the council ought not to be called upon to undertake liabilities that it could not possibly meet.

At the 'return' hearing on 20 June, the council's barrister, Henry Slesser[244] KC,[245] presented the stark facts about Poplar's plight. 15,574 of a population of 160,000 were unemployed. The Borough's rateable value was so low that if it raised the rate by one penny, it would generate only £3,800. The guardians were spending £4,500 per week on relief. If Poplar council were to meet all its liabilities, it would have to charge a rate of £1.18s.8d (£1.93) in the pound!

Alexander Macmorran KC, representing the LCC, argued that all councils were in the same boat, all found it difficult to pay. But this could equally have been an argument for other councils to take the same stand as Poplar! Slesser told the court: 'It comes to this, that the Borough of Poplar is practically insolvent and cannot pay its debts. It is like the man who, being unable to pay, has to have his furniture sold.' The councillors were in fact more proactive and defiant than their barrister made out. They were more like the person who, impoverished by an unfair system, refused to pay his bills in order to avoid having his furniture sold. It was not just a case of 'Can't Pay' but also 'Won't Pay'.

Slesser argued that the court should not issue a mandamus because it had not exhausted other avenues, and perhaps it should levy 'distress of goods' on the council, forcing it to sell its assets to pay its debts. The court thought this impractical, since the council only owned such things as dustcarts, horses and chairs, and would have to buy new ones in order to carry out its legal duties!

The Lord Chief Justice[246] could not imagine the reasons for Poplar's action, 'unless it be popularity'. Slesser replied, 'No, my Lord, I am afraid it is poverty'. The court granted the mandamus, clarifying that failure to obey it would lead to a charge of contempt of court[247] and ultimately to prison. Macmorran hoped that 'after this the borough council of Poplar will take a saner view of things, and I do not expect that they will refuse to obey an order of the court and be attached for contempt.'[248] He expected wrongly. Poplar's opponents did not yet appreciate the councillors' determination to see through the fight that they had started. Sam March told a local newspaper that the threat of action for contempt would not cause the councillors insomnia.[249]

Between the various court hearings, Poplar's Labour representatives tried to win over the London County Council. With only 15 Labour LCC members out of 124, and with a Municipal Reform (Conservative) overall majority, they were always going to fail, but that did not deter them from assertively stating Poplar's case. Sam March told of Poplar women who had pawned the pictures on their walls and even their wedding rings to get money to pay the rent. Susan Lawrence argued that Poplar was in a position of 'absolute desperation'.[250]

That month Susan, along with George Lansbury, was re-elected to the Labour Party's National Executive. Biographer John Shepherd reports that Lansbury was 'a popular member of Labour's NEC, regularly heading the poll at the party conference during the 1920s'[251]. Even as Labour's leaders were keeping their distance from Poplar, it seemed that its rank and file admired Poplar council's stand.[252]

Also in June, boilermaker John Suckling resigned his seat as Labour councillor for Poplar East ward, ostensibly due to 'pressure of business' but possibly because of the pressure of the rates rebellion. Poplar Labour Party had deep roots in the community and plenty of activists willing to step into any vacancies in the ranks. William Lyons did so, and on 23 June was elected with over a thousand votes, an increased majority on a higher turnout.[253] Poplar residents were endorsing their council's actions at the polls as well as at meetings and marches.

A quarter of the year had passed since its original defiant decision, so the time had come to set the rate again. On 29 June, the council repeated the procedure it had followed in March. The Finance Committee reported on the court actions, and proposed a rate of 9s10d (49p), including the precepts to the cross-London bodies. Charles Key moved an amendment to delete the precepts, giving a rate of 5s3d (26p). Labour councillor James Jones expressed some doubts about excusing people a portion of their rent now if it would mean they had to pay more in future, but firmly supported not handing it over to the LCC and other

Right table: Crs. C.J. Kelly, Walter Green, W. Lyons, B. Fleming, J. Rugless, A. Baker,
J. O'Callaghan, J.A. Hammond. Right centre table: Crs. Goodway, J. Russell,
George Lansbury, Ald. Mrs. M. Lansbury, Ald. Susan Lawrence, Cr. J.H. Jones, Ald. Hopwood.
Left table: Cr. Rev. K.J. Kitcat.

Outside council offices after the meeting.
Front row: Cr. George Lansbury, Mrs. Lansbury, the Mayor Cr. S. March, Cr. Mrs. Mackay,
Cr. Mrs. Cressall

bodies. In the debate, Jones' colleagues won him over to continuing the policy of neither collecting nor paying the money, and Key's amendment passed with just one vote against, that of PBMA councillor Cowl. Edgar Lansbury argued that Poplar council 'had the government on the run, and to get over the difficulty they would have to bring in a measure for the equalisation of rates in the Metropolis'.[254]

On 7 July, the judges from June's court hearings delivered their judgment in writing. In granting the LCC and the MAB their mandamus, they stated that 'We cannot help expressing our sympathy with the inhabitants of Poplar, but we believe and regret that there are other districts suffering from similar disabilities'. So why were these other councils not joining Poplar's fight? Some Labour councils were led by men such as Hackney's Herbert Morrison, who opposed any illegal action, believing instead that Labour should prove itself responsible in power. In others, such as Shoreditch, even if a majority of Labour councillors wanted to follow Poplar's example, the cautious minority could unite with opposition councillors to vote them down. Some Labour councillors admired Poplar but did not think it would win; still others supported Poplar in theory but would not make the personal sacrifice involved. But if Poplar council kept up its fight, other councils might yet follow its lead.

The day after the judgment, the King and Queen visited Poplar to open a new extension of the Royal Albert Dock. On Charlie Sumner's suggestion, Poplar council arranged for a banner to be displayed on the dockside for the royal couple to see as they sailed past: 'Poplar Borough Council expects this day the King will do his duty by calling upon His Majesty's Government to find work or full maintenance for the unemployed of the nation.'[255] John Scurr had proposed that, in addition to the banner, the council present a special memorial to the King to draw attention to the plight of the borough. He dropped the proposal though, as disagreement emerged between councillors including Charles Key, who described himself as 'a loyal subject of the King', and others, including communists Minnie and Edgar Lansbury, who said they were 'nothing of the sort'.[256] The Mayor and councillors stayed away from the royals' reception.

Meanwhile, the unemployed movement continued to mobilise. In June, 200 jobless marched from London to Brighton, where they addressed Labour Party Conference.[257]

HEROICS, JUSTICE AND COMMON SENSE

After two more attempts by the council to delay legal proceedings had met with little success, on 25 July the LCC and MAB applied for the court to issue writs against the councillors[258]. The MAB's list of 29 councillors excluded opposition councillors who, despite earlier support, were now willing to levy the precepts.

The LCC's counsel, though, said that 'The LCC intend to take no risks and serve the lot'[259]. Although greeted with laughter, this was not true, as the LCC applied for writs against 31 of the 49 councillors. The two bodies never explained the reasons behind their choice of names. Councillor Albert Easteal, who was left off both lists, speculated that perhaps the intention was to pick on prominent members of the council and leave out others 'in the hope that they will rat on their leaders'.[260] If so, there were two odd omissions: Charles Key, who had personally proposed the deletion of the precepts, and Jack Wooster, chairman of the works committee. Some may have escaped a writ simply because they were not at home when the legal official called on them.

Ironically, John Clifford, a Labour councillor who had voted for the action but resigned when the pressure mounted, was included in the writ despite having jumped ship. He was dismayed, his former colleagues amused, when the judges told him that, 'You supported the resolution and your position is a very unpleasant one'[261].

The Court granted the writs, Lord Chief Justice Scrutton dismissing the suggestion of selling the council's goods instead as 'ludicrously inapplicable'[262]. Mayor Sam March remained defiant: 'The spirit of the council is that we are determined to fight it out, even if we are committed to prison.' [263] The court awarded the writ, meaning that the councillors would have to personally attend court on 29 July to explain themselves.

Three days before that, the LCC met late at night to discuss Poplar's non-payment. Coming to Poplar's defence, Labour member Harry Snell[264] said that, 'Poplar did not ask for clemency, but only justice for the locality in which the people lived.' But George Hume, leader of the Municipal Reform group, instead 'hoped that this attempt at heroics would not be carried on further, but that the common sense of those concerned would prevail'.[265]

Was Poplar's action just 'an attempt at heroics'? And what is wrong with 'heroics' anyway? Working-class struggle against the odds *is* heroic, despite Hume's efforts to belittle it. Whether it was 'heroics' in the negative sense – an empty gesture, or personal attention-seeking – would be shown by whether the councillors would prove themselves genuine heroes by seeing their fight through to victory. Hume also appealed to 'common sense', a phrase that tends to mean whatever the person saying it wants it to mean. 'Common sense' to Hume was to obey the law. But it was equally 'common sense' to Poplar that if you cannot pay a precept then you do not pay it, and if a law is unjust, you defy it. J.M.Gatti, Chair of the LCC's Finance Committee, referred to Poplar's strategy as a 'mad scheme'[266]. But were it to win, it would not seem mad at all.

On 28 July, the LCC took an urgent deputation to the Minister of Health, Liberal Sir Alfred Mond, who had taken up this position only in April, replacing

Christopher Addison, who had attempted a house-building programme that appeared radical but quickly lost momentum, and which the government unceremoniously dumped when slump set in. Kenneth Morgan argues that Mond replacing Addison was the symbol of the coalition government's new course for 1921, as it became 'determined that financial considerations alone should be the yardstick for dictating the pace and scope of its social programme.'[267] Mond was a powerful industrialist and a member of many clubs popular with upper-class gents,[268] a 'rather flamboyant specimen of a certain class of very rich men',[269] and 'the very epitome of the capitalist in politics'.[270] He advocated conciliation between capital and labour, perhaps one of the earliest champions of 'partnership', but was 'Blunt, direct, sometimes rather blustering, and occasionally distinctly ill-mannered.'[271]

The LCC representatives had finally realised that the Poplar councillors were serious about their defiance and were prepared to go to prison. Legal action was going ahead, but it would not get them their money. They were also worried that other councils may soon follow Poplar's lead. They asked Mond to put a Bill quickly through Parliament enabling him to appoint a commissioner to collect their rates. But the Home Affairs Committee declined on the grounds that it would be 'impossible' to do so and 'that such a Bill would in any case be treated as controversial and would provide an occasion for discussion of such questions as the equalisation of London rates &c.'[272] The government was showing its fear not just of the rebel councillors, but of even discussing the issue of the unfair rating system.

On 28 July, the day before the councillors were due to appear in court, Municipal Alliance councillor Cowl proposed that the council obey the Court's mandamus because it had no hope of winning in court nor of persuading the government to change the law through illegal action. His colleague Alderman Knightbridge seconded, arguing that although he had voted for the action at the outset, the council should now accept that it had made its protest and had been beaten. Once again, the opponents of Poplar's action had not doubted the justice of the cause for which the council fought. Cowl, Knightbridge and the two who voted with them – Cohen and Kitcat – had argued for surrender and done enough to save their own skins in court the next day.

George Lansbury found time before the court hearing to write a tribute to his comrades:

> Nobody who has served in public life so many years as I have could but feel proud of the splendid band of men and women councillors who in face of all the threats of Courts and Judges, decided once more to burn their boats and tell the Court in plain unmistakable terms that, so far as

they were concerned, the poor of Poplar should not be forced to pay. The Courts may send us to prison, but this will not get the money, for whether our period of detention be short or long we shall not give way. Here and there a comrade may for one reason or another, fail us, but the mass is as solid as a rock.[273]

By this time, the councillors were feeling the pressure. Edgar Lansbury later recalled, 'Over every meeting of the finance committee hung, like a sword of Damocles[274], the threat of bankruptcy. Heavy rates, deficits, bank overdrafts and the increasing demands made upon the borough funds by the guardians by reason of the ever-increasing unemployment and destitution in the locality caused the councillors sleepless nights and nightmare days.'[275] Robert McKee, author of the scriptwriting manual, 'Story', advises drama writers to put their main character in a dilemma. 'True character', he says, 'is revealed in the choices a human being makes under pressure – the greater the pressure, the deeper the revelation, the truer the choice to the character's essential nature.'[276] It is good advice for creators of fictional characters, and also true of real-life individuals and political movements. Facing the pressure of looming imprisonment, the dilemma of whether to fight or surrender, the Poplar councillors chose to fight. They revealed their true characters as brave and principled human beings, and also the character of their movement as one that would stand up for its class no matter how obstinate and repressive its opponents.

As the councillors prepared for prison, they also prepared to sustain their campaign outside the prison walls, forming a committee to organise publicity and agitation if and when they were jailed, to include 'Very striking posters and leaflets'[277]. On the morning of their court appearance, 29 July, the councillors assembled outside Poplar Town Hall. George Lansbury told the crowd of supporters: 'If we have to choose between contempt of the poor and contempt of court, it will be contempt of court.'[278] Two thousand people, including 3-400 dock trade unionists carrying banners, marched with their councillors the five miles from Poplar to the Court. Mayor Sam March having gone ahead to the court, Charlie Sumner led the procession, wearing the official chain of office and accompanied by the council's mace-bearer. Having shunned the use of such paraphernalia in the council chamber, the councillors now paraded them as symbols not of pomp and high office but of a council that had taken to the streets. Leading the march was a band and a banner, carrying the words: 'Poplar Borough Council marching to the High Court and possibly to prison to secure equalisation of rates for poor boroughs.' Other banners read 'Let Justice Prevail Though The Heavens Fall' and 'Westminster gets £29,000 for a penny rate; Poplar gets but £3,200'.[279]

The council marches in solemn procession to obey the summons of the High Court.

Photographs show that nearly all the marchers were men. Some of Richman's 1974 female interviewees told him that their husbands would not let them march. Even at a point of such great mobilisation, in a campaign where women were playing a crucial role from grass-roots through to leadership level, the labour movement was allowing sexism to limit its strength.

In the largest courtroom in the building, 'crowded to suffocation'[280], the opposition councillors got the writs against themselves dismissed by promising to levy the precepts. Of the five, only Kitcat expressed sympathy with the cause for which Labour was fighting. But history does not remember those who saved their own skins as fondly as those who were prepared to make personal sacrifice for worthy ends, and the Labour councillors took the stand, refused to concede or grovel, and argued their case. The *Daily Herald* reported that,

This was no case of professional oratory by barristers or stage theatrics but the impassioned pleadings of men and women whose liberty was at stake for the remedy of the intolerable conditions under which the persons whom they represent are forced to exist. In simple language councillor after councillor, some of them unemployed, some ex-Service men, told of the terrible conditions prevailing in Poplar and explained why it was impossible to pay the precepts.[281]

One councillor invited the Lord Chief Justice to spend a week on the Poplar docks, where he would witness how 'men scrambled for work like dogs after bones.' Mayor March explained that the council had taken its action 'as an emphatic protest against burdens put upon the poor people of Poplar by the government'. George Lansbury argued that 'Unemployed, like animals, became dangerous if not fed, and for 15 months they [the council] had done nothing less than struggle to keep the peace'.[282] Apart from Lansbury, the councillors, in the words of the Master of the Rolls, 'directed their attention almost entirely, not to the legal point at all, but to justifying to the court, or to the public, the motives and the reasons for their actions.'[283]

As they expected, the Court ruled against Poplar, serving writs on the councillors that gave them 14 days to pay up or go to prison. The Lord Chief Justice was 'impressed by the earnestness and honesty of the men who have addressed us' – perhaps he had forgotten that Susan Lawrence had spoken! – 'but the council were misdirected in the action they took. They are looking through a microscope at the suffering around them. The resolution they have adopted is pure anarchism, and persistency in it will lead London into a helpless state.'[284]

George Lansbury asked what class of imprisonment the councillors faced. This may have been a defiant display of their readiness for jail, or perhaps concern for their well-being fuelled by his own previous experience of prison.

The *Herald* declared that, 'This case will become historic, and will be followed by a very great upheaval in East London. Other borough councils will find it difficult not to follow Poplar's example.' But no other council had yet followed Poplar.

THE SCENT OF VICTORY

Poplar's councillors remained committed to their direct action. They could have chosen to back down, obey the law and know that they had gone further than anyone else in fighting for a just rating system. But where would that leave them? If they disarmed their big cannon, the only weapon left in their arsenal would be representations to decision-makers. As George Lansbury wrote, 'The people of Poplar for many years have starved and suffered; those in work have been forced to keep those out of work. Over and over again they have sent deputations to King and Queen, Ministers of the Crown, and the LCC. Nothing, absolutely nothing, has been done.' They accepted without shame that they had become law-breakers. George wrote, 'So far as we are concerned, the question is, not whether what we are doing is legal or illegal, but whether it is right or wrong.'[285]

On Saturday 30 July, the Metropolitan Asylum Board's meeting was livelier than usual. In solidarity with Poplar, Reverend A.G. Prichard proposed that the MAB reduce the precept assessed on several parishes by the amount due to be levied on Poplar[286]. MAB Chairman Canon Sprankling ruled this 'absolutely out of order'. So Prichard spoke against the Board's recommended levy, arguing that, 'the Board should express their sympathy with the terrible position in which Poplar is placed by rendering a public service.'[287] Prichard lost and the MAB maintained its legal action against Poplar council.

The councillors' robustness had the government shaking. On 2 August, Sir Alfred Mond announced that he was ending the wartime 'stereotyping' of the Metropolitan Common Poor Fund (MCPF) payments, benefiting Poplar and other poor London boroughs. No-one doubted that Poplar council's stand had won this concession. The Clerk to the Whitechapel guardians told his Board that, 'in all probability the extreme action of the Poplar Borough Council was responsible for the readjustment'[288]. According to one local newspaper, the LCC had called for this measure 'Again and again' but had received no answer. 'Now, under the pressure of Poplar's refusal to pay, the Ministry of Health suddenly climbs down, and last Friday agreed to re-adjust the fund. It is little things of this kind which make one so tired of Whitehall ways.'[289]

Mond's move saved Poplar 10d (4p) on the rates. The Minister thought this enough to placate the council and announced in the House, 'This will afford substantial relief to the poorer boroughs, including Poplar ... I trust that the Poplar Borough Council having made its protest, will obey the Order of the Court.' He trusted wrongly. Poplar's councillors had come too far, the stakes had risen too high, for it to give up for the unprincely sum of ten pence. Mond's readjustment had given them not satisfaction but a taste of how much more they might win if they kept up their fight.

Most importantly, 10d (4p) was simply not enough to address the plight of Poplar's poor, an example of which was described in the *Daily News* that same day. The Stokes family lived at 42 Woolmore Street, their home a 'wretched' single room with one small window, torn wallpaper, almost no furniture and 'utterly devoid of any comforts'. Mr and Mrs Stokes shared their one bed with their four children, had to make a paper fire to heat water, and were both ill through lack of food and poor living conditions. 'Yet Mr Stokes is one of the heroes. He served in the Royal Fusiliers, and was honourably discharged. His home is not fit for a dog – much less for a hero.' Solidarity with the Stokes family, anger with the ruling class which exploited and then discarded them, determination to raise working-class life out of squalor and offer the vision of a different, class-free system, and 100 per cent belief in the justice of their cause – these things gave the councillors a passion for their battle that no crumb from the table of the rich would satisfy.

On 4 August, for the third successive quarter, the council set a rate which excluded the precepts for the cross-London bodies. The rate was now even lower: 4s 4d (22p). The council had taken Mond's concession and turned it back against the authorities by using it to cut the local rate yet further! This new rate was for the quarter 30 September to 30 December, so the council would not ordinarily have set it at the start of August. It did so because two-thirds of its members might soon be in prison, and the councillors were not going to let imprisonment get in the way of their fight!

That same day the Appeal Court had rejected the council's final appeal but extended the 14-day deadline to one month, not wanting the councillors to go to prison without time for due reflection. Once again, the authorities failed to grasp the political commitment of Poplar's socialist councillors and hoped in vain that they would change their minds. And once again, the court had proved which class it served. Lord Justice Younger felt that the councillors had 'magnified their subordinate office, and in a sphere in which it is their duty to obey they have arrogated to themselves the right to rule'[290]. The court, apparently, must remind these upstart socialist councillors of their place.

George Lansbury wrote that, 'It is well that organised labour should understand that in the Courts of law all the scales are weighted against us because all the judges administer class-made laws, laws which are expressly enacted, not to do justice but to preserve the present social order.'[291] The councillors were leading the working class through a learning process. Pamphlets, newspapers, study classes and speeches are crucial to socialist education, but there is no steeper or more effective learning curve than direct participation in class struggle.

The Appeal did, however, reverse an earlier award of legal costs against the council. The councillors welcomed this at their meeting that evening, not just because of the financial saving but also because it proved wrong the Municipal Alliance and other fainthearts who had said that the council's defiance would land it in deeper debt due to legal costs.

There were even such fainthearts in the Labour Party's own ranks – indeed, in its leadership.

THE TWO SOULS OF SOCIALISM

Poplar's labour movement continued to mobilise support. The *Daily Herald* reported every development and day after day made Poplar's case to its readers nationwide. Poplar Trades Council sent a circular to other London trades councils asking them to pressure their local Labour councillors 'to support the action of Poplar by all means in their power'. But London Labour Party Secretary Herbert Morrison was drafting a circular saying the opposite.[292] He wanted London Labour to write to all Party branches and trades councils, giving a detailed repudiation of Poplar's action, itemised in seven points.

Firstly, he wrote that the way to achieve rates equalisation was to educate people to vote Labour. However, people in Poplar and across London had voted Labour in 1919, only to see their chosen representatives hemmed in by structural discrimination against working-class areas. If Morrison meant that the only solution was to elect a Labour government, then he was asking a starving borough to wait for something that had never yet happened.

His second argument was that the rates that Poplar was withholding were those that were already pooled, so their action made no sense. Later, he explained: 'the real people we were after were in the government, rather than the LCC, which, in running services for the whole county, was following a policy of equalizing rates, quite apart from its modest equalization fund.'[293] But the funding system meant that a borough council could take direct action against the LCC more effectively than against central government - both of which, with their Conservative majorities and Liberal supporters, were run by the same political parties. Mond's concession showed that Poplar's action was putting pressure on the government.

Thirdly, Morrison feared that Poplar's action would encourage a future aggrieved Tory council to take similar action against a Labour LCC or government. George Lansbury's counter was that, 'If we do anything so unjust to others as the present rating arrangements are to us, I hope there will be a revolt'.[294]

The fourth point in Morrison's draft circular was that Labour had nothing to gain by creating chaos. His words echoed the judges', concerned to preserve the status quo and overlooking that underfunding had already created chaos for Poplar's people and council. The council's action had brought relief to its overburdened ratepayers, and had brought hope and confidence to its community.

The Appeal Court was disproving Morrison's fifth argument on exactly the day that he presented his draft to a London Labour Party meeting. The ratepayers, he said, would have to pay in the end through legal costs.

Point six was that having accepted office, Labour had accepted responsibility for administering local services. This seems somewhat unfair, given Poplar council's dramatic improvements in local services. The councillors' action showed a deep sense of responsibility towards services, as without it the council's services would be doomed. Moreover, Poplar's administration was continuing to provide services even whilst fighting its battles. The guardians engaged in near-daily correspondence with the Ministry of Health about its provision of relief to Poplar's needy.[295]

Finally, Morrison argued that Poplar's tactic would help those who wanted to strip power from local government. However, one of Poplar's key demands was that poor relief should be paid for centrally rather than locally. Funding the guardians was a power – or a burden – they were willing to have stripped from them! For Poplar, the notion of local government power was hollow if they did not have the power to carry out their policies or even lift their people out of destitution. Nevertheless, Morrison's fear of ruling-class reprisals had some substance. Anyone who stands up to a bully runs the risk that the bully might hit them back harder. But if they refuse to take that risk, they accept being bullied forever.

Herbert Morrison was also annoyed with Poplar council for not consulting the London Labour Party before deciding to withhold the precepts. Had Poplar done so, it may have persuaded other councils to take similar action. But perhaps more likely, other Labour councils with more moderate politics and without the depth of Poplar's poverty crisis may have blocked its rebellion.

The divide between Poplar and Hackney, between Lansbury and Morrison, ran deeper than irritation at a lack of consultation, or Morrison's list of seven objections. Their views of socialism were at opposite ends of the spectrum.[296] Poplar councillor Charles Key had said, 'We have come to make a change', George Lansbury said that 'Labour councillors must be different'. In contrast, Herbert Morrison contended that, 'the ultimate justification for Labour policy is not that it is *different* but that it is *sound* in the interests of the people'.[297]

Morrison believed that Labour councils must prove themselves efficient, acting responsibly and lawfully. His favoured attack on the Conservatives and Liberals was to accuse them of 'muddle' rather than indicting them for serving the rich at the brutal expense of the working class. Labour leaders do similar today, jousting with other parties about their 'ill-conceived' or 'poorly-thought-out' policies, avoiding fundamental political clashes and implying that capitalism would be fine if only a more competent hand steered it. Edgar Lansbury remarked that his father 'hears daily many a story direct from the victims of economy and efficiency'.[298]

Morrison made a different choice to that made by Poplar. He obeyed the law and lobbied unsuccessfully for fairer rates. When high unemployment hit Hackney, Mayor Morrison appealed for public donations to help the unemployed, and booked a room in the Town Hall to hold a whist drive to raise funds.[299] He would beg the public, beg the government, but not take action. He would ask the poor to help each other rather than confront the authorities, redistributing poverty rather than wealth.

On 4 August, Herbert Morrison presented his draft to a meeting of the London Labour Party Executive and London Labour Mayors.[300] Sam March was present as Poplar's Mayor, Susan Lawrence and John Scurr as members of the London Labour Party Executive, and George Lansbury by special invitation. The majority at the meeting agreed with Herbert Morrison or, even if they sympathised with Poplar council, did not want to get involved in that sort of thing themselves. However, Poplar's representatives persuaded them that circulating such a detailed and damning document could expose Labour's divisions to their political opponents. So the meeting decided not to communicate with the press, and agreed to send out a brief private circular advising councils not to follow Poplar's lead. [301]

The circular's lack of support for Poplar met an 'indignant' response in some areas,[302] and may have spurred Poplar's sympathisers in other boroughs to take a firmer stand. They would meet the following month to counter Morrison and the official London Labour line of leaving Poplar isolated.

SAVE THEIR SKINS?

The *East London Advertiser* implored the councillors to 'save their skins by levying the rate' and urged the government to find an alternative agency for collecting the precepts.[303] Despite having some legal power to collect the precepts 'over the heads' of the council, in particular the 1829 Police Act, the government chose not to, fearing the scale of likely resistance. The *East London Observer* urged the government to empower itself to create a substitute authority for the disobedient council. Such a power had existed previously,[304] but had lapsed.[305] The *Observer* could only assume that this was 'by some oversight', as at that time 'such an idea as a local authority in revolt never entered the unimaginative mind of the Legislature. In those days we were all well behaved and orderly'.[306] 'Those days' were the days in which many working-class people did not have a vote, before the great 'cycle of revolt'. The days before Poplarism.

The councillors were not going to levy the precepts short of victory and the government could not find a way out. The newspaper observed that:

> It really is a most remarkable circumstance that in modern conditions of politics and administration, authority can never be got to do anything, or to make the slightest step towards reform, until aggrieved parties have made themselves a perfect nuisance, and indulged in all sorts of threatenings. The Government has really got to be intimidated.

The government made one more concession, setting up a Royal Commission to look at local government in Greater London. It was another of those demands that the government had previously ignored for years. 'Only fine promises were received', noted one local newspaper,[307] 'but now that Poplar has taken the law into its own hands the Royal Commission is reluctantly granted.' But the promise of a Royal Commission does not put food on the tables of the poor, and its outcome was not guaranteed. The best way to get a result from the Commission was to keep up the fight.

Everyone now knew that the thirty Poplar councillors would go to prison. The Cabinet decided to let them go right ahead, after Sir Alfred Mond gave his view that the councillors 'were quite determined to be martyrs … it was known to be the policy of Mr. Lansbury to make administration of the borough impossible in order to secure complete equalisation of London rates'. The question now was 'whether any effort should be made to prevent the members of the council from going to prison … on the whole it seemed desirable to let matters take their course'.[308] Maybe Mond was banking on the councillors changing their minds at the last minute. Or perhaps he thought that a spell inside would make them see sense, since they would be released not after a fixed term but only when they agreed to collect the precepts. Maybe he thought they should go to jail and stay there and the whole problem would go away. Or perhaps he just did not know what else to do. Because Poplar council had stood its ground, its opponents were floundering. The LCC and other bodies were no closer to getting their money. The Metropolitan Police had written to the council asking if they intended to pay their precept. The council replied no – we have not collected it, so we cannot pay it.[309]

The two local MPs, Yeo and Blair, challenged Mond in parliament, incredulous that the minister seemed neither willing nor able to act. The government had considered methods to collect the monies, but as Ministry of Health official Sir Aubrey Symonds put it, 'The inhabitants of Poplar, even the more prosperous classes, were inclined to sympathise with the borough council, and resistance was therefore not unlikely'.[310] The government had a legal mechanism to collect the police rate, but chose not to use it for fear of the protest it would provoke, deciding 'that no endeavour be made to raise the amount due by the appointment of occasional overseers'.[311] That protest would have come from a well-organised labour movement that involved the working-class population, took its decisions collectively and democratically, and continually publicised the issues and arguments, thus rendering the legal powers against them ineffective.

On 17 August, Symonds issued a statement on Mond's behalf, explaining why he would take no further action. He had already met some of Poplar's demands. He could not award the grant for the public works scheme because Poplar council had chosen not to prioritise ex-servicemen. Any further equalisation of rates would require legislation, which the Royal Commission was considering. Poplar's heavy rates were caused by its own 'extravagances', primarily outdoor relief, which the ministry apparently saw as a consequence of extreme generosity rather than extreme poverty.

It was a long, hot summer, horribly uncomfortable in the overcrowded East End, and accompanied by a drought which drove up the price of milk. The Poplar councillors' liberty would last only until the end of August, and they spent that time not 'reflecting' as the appeal court wished them to, but building their campaign. The council wrote to all ratepayers explaining the situation, and held twelve public meetings between 22 and 31 August. 'Ye Old English Fayre' in the East India Dock Road recreation ground raised £334 towards the legal fund.[312] On Sunday 28 August, 4,000 supporters marched from Poplar to Tower Hill, where contingents from Stepney, Bethnal Green, Shoreditch and elsewhere met them.[313] Their banner read 'Poplar Borough Councillors are still determined to go to prison to secure equalisation of rates for the poor Boroughs'. George

Demonstration on Tower Hill in support of the council's action.
Sitting: Cr. B. Fleming, Cr. Mrs. J. Mackay, Ald. Susan Lawrence. Standing: Cr. C.J. Kelly, the Mayor Cr. S. March

Lansbury urged the crowd to step up the campaign by paying 'No rent, no rates, no taxes until the fight is won'.

The *Daily Herald* commissioned an oil painting of Lansbury, 'as a sort of riposte to our anti-Bolshevik friends who think he ought to be boiled in oils!'[314] The painter John Flanaghan said of George, 'there is no getting away from the fact that he possesses extraordinary force of character and, what is rather rare these days, intense sincerity. This and his obvious idealism make him a unique personality, as interesting to the painter as to the politician.'

On Wednesday 31 August, the council met for the last time before prison, 'to wild applause from the multitude outside'.[315] Press reporters and photographers packed into the town hall, in contrast to their lack of attention to Poplar's sufferings when the councillors were behaving themselves! The meeting lasted just half an hour, consisting entirely of arrangements to keep the borough functioning. The council granted leave of absence to those thirty of its members who were going to prison. It reconstituted its committees with those who were not to be jailed, and appointed Charles Key to act as mayor. It passed a resolution to stop council workers' wages falling for the next four months. It was all very formal and proper for a council accused of anarchism and chaos!

The meeting ended with the singing of The Red Flag, with councillors and supporters bringing particular passion to the lines, 'Come dungeon dark or gallows grim, This song shall be our parting hymn'. Outside the town hall, 6,000 people waited in support, packing alleyways and standing on window sills, from where they heard speeches from Sam March, John Scurr, James Rugless and George Lansbury. Scurr explained how Poplar's choices had forced the government's. [316] 'The Government is on the horns of a dilemma. If they send us to prison they will not get their money; and if they do not send us to prison, they will bring the law into contempt. Poplar does not care on which horn they choose to impale themselves.'[317]

3. IN AND OUT OF PRISON

ARREST

Arrests began on 1 September. The *Daily Herald*'s headline that day was "Over The Top' for the Workless', stirring working-class people to fight for those betrayed by the government that had sent them to a bloody war in the trenches. The *Herald* would give its prime front-page slot to the councillors for the next seven issues.

Thousands of local people were willing to physically prevent the arrests, but that was not part of the councillors' strategy. Minnie Lansbury wrote to *The Times*, explaining that they had no wish to be martyrs but, had they so desired, 'nothing short of a machine gun detachment' could have got them to prison.[318] So the thousands gathered at the councillors' homes to show their support. Minnie's sister-in-law Annie Lansbury recalled that after the initial arrests, 'As the news spread round the borough, crowds poured into the streets. The people themselves posted guards at the houses of the 27 other [non-Lansbury] Councillors threatened with arrest, and announced that they would permit no arrests after dusk.'[319]

Unemployed ex-servicemen thronged to Minnie's house, appreciative of her work as chair of the War Pensions Committee. The house, 6 Wellington Road in Bow, was, according to fellow councillor Thomas Blacketer, 'the well-known centre of her great public activities ... To the many poor people of this wide East End district, No.6 was a House of Hope ... They knew they were always sure of sympathy and assistance in their troubles from Minnie Lansbury, and no needy one was ever turned empty away.'[320]

Poplar council issued a statement:

> Thirty of us, members of the Poplar Borough Council, have been committed to prison. This has been done because we have refused to levy a rate on the people of our Borough to meet the demand of the L.C.C. and other central authorities. We have taken this action deliberately, and we shall continue to take the same course until the Government deals properly with the question of unemployment, providing work or a full maintenance for all,

and carries into effect the long-promised and much overdue reform of the
equalisation of rates.[321]

Even at this late hour, the councillors could have backed down and agreed to
levy the precepts. They could have been satisfied that they had made their point,
won a small concession already and could always ask for more. But no. They
had come this far and, as councillor Joe O'Callaghan told the crowd outside his
house: 'We will never give in. If they keep us for twelve months and a day, when
that time expires I am willing to go back for another such term.'[322] In the 21st
century, politicians frequently talk of 'tough choices', but few are as genuinely
tough, and courageous, as those of the Poplar councillors.

The arrests began with the sheriff's cars pulling up at Poplar's Labour Hall
and driving away with George Cressall amid cheering crowds. The cars then
proceeded to Mayor Sam March's house, where the family had just finished
dinner and was listening to Sam's sister-in-law singing. The sheriff's officers
let her finish her song and the Mayor pack his attaché case before taking him
away. The next stop was Josiah Russell's house, then on to arrest James Jones,
who was busy with 'a little carpentering job. He put his tools down and joined
the prisoners.'[323]

Having next picked up Chris Williams and Ben Fleming, the cars went to
John Scurr's house, but he had become bored of waiting and had gone for a
walk, so unintentionally avoided arrest for another day. Dave Adams was also
'not at home' when the cars called for him at the Dockers' Hall, where they
were greeted instead by a huge crowd which applauded the councillors in the
cars.[324] The *Herald* reported that, 'Cheered by crowds of patriotic ratepayers,
the councillors accepted complacently the law's reward for their championship
of the poor and the unemployed, confident of the ultimate triumph of their
cause'.[325]

On 2 September, the sheriff's officer arrived at the Scurrs' house again, greeted
by crowds who had been there all night. As the officer went to the house to
arrest John Scurr, Joe O'Callaghan, arrested earlier, emerged from the car to tell
the throng that he was not going to Brixton because he wanted to but because
he had made a promise and intended to keep it. 'I do not care if I hang', he
said.[326]

Scurr urged the crowd to remain calm and not to riot, but Susan Lawrence did
not want them to remain too calm: 'Let their fervour', she said, 'be maintained
while their representatives were still expressing their contempt of the law within
prison walls.'[327] Six male councillors went to Brixton prison that day and on
Saturday 3 September another five joined them. One was George Lansbury, who
had phoned the sheriff and made an appointment for his arrest. He and Edgar

Alderman Hopwood surrounded by his bodyguard.

Mobilization: Bodyguard of the people outside home of Alderman John
and Councillor Julia Scurr.

posed for a photograph in the garden while they waited for Dave Adams and Albert Baker to come to the house for the officer to arrest all four. The sheriff's officer chatted pleasantly with the councillors for ten minutes before arresting them, and the Lansbury family parrot laughed and interjected throughout the proceedings.[328]

It is little wonder that George Lansbury thought the whole affair 'a screamingly funny farce', adding that 'If only we could put it on the 'movies' all the world would be laughing.'[329] Cinema newscaster Topical Budget broadcast a short bulletin, 'Farcical 'Revolution' which may be Serious if it Spreads'.[330]

Several of the councillors had young families. James Rugless had a newborn son. A group of the councillors' children went to stay at the holiday home of the Fellowship of Reconciliation[331] in Kent; relatives or supporters cared for others. Charlie Sumner's son stayed with solicitor Thompson's family.[332] Everyone had to make arrangements for rent to be paid, work to be taken care of. The Poplar councillors' determination to pursue their fight despite family hardships contrasts with decisions taken by other councillors in similar situations since then.[333]

Crowds waiting at Newby Place for the arrival of the women councillors.

The crowd listening to Mrs. Cressall.

Women councillors speaking from the balcony of the town hall.

Councillor Mrs. Julia Scurr advocates 'no surrender'.

Alderman Mrs. Minnie Lansbury.

Preparing to depart. Mrs. M. Lansbury (at window), Mrs. MacKay,
Miss Susan Lawrence, Mrs. Cressall.

On 5 September, the five women councillors were to gather at Poplar town hall for their arrest. But a last-minute change of plan saw Jennie Mackay arrested at home and Julia Scurr and Nellie Cressall at the Scurrs' house. The car made its way to the town hall accompanied by a huge crowd headed by a band and local trade union branch banners. So many supporters packed the streets that those who could get into Poplar town hall were for a time unable to get out. One well-wisher gave Minnie Lansbury a bouquet of roses, and all five women spoke to the massive crowd from the town hall balcony. Susan Lawrence told them, 'We are in one of the biggest struggles this country has ever seen ... Poplar has aroused the whole country, and Poplar is going to lead to victory.'[334] Some in the crowd suggested that they physically prevent the women being taken, but Susan, who had returned from the annual Trades Union Congress early to go to prison with her comrades and sisters, insisted, 'we want to go ... I am going even if I have to walk all the way to Holloway'.[335]

Poplar council's enemies knew that the councillors had the upper hand in their battle, despite – or perhaps because of – their imprisonment. The Municipal Alliance raged at the displays of pride and support, complaining to the Home Secretary that,

For the past six days the Borough has been in a condition of ferment and upheaval and why those in charge of the Sheriff's Department could not in the exercise of their duties have arrested these persons if not in one body at least on one day passes our comprehension. The course pursued has been one to give a cheap advertisement and notoriety to those responsible for the present condition of affairs, with the consequent result that the passions of their followers have been inflamed and aggravated; and a feeling of much disgust occasioned in the minds of those entirely opposed to their unconstitutional procedure.[336]

The 'passions' and 'advertisement' continued on that September Monday, when after tea, bouquets and waving from the balcony, the Sheriff arrested the women councillors and took them for a meal in a restaurant en route to Holloway Prison, knowing that prison food would not be good. They proceeded slowly along the East India Dock Road in a motorcar, which allowed the biggest demonstration of the campaign so far – up to 15,000 supporters[337] – to follow them along Poplar's most important highway, complete with Irish band and a sardine tin on a pole instead of the mace.

The next day, six more men were arrested. The sheriff's officer called on councillors Green and Oakes at 6 a.m. Both were in bed and at their request, he returned to arrest them after breakfast at 9 a.m. Walter Green had three young children and his wife had recently died. When he was arrested, his children repeatedly asked when he would return.[338] When councillor Albert Farr got home from his day's work as a postman at 5 p.m. on 6 September, he found the sheriff's officer having a cup of tea with his wife and friends. The officer took him away in a car on the front of which were attached two *Daily Herald* boards.[339] Huw Richards argues that Poplar's rates rebellion 'was a quintessential *Herald* story, with Labour people carrying their struggle for justice against uncaring and overbearing authority to dramatic and self-sacrificing lengths. The paper's coverage of Poplar epitomised its priorities and outlook.'[340]

The last councillor arrested was Charlie Sumner on 8 September,[341] who had been away at the annual Trades Union Congress, accompanied by Susan Lawrence for a short time and by free councillors Wooster and Blacketer. The councillors sent 1,000 copies of their circular letter for Congress delegates.

TRADES UNION CONGRESS 1921

The unemployment crisis dominated the Congress, meeting in Cardiff. President E.L. Poulton described its effect in human terms:

One of the saddest things to me is to see a man or woman in full physical health and strength, with mental abilities fully alive, finding himself or herself suddenly deprived of employment ... The first few days, or even weeks, they will carry themselves as erect as when they had a regular income. In the course, however, of a few weeks those who have eyes to see begin to see in that man or woman a gradual deterioration. Instead of carrying themselves erect, you begin to see them drooping. You begin to see less lustre in their eyes. Their feet begin to shuffle along rather than to get along briskly. See that man or woman in another week. He is not then slightly drooping, but his eyes have lost practically all their lustre. His body is bent, and he is shuffling along the streets trying to avoid his former workmates, although he himself has done nothing whereof he need to be ashamed.[342]

On the first day, Monday 5 September, the Trades Union Congress listened to a deputation of the unemployed, including J.W. Holt, Chair of the National Council of the Unemployed, and Clydeside socialist John McLean. Holt pointed out that 'it is not much good passing pious resolutions … It is the business of the Trades Union Congress to do something.' McLean was the first Congress speaker to mention Poplar, praising the imprisoned councillors and setting the stage for the following day's debate on 'Unemployment and the Poplar Situation'.

In that debate, speaker after speaker praised Poplar's actions. Ben Tillett pointed out that 'there is one law and one privilege for the rich and one law and no privilege for the poor'. Waterman's Society delegate Harry Gosling said, 'I believe you cannot get anything done unless you rebel, otherwise they do not believe you are in earnest … in other words, if you want to amend the law it almost seems as if you must break it'. Jack Jones, MP for Silvertown: 'We have exhausted the possibilities of constitutionalism … Where do we find ourselves? The law leaves us in the lurch and tells us that the poor must keep the poor. We must feed the dog from its own tail!' The only criticism was from George Barker MP, who complained that Poplar was getting too much attention, and referring to the many unemployed, argued that, 'the condition of these people is very much worse than the position of those people that have been honoured by being able to go to Poplar prison'.

Congress unanimously passed a resolution that included their opinion that: 'the Poplar councillors in the stand which they believed to be the best to take under exceptional circumstances to call public attention to the distressful conditions of the unemployed, have rendered a real national service.' Whilst supportive, this resolution is careful to state that it was the Poplar councillors' belief – not the TUC's – that theirs was the best course of action, and that their circumstances were 'exceptional' rather than representative of a nationwide crisis. J.H. Hayes of the Police and Prison Officers' Union criticised the resolution for failing to demand the immediate release of the Poplar prisoners.

The TUC parliamentary committee met with Poplar council representatives and London Labour Party officers at the Congress. Herbert Morrison reported that, 'the Parliamentary Committee was very anxious that it should in no way appear that they were suggesting that other Boroughs should take action similar to that taken by Poplar, or that they were in any way censuring the other Labour Boroughs for not adopting the Poplar policy'.[343]

Poulton described the effect of unemployment as 'driving on the one hand many to despair, others to apathy and a fatal submission, that the circumstances are above and beyond alteration; to this attitude and frame of mind we must resolutely set ourselves against, and by vigour of attack and assault upon conditions that produce such deplorable results bring about their abolition'. In Poplar, despair, apathy, and fatal submission had not taken hold, because of the vigour of the campaign spearheaded by the councillors who were now behind bars.

A COUNCIL BEHIND BARS

The gates closed behind Poplar's prisoners of conscience, now dubbed the 'Fighting Thirty',[344] the party atmosphere of the arrests fell away, and incarceration began. Before the First World War, people imprisoned for contempt were automatically given 'first division' status, placing them under a less tyrannical regime. But in 1914 parliament had changed the law.[345] Whilst most still received this rating – including a group of Sinn Fein men in Brixton – some did not. Poplar's prisoners were placed in the second division. The Home Office argued that the law stipulates that those imprisoned for contempt were treated as debtors, but the *Daily Herald* quoted three standard law books that they should be in the first division.[346]

Wives visited imprisoned husbands before some of them were themselves imprisoned. Julia Scurr reported that, 'Food unfit for any human being is offered to the councillors ... Fish was given on Friday, they told us, that was uneatable; in fact, it was in an advanced state of decomposition.'[347] Minnie Lansbury, after visiting her husband and father-in-law in Brixton prison before her own arrest, accused the prison authorities of mistreating them out of 'political spite'.[348] No-one knew then that Minnie would pay a higher price for the prison conditions than any of the other councillors.

The Poplar inmates spent most of their time locked in dark, airless cells; were fed stale bread and lumps of fat masquerading as 'food'; served 'vile pestilential stuff called tea' and 'fresh vegetables [that] baffle description';[349] and had a chamberpot for a toilet which they had to 'slop out'. All the councillors lost weight; some became seriously sick and were in the hospital wing within days.

They were allowed only one letter in or out and two 15-minute visits per week. George Lansbury became ill one night, rang the bell, and saw the warder come and quickly go. He later recalled that, 'I rang again, the door opened and a man leaned across me and said he would smash my bloody head in if I did not stop it'. George shouted to alert his fellow inmates, prison officials attended, and the warder was punished.[350] George told his wife Bessie: 'What makes it possible for us is the thought that our hunger in gaol is saving people from being hungry outside.'[351] Free councillor Jack Wooster told a supporters' rally that Battersea Dogs' Home was a mansion compared to that 'hell-hole of Holloway'.[352]

But prison could not break the Poplar prisoners' spirits, and the solidarity and fighting spirit that had brought them to prison in the first place would now help them to improve the conditions of their stay. Minnie Lansbury even 'enlivened the occasion by sliding down the banisters to the horror of the wardresses'.[353] Alfred Partridge kept spirits high at Brixton, described by one of his fellow councillors as, 'a perfect treasure, [who] can always be relied upon in time of trouble to come up with a smiling face, and whose good temper, pluck, and determination are unfailing'.[354]

The councillors threatened a hunger strike to win better treatment. When the warders gave them orders, they asked to see their union cards. They reported sick every morning, demanding a full medical examination. They studied the prison regulations and demanded all they could: open doors, newspapers, footballs. At Brixton they even challenged the Sinn Feiners to a match.[355] And – just as they had with the rates – they simply refused. They refused to wear prison clothes or do prison work. Edgar Lansbury reports that they refused to walk in single file during exercise periods, and instead 'strolled about the exercise yards arguing and debating and causing great disaffection amongst the other prisoners'.[356] Looking back from 13 years later, writing in an affectionate and upbeat biography of his dad, Edgar stays silent about the appalling conditions in prison. It was not a holiday camp for recalcitrant councillors, but a genuinely gruelling experience made less unpleasant by the power of solidarity and by their 'challenging humour and bravado'.[357]

Brixton prison's governor, instead of deciding on each of the prisoners' demands, insisted that the formal way to ask for changes was to petition the Home Office. So the councillors did so – repeatedly, both for the demands themselves, and as a deliberate strategy to bug the authorities. They petitioned[358] for: the women councillors to join them for meetings; extra visiting hours; food, recreation, tobacco and newspapers; and for a basket of apples sent by well-wishers to be given to the councillors.[359]

George Lansbury personally petitioned for: first division status; consultation with his own doctor; permission to buy his own food; and a daily visit by the

Herald's editorial staff.[360] The *Herald* contrasted the denial of this to Lansbury with the case of W.T. Stead, who was allowed to edit the *Pall Mall Gazette* from prison in 1885.[361] George wrote to Bessie, telling her his experiences and outlining his views on the prison system. The prison authorities stopped and confiscated the letter, refusing even to return it to George on his eventual release.[362] A prison official's notes summarised the letter's contents and justified its confiscation on the grounds that the Rules forbade allegations of unfair treatment and required complaints of prison conditions to be deleted. The official noted that,

> This letter is ... evidently intended for publication ... Mentions diet. Has not been well but is better ... Speaks of the prison system as a damnable one. Everything is as bad as it is possible to conceive. Torture to a sensitive mind and leads to utter complete moral depradation to those who have become inured. Officers have an impossible task as the abominable criminal system is the last word in refined cruelty ... The vilest and most blasphemous place is the chapel ... Diatribe about the travesty of religion in Prison.[363]

By 9 September, the *Daily Herald* was able to report improved conditions: better food, and the right to talk and associate freely. Within a week, George Lansbury had won the right to visits from *Herald* staff,[364] and although he would not be allowed to edit the paper from prison, he 'managed to get articles out' and ensure that 'my view on what was to appear in the paper day by day was always heard at the [*Daily Herald* editorial] conference'.[365]

The councillors even won the right to hold council meetings in prison. The first, on 11 September, is recorded as taking place in 'George Lansbury's cell no. 5, H.M. Prison Brixton'. However, the following day's meeting agreed 'that the Governor be informed that it is impossible for us to discuss matters collectively in one Cell, and asked if it would be practicable to arrange for us to have the room downstairs for about an hour from 5 p.m.'[366] The governor let them use the prison's board room. On September 23, Charles Key and other free councillors came to the meeting. From 27 September, the women councillors came from Holloway to join the meetings, confounding the authorities' earlier insistence that there was no way by which the imprisoned husbands and wives could visit each other. For neither the first nor the last time, rules became flexible under the pressure of resistance. Guests at other meetings included the town clerk, the TUC parliamentary committee and LCC Labour leader Harry Gosling.

A total of 32 borough council meetings were held within the walls of Brixton, their minutes later entered into the official records[367]. They are a fascinating insight into a Labour council continuing to fight for socialist politics in extreme circumstances, discussing their ongoing campaign, prison conditions, and the more mundane business of the borough, from surveys for paving works to rats on Ellerthorpe Street. During the early weeks of September, the free councillors had run council committees in the prisoners' stead, for example when councillors Easteal, Rawlings, Lyons, Hammond and Mrs March met as the baths and wash-houses committee and discussed requisitioning supplies, winter opening hours and other issues while their colleagues were in jail.[368] By the end of the month, councillors carried out their committee business from behind bars, and baths superintendent Mr Jefferson Hope attended Brixton prison to meet committee members.[369]

The ILP had marked 25 September as a day to commemorate James Kier Hardie, and the councillors did so, listening to a talk by John Scurr. A week later, Scurr and Edgar Lansbury gave a talk about 'William Morris, Artist and Socialist' and again, the councillors stood in silent tribute. While imprisoned, Scurr had secured selection as prospective Labour candidate for Mile End and Stepney constituency, earning him the 'hearty congratulations' of his fellow councillors.[370] The councillors had the borough's library service deliver books to them in prison. Voracious readers committed to self-education, some ordered dozens, ranging from studies on poverty to works on socialism, popular novels to classics by Thomas Hardy, Charles Dickens and others, *Quo Vadis* to *The Ragged Trousered Philanthropists*.[371] Susan Lawrence set about writing a pamphlet about taxation, and got permission to have books to assist her research.[372] George Lansbury later felt able to describe their treatment as that of 'a species of special visitors who did pretty nearly what we pleased'.[373]

Vincent suggests that the councillors campaigned only for their own comfort, seeing themselves as better than the common criminals in custody alongside them.[374] Indeed, George's daughter Daisy Lansbury complained that the councillors were 'being treated as common debtors – and this they are not'.[375] However, Daisy seems more concerned at the contrast between the Poplar prisoners' conditions and the 'very lenient treatment' of one Mr. Kiley, son of a wealthy MP, recently convicted of swindling, suggesting that 'there is one law for the rich and one for the poor'. And the *Daily Herald*'s outrage at the prisoners' treatment as 'common debtors'[376] is accompanied by a clear statement that 'The treatment of ordinary criminals in British gaols is, in any case, a scandal and an offence'.[377]

Other evidence also suggests that Vincent's criticism of the councillors may be unfair. When the councillors won some improvements in their conditions, other prisoners sent a deputation to the governor to ask for the same; the governor summoned George Lansbury to explain to them why they should not;

George attended as requested, but stated clearly that the other prisoners should have the same conditions![378]

On their eventual release, the councillors issued a statement including the words, 'In spite of the privileges granted us and taken by us, we are of the opinion that prison is hell. No one is bad enough to be treated as men and women are treated in these modern Bastilles.' Imprisonment intensified the councillors' commitment to – and ability to campaign for – prison reform. Alf Partridge told friends, 'When we come out of prison, we'll have something to say about the prison system. There are young boys in here who make your heart ache when you think of the little chance they'll have of leading a straight life after. From the point of view of propaganda it's excellent that we should be here.'[379]

Moreover, the councillors did not want a crusade for rates equalisation to become a crusade for their own comforts, and quickly made this clear. Harry Gosling told the Trades Union Congress on their behalf: 'Do not allow this thing to be camouflaged by what is being done to those in prison ... whilst we have to see that they get that treatment to which they are entitled, they do not want you to lose sight of the greater and more important principle involved.'[380] George Lansbury wrote that, 'All of us are anxious that the issue for which we are fighting should be kept clear and distinct. We do not desire that our treatment in prison should be allowed to fog the position'.[381] The *Daily Herald* affirmed that 'the councillors themselves are not "squealing", and are prepared to face anything rather than give way'.[382]

Vincent also attempts to reduce Poplar's rebellion to 'political theatre',[383] echoing the Webbs' view of it as 'a long-drawn-out administrative comedy'.[384] Indeed, George Lansbury's biographer John Shepherd compliments him on his 'political adroitness in stage-managing popular protest in the East End', pointing out that Lansbury had earlier illustrated this skill when arrested for pro-suffrage activities in 1913.[385] However, the undeniable fact that Poplar's campaign involved an element of 'theatre' does not mean that the campaign itself was merely theatre. As TUC President Poulton said in his Congress address:

Our friends at Poplar ... have ... exhausted all the means at their disposal, and not having been listened to by the Government, felt they were bound to take the action they have taken. Then what happens? ... All the newspapers give us all kinds of news about what is happening in Poplar, how this and that councillor is being followed around by record crowds. This is not being done from our standpoint and for theatrical display. The position is too serious for theatrical display. If Governments, however, will not listen to duly-elected representatives we feel bound to take some action.[386]

The Brixton prison authorities offered to transfer the Poplar prisoners to another cell block with better facilities. But they refused, as it would take them away from their outer cells and they would no longer be able to hear, or speak to, the crowds of supporters who gathered outside every day.

SUPPORT ON THE OUTSIDE

Edgar Lansbury recalled that:

> Enormous processions marched with bands and banners round the prison walls. Leather-lunged orators addressed the crowds from the upper windows of houses facing the prison. We could see them plainly over the prison wall, and they could see us peering between the bars of our cell windows. We all sang the Red Flag, the Internationale, and other socialist songs, shouted greetings to each other over the wall, and as a rule father would wind up the demonstrations with one of his rousing speeches which could be heard throughout the prison.[387]

The day after the women's imprisonment, 15,000 people assembled outside Holloway prison to cheer them. On 7 September, 5,000 men and women marched to Holloway in 'the most remarkable demonstration of loyalty to the cause of the suffering poor ever seen in the East End'.[388] North Lambeth Labour Party organised nightly demonstrations outside Brixton. Evening protests usually concluded with open-air meetings, with speakers, appeals and votes on resolutions of support.[389] These mass demonstrations contributed to building the momentum of the campaign; sustaining the prisoners' morale; keeping the issue in the public eye; and convincing the government that opposition to the unfair rating system would not simply go away as Mond had perhaps hoped. Herbert Morrison, by contrast, had become 'dissatisfied' with demonstrations as a tactic, because 'They won no votes and were valuable only as emotional outlets for the activists'.[390] Poplar's protests proved to have a wider value.

Audible support was particularly important to the women, fewer in number than the men, and two of whom – Minnie Lansbury and heavily-pregnant Nellie Cressall – were soon in the hospital wing. Holloway's regime was even more officious and restrictive than Brixton's.[391] Islington Labour Party and local NUR activists made sure that well-wishers besieged Holloway every evening, while Shenfield Training School's band performed special recitals. Poplar's board of guardians paid the band's expenses, provoking a legal row with District Auditor A.Q. Twiss which would last for the next two years and result in guardians A.A. Watts and Joe Hammond paying a surcharge.[392]

A group of eight well-known writers, including H.G. Wells, petitioned for the councillors' release and for better conditions meanwhile.[393] Even their longstanding local adversaries, Sir Alfred Warren and councillor Rev. Kitcat, urged the authorities to improve their conditions. Kitcat helped run the maintenance fund for the councillors' families, whose Treasurer was solicitor W.H.Thompson and which attracted donations from Women's Co-operative Guilds,[394] trade unions, Communist Party and ILP branches, and even from the Poplar Chamber of Commerce. MPs, union leaders, magistrates and bishops visited the prisoners. Each issue of the *Daily Herald* carried news of resolutions and messages of support from working-class bodies far and wide. Messages of support arrived from the Poplar Costermongers' and Street Traders' Association, the Boot and Shoe Operatives' Union, and many, many more. J.R.Clynes, leader of the Parliamentary Labour Party and a member of the TUC General Council, brought £25 and a message of support.[395] A large meeting in Woolwich, held to protest against unemployment, unanimously passed a resolution demanding the prisoners' release.[396] Support was even showing within the ranks of the Metropolitan Asylum Board, member Rev. Prichard unsuccessfully proposing that the board adjourn its meeting as one of its members, Charlie Sumner, was in prison.[397]

Sunday 4 September had seen the first public meeting in support of the councillors since arrests began. The venue, Bromley town hall, burst its capacity nearly an hour before the scheduled start, and an overflow meeting was hastily arranged.[398] On Sunday 11 September, a huge demonstration gathered at the Obelisk in Bow and at Poplar's dock gates.[399] The following Saturday, four bands accompanied a great march through the borough.

In response to 'a number of extraordinary letters' the councillors wrote to Poplar school children, explaining their actions and urging the youngsters to join a trade union when they leave school, telling them that, 'We want you to grow up strong, active, loving men and women. We want you never to be contented while there is one single man or woman starving.'[400] Mayor Sam March issued a statement from prison outlining the councillors' case, emphasising that 'above all we are fighting for the establishment of the principle that men and women willing and able to work shall either be found work or be given adequate maintenance, and that in either case the means shall be provided from National Funds'.[401]

Such support sustained the councillors, in particular because it was support from their own people. George Lansbury wrote that, 'It has been my good fortune to live with the poor all my life. Like others, they have their faults, and so have I, but they are of me and I of them. In prison I shall hear their cheers, think of their stories of hope and despair, and all the time be conscious that, though the cell door is locked, I am not alone.'[402]

On Saturday 10 September, thousands rallied in Trafalgar Square and cheered a letter from George Lansbury which argued that, 'It may be that hundreds of days will have to be passed in prison by us and others before victory comes. But it will all depend on people like you. If you keep the flag flying, if you never drop your colours, then sure as the sun rises victory will come to our people and so to us.'[403] Back in Poplar, residents had already taken up this call, responding in their thousands to the following notice:

Fellow Citizens, – The Poplar Borough Councillors, by their heroic resistance, are saving you from an additional rate that would amount to 9s.2d. in the pound.

Efforts may yet be made to over-ride their decision and to levy the rate despite them. To meet any such action we are setting up a Tenants' Defence League in each ward of the borough.

The League will be absolutely non-Party, and open to every ratepayer, tenant, and householder.

The imprisoned councillors now ask you to begin organising through these Defence Leagues without delay, so that all may be prepared to act together when the time comes. Organise at once – and then wait for the word from prison.[404]

It is notable that this new organisation was not the Prisoners' or Councillors' Defence League but the Tenants' Defence League, its focus on working-class community self-defence not on cheerleading heroes. The League quickly recruited 10,000 members, and within a short time 'Hardly a house [was] without its window-card denoting membership of the League',[405] which had produced a leaflet in the style of a large postcard, headlined 'Souvenir of Poplar's Plucky council – in prison for protecting the local ratepayer' and explaining the council's case, giving figures for how much rent the council's actions had saved Poplar's tenants. The rating system, it said, was 'robbery': if rates were equal across London, they would be 16s 6d (82½p) per year. Even without the precepts, Poplar was having to levy 19s 2d (96p) – '2s 8d (13½p) more than her fair share' – and now the court had ordered the borough to pay an extra 9s 2d (46p)!

The League's first week saw a constant queue of people waiting outside its office to sign up, and culminated in a public rally at Poplar town hall, addressed by free councillors and Jack Jones MP.[406] As Poplar people rallied to the Tenants' Defence League, they also dug deep for the councillors' families. The

Daily Herald listed donations in a regular column, 'Councillors' Kiddies', the list often running to more than a hundred donors.[407] The paper reported that 'Most of the contributions are from people able to give only small amounts, their letters telling of self-denial'.[408] One letter contained two guineas and a box of chocolates for Councillor Green's motherless daughter. Another contained half-a-crown from a widow struggling to support her own kids, who wrote: 'I am sorry I cannot send more to help to crush those who are making our lives and those of our children a misery after we have given up our dear ones. This rotten Government has aroused the women as never before.'[409]

The jailed councillors oversaw publicity and campaigning on the outside. One meeting expressed concern as to whether the publicity committee was doing enough to spread the word, resolving to write to the committee 'with reference to lack of meetings and speakers in Bow and Bromley'.[410]

The local Labour Party enjoyed a boost, as future Poplar Labour chair, Bill Brinson, described: 'In 1921 it began to build. We built up a huge membership – practically every street had a collector ... We got a big lift up over pinching the rates because every night we used to march to Holloway Prison and Brixton with bands and work up some enthusiasm.'[411] Herbert Morrison admitted that Poplar's fight 'evoked enthusiasm among many of the rank and file, but speculated that 'they may not have reflected upon the social, political and constitutional aspects of the matter'.[412]

The Tenants' Defence League was ready to organise a rent strike if and when the state intervened to collect the precepts, piling more pressure onto the government.

GOVERNMENT UNDER PRESSURE

George Lansbury had predicted before his arrest that the government was 'sowing dragon's teeth'.[413] Sir Alfred Mond now faced the same sight as the teeth-sowing Cadmus: an army rising up from the ground to fight back against him.

Unemployment was rising across the country, and the jobless rioted in Dundee, Bristol and Liverpool. Ten thousand unemployed people besieged the Woolwich guardians in their office overnight. In late August, unemployed workers held mass deputations in Shoreditch, Clerkenwell, Hackney, Holborn, Lambeth, Hammersmith, West Ham and St. Pancras. By September, jobless residents were marching in Bermondsey, Brighton, Lewisham, Stepney and Orpington too.[414] The *Daily News* reported that 'Mass meetings of the workless ... are being held and organised in every industrial district, and every board is to be tackled in turn'.[415] Some guardians responded by increasing their relief payments, and the first of these, the 'Islington scale', became a rallying point for both supporters and opponents. Egged on by *The Times* and the Middle Classes Union,[416] Mond vetoed the Islington scale on 9 September.

The Directorate of Intelligence sent reports to the Cabinet alarmed by the mass demonstrations, the role of communists and the threat to law and order.[417]

The *East London Advertiser* advised the government to 'order the unconditional release of all the Poplar prisoners, and leave the solution of the civic problems at issue to reason and not to force – to peaceful persuasion and not to violent terrorism. Force never succeeded in these cases; it is always met by force; nothing is gained and all is lost'.[418] The *Advertiser*'s fear of working-class uprising was real, but the concern about 'violent terrorism' was somewhat alarmist. George Lansbury was well-known as a pacifist and had stated earlier in the year that 'We cannot go in for violence, even if we had the means, because most of us do not agree a bit with killing or destruction of any kind; so we adopt what, to us, is the more excellent way – we fold our arms and refuse to levy the rate.'[419]

The *East London Observer* also decried the government's tactical hamfistedness: 'If the action of the central authorities in executing the writs of attachment at this stage is interpreted as spiteful and vindictive by large masses of the people, those responsible for the sorry business have only themselves to thank.' The *Observer* also saw that the cause of the crisis was the unfair rating system, reform of which was 'delayed by the obtuseness of detached representatives and the apathy of officialdom'.[420]

What was the government to do? Dismiss the councillors from office and order new elections? No, because the voters were certain to elect candidates pledged to exactly the same course of action. Perhaps the Receiver[421] would withdraw the Metropolitan police from Poplar. However, the Police and Prison Officers' Union had already told Poplar council that it would supply the borough with a trade union police force, drawing only the average wage of local workers.[422]

The *East London Observer* had urged the government to rush a short Act through Parliament empowering itself to create a substitute authority for the disobedient council. Considering this possibility, Sylvia Pankhurst believed that a rate strike in protest would be easy to organise; a rent strike may be harder, but was nonetheless still possible and desirable.[423] The government realised this too, and chose against this course. Mond considered a new law allowing the LCC to collect its own rate, although the LCC itself did not want to do so. George Lansbury pointed out that 'such legislation will only transfer the dispute from the councillors to the ratepayers – from 30 to more than 30,000'.[424]

Part of Herbert Morrison's objection to Poplar's strategy was that 'the logical consequence of refusing the precepts would be to hold up such public services as education, school meals and medical treatment' and that the government would appoint a commissioner to run the borough.[425] His fears were not realised.

Paralysed by his anxieties, Morrison showed little fear of what might happen to working-class people, or to the Labour Party, if Poplar did not fight back. Morrison's *London Labour Chronicle* did not even mention the councillors' imprisonment in its September issue. A small item appeared in October, not praising or supporting Poplar but reporting the efforts of Morrison and his allies to secure their release, and reassuring readers of his determination to achieve not a victory but 'an amicable settlement' and 'an end to the deadlock'.

The Government held back from taking action, and made concessions on the issue of unemployment. Mond chaired a Cabinet meeting on 12 September, which agreed to extend state assistance to needy Poor Law authorities, provide more capital for public works schemes, and widen the scope of unemployment insurance.[426] But with no sums announced, there was little confidence this 'extra help' would be more than nominal. Mond sent out a circular to boards of guardians allowing them to pay out-relief to able-bodied unemployed without forcing them to the workhouse or the labour test.[427] But Mond's move simply legally endorsed what was already happening, and did not address rates equalisation, so would not budge the councillors. Edgar later recalled that during the councillors' time in prison, 'the government made many unofficial promises to deal with the question of the rates in London on the lines of our demand if only we would first purge our contempt of Court by levying the rate. Father was too wily to be caught in this way. Most of us took the line that the Government having allowed us to get into prison through their own neglect should find some means of getting us out again.'[428] This quote reveals two of the councillors' important strengths: you do not trust your enemy; and you do not take responsibility for your enemy's mess.

OTHER COUNCILS ANSWER THE CALL

The imprisonment and stubborn determination of Poplar's councillors finally spurred other councils to act. Neighbouring boroughs Bethnal Green and Stepney were ready to follow Poplar's lead and withhold the precepts. Bethnal Green made its decision by 16 votes to 10 on 22 September. Mayor Joe Vaughan, though not present at the meeting, said that 'Poplar did the right thing ... I am determined to back Poplar to the limit, and, if the council consents, am ready to join Lansbury and his colleagues in prison'.[429] Given that he was a Communist Party member of high standing, it is perhaps disappointing that he did not act earlier in the year.

On 13 September, Stepney Borough Council held a special meeting during its recess period. Mayor Cahill reported on his visits to Brixton prison and 'how profoundly he had been impressed with the sorry plight of his fellow Mayor and colleagues of Poplar'. Loud cheers met his description of the prisoners as 'those

The mayor and deputy mayor of Bethnal Green call to say goodbye and good luck!
Deputy Mayor Ald. T. Boyce, Mayor Cr. J.J. Vaughan, Ald. John Scurr, Cr. Mrs. Julia Scurr

who were prepared to sacrifice their liberty, and even their lives, for the benefit of the workers of Poplar'.[430] Many Stepney Labour councillors were now ready to follow Poplar's action, but since such a proposal was not on the agenda, they settled for passing (without opposition) a resolution demanding the prisoners' release and warning the Home Secretary that if this were not done, Stepney would refuse to levy the precepts. It seems a shame that while Poplar had broken the law and was at that very time suffering the brutal consequences, Stepney allowed itself to be hamstrung by bureaucracy.

Stepney Trades and Labour Council called a special conference to protest against the London Labour Party circular which had advised local Labour Parties not to follow Poplar's example. The conference took place on 24 September, attended by 27 London Labour Parties, and unanimously passed two resolutions: one protesting against the circular; the other calling on councils to repeat Poplar's action. The conference was chaired by Stepney Alderman[431] Clement Attlee, who told the gathering, 'I have always been a constitutionalist, but the time has come when it is necessary to kick'.[432]

Receiving no satisfactory answer from the Home Secretary, Stepney carried out its threat on 5 October, voting 29-21 in favour of Attlee's resolution to disregard the precepts. On other London councils, the call to emulate Poplar was defeated. Battersea council voted down a resolution to refuse to levy the precepts by 26 votes to 25. Shoreditch council voted down the same proposal, also by one vote, when right-wing Labour councillors 'crossed the floor' to vote with the opposition against the Labour majority's support for defiance.[433]

Tottenham council voted to admire rather than imitate Poplar's action, voting down those councillors who expressed readiness to go to prison with Poplar.[434] Finsbury Borough Council voted down a resolution that the Poplar councillors were legally wrong but morally right; Islington council decided to hold a Town's Meeting to consult local opinion.[435] West Ham council gave its full support to Poplar, but could not take the same action because it was outside the area of the London County Council.[436]

Although unwilling to confront the unfair rating system, Shoreditch, Edmonton and others were happy to condemn it, endorsing a resolution that called on 'all local authorities to bring home to the Government its responsibility by standing for the equalisation of rates of all Borough and Urban District councils of Greater London, and by so doing, remove the scandal of the poor having to keep the poor. It demands that the Government shall immediately summon Parliament to take adequate steps to deal with the urgent unemployment crisis, and to redistribute the burden of the rates over the Greater London area, so that the wealthy shall pay in proportion to their means.'[437] It was clear by this time, though, that Poplar's action had done more than anything else to 'bring home to the Government' the need for rates equalisation. Little wonder that Edgar Lansbury said a year later that 'We all ought to be judged politically by our deeds, not by our looks or our speeches and promises.'[438]

Hackney council decisively rejected Poplar's strategy, refusing even to support a demonstration for rates equalisation lest it associate them with Poplar. The town clerk of Poplar had written to east London borough councils asking them to support the protest rally, and Councillors Sherman and Good proposed that Hackney do so. But Hackney Labour leader W. Parker opposed, arguing that although Lansbury and his colleagues were sincere they had made a mistake. Sherman pointed out that hungry people do not care much for constitutionalism: 'They want to be fed, and some of them are going to be fed by hook or by crook.'[439] Alderman Anning added that the decision not to support the demonstration was 'a flagrant betrayal of the people of Hackney.' At this meeting, as at several meetings of several councils, Poplar supporters were present in the public gallery cheering on those who were prepared to follow their course. Mayor Herbert Morrison threatened to clear the gallery. Sherman and Good's proposal was defeated.

On 28 September, after Hackney council had heard a deputation of local unemployed, Labour councillors Eldon and Sherman proposed an amendment to the finance committee's report 'to consider what action can be taken to lessen the burden of the rates, that presses so heavily on the poorer residents of the borough, a large number of whom are unemployed'. It was intended to lead to refusal to levy the precepts, but received only nine votes in favour, 46 against.[440]

Messages and money aside, tangible support for Poplar's stand came only from its local labour movement and population, the *Daily Herald*, the LDCU, and some municipal next-door neighbours. Herbert Morrison told Hackney council that he was 'very determined, in this question or any other question, only to uphold constitutional action and action within the law', but that 'a duty has been imposed on us to do everything possible within the limits of our Constitution to secure the release for our fellow citizens [the unemployed] from the hardships under which they are suffering'. He would now go as far as the law allowed him, and find out just what limits it placed on the effectiveness of working-class campaigns sworn to remain within the constitution. For Morrison had an alternative strategy. He had demanded an audience with the prime minister himself, Lloyd George.

PURSUING THE PRIME MINISTER

Morrison may well have been sincere in his desire to see the rating system changed and the suffering of the unemployed alleviated. But he was also, perhaps primarily, concerned to see constitutionalism restored as Labour's way of working. With the jailings, marches and clashes with the police, confrontational methods were getting the upper hand. 'It seemed as though Labour's responsible image had been submerged in a sea of direct action ... He had to prove that orthodox and constitutional methods of political campaigning could succeed where "direct action" had failed.'[441]

So Morrison put together a deputation of London Labour Mayors to travel to Scotland, where Lloyd George was taking a 'recuperative holiday' following a breakdown earlier in the year.[442] Bethnal Green's Mayor Vaughan took part. Shoreditch's Mayor Girling declined an invitation to France in order to attend, saying, 'The situation is so serious that we have no other alternative but to go to Inverness.'[443] However, Fulham's William Gentry, secretary of the London Labour Mayors group, refused to even ask the Home Office if Poplar Mayor Sam March might be released to join the deputation.[444]

The Prime Minister told the Mayors that he did 'not consider any useful purpose would be served by their suggested conference in Inverness',[445] but undeterred, they took the train to the Scottish city, then travelled round the Highlands in pursuit of Lloyd George, finally pinning him down in Gairloch on 22 September. Woolwich council leader William Barefoot's report of the trip explained that 'the desperate situation ... demanded desperate action',[446] but did not mention the Poplar councillors' desperate action. Barefoot even complained of the 'discomforts' of the journey to Gairloch, which we can be sure were less severe than the discomforts of Brixton and Holloway prisons, or of the unemployed! Morrison recalled that 'We went to the house where he was staying, and I was elected spokesman for the deputation. Our number sorely taxed the local taxi service, and I travelled sitting on the knee of Sir Alfred Mond, the Minister of Health'.[447]

Charles Key telegrammed Gentry asking him to ensure that the deputation demanded the release of his fellow councillors. But Morrison was in no hurry to do so. He began by putting suggestions to Lloyd George as to how he might tackle unemployment. The Prime Minister either refused or sidestepped every demand, telling them that 'the only real remedy for unemployment was simply to wait for better times'.[448] Morrison pleaded with Lloyd George that inaction might lead to unemployed movements turning to violence and falling into 'irresponsible' hands, and stressed that he and the labour movement were as alarmed by that prospect as the government would be.[449] He raised the issue of the Poplar prisoners only at the tail end of the meeting. He did not even ask for their release, instead stating 'I express no opinion with regard to it ... we want to raise the question whether it is not possible for some discussion to be raised for the purpose of securing that this deadlock be ended'.[450] Lloyd George did not want to talk about the troublesome prisoners and told Morrison to talk to Mond instead.

Morrison did so, and suggested to Mond that imprisonment might be ended by an amicable settlement. But Mond insisted that release was in the power of neither himself nor the Home Secretary Edward Shortt[451], a Liberal described by Morgan as 'mild-mannered and somewhat colourless'[452]. Mond flatly stated that, 'they were committed to prison for contempt of court, and they can only be released by a judge of the High Court when they obey the order of the court'.[453] We will see how much more flexible the government's apparently limited powers would become as the crisis intensified over the following weeks. Mond thought that 'the prisoners should now be content with the protest they have made', missing the point that the councillors intended not to protest but to win.[454]

Susan Lawrence had previously suggested to the LCC on several occasions that it convene a conference to discuss unemployment and unequal rates. Before imprisonment brought the issue to a head, nothing had been done. Now Morrison suggested a conference and Mond considered it. The Poplar councillors smelt a rat, believing not only that Mond 'evidently wants to be relieved of the embarrassment of keeping the councillors in gaol'[455] but also that Morrison might be trying to arrange a conference for some of them to attend whilst the others remained in prison. At their meeting of 23 September, the men resolved 'That the imprisoned Aldermen and councillors reaffirm their determination not to enter into any negotiation or discussion as to future action until Poplar Borough Council was able to meet as a corporate body, as free men and women in their own Council Chamber'.[456]

They suspected that wheeling and dealing was going on behind their backs and that Herbert Morrison was trying to wrest control of the situation from their hands by appointing himself intermediary between them and the government. So the *Daily Herald* made the point that 'The men and women in prison have learned who their friends are. They understand quite well the underhand intrigues which have been carried on against them, and they are not willing to hand over their future to any but friends who are trusted, tried and true.'[457] The prisoners sent a telegram to the Prime Minister clarifying that 'We are prepared to enter into a conference of all parties concerned only as free men and women. No one has had or has authority to suggest any other course.' The women councillors gave visitor Charles Key a message for the outside world: 'They desire it to be known that they decline to take part in any conference or negotiations unless they can do so as free women. They prefer the alternative of continued imprisonment.'[458] George Lansbury wrote that 'no neutral person, no good offices are needed to ensure the attendance of the Poplar councillors ... All that is needed is [our] freedom ... It is also necessary to remind friends and enemies that Poplar is governed by democrats, and that as such we do not intend handing our future over either to a few selected delegates or friends.'[459] Morrison defended himself in a letter to the *Herald*,[460] but continued trying to cajole the councillors into accepting a worse deal than they would eventually win through remaining resolute. He acted like the trade union bureaucrat who responds to strike action not with support and encouragement but with panic-stricken efforts to settle everything down and return to business as usual.

Edgar Lansbury would later write that 'Morrison and his followers first save money by ill-treating their unemployed ... then refuse to follow those who make a revolt, but try to do them as much harm on the quiet as they can..[461]

On 27 September, eleven London Labour mayors visited Brixton prison and met with the Poplar councillors. As anticipated, Morrison suggested that a Poplar delegation attend the proposed conference, leaving their comrades incarcerated and themselves returning to their cells once the conference closed. George Lansbury denounced the very suggestion as 'outrageous'; the councillors unanimously dismissed it and instead asked the mayors to liaise with their solicitor, W.H. Thompson, to apply to the high court for their release. The mayors agreed. The London Labour boroughs refused to submit proposals to the conference unless the Poplar councillors were free.

NELLIE CRESSALL RELEASED

Immediately on her imprisonment, Nellie Cressall was put into the hospital wing, unable to eat, and in the eighth month of pregnancy. The prison authorities neglected her, not letting her out for exercise, and giving her food that should could not eat. Three days later, Minnie Lansbury was also in the hospital wing, where she tried hard to contact Nellie and complained about her treatment, leading to a little improvement.[462] Stepney councillor Cahill said that, 'The Government ought to be ashamed of themselves in arresting a woman in Mrs. Cressall's condition. If they were not, then all the devils in hell would not shame them.'[463] Nellie was popular among local working-class people. 'She helped us with the ration coupons. We went to her if there was trouble. If you went to a social or the Docklands' Settlement she was there. She lived in one of the council houses. She was one of us – rough and ready not highty-flighty.'[464] Facing a huge public outcry, it was untenable for the authorities to keep her locked up.

Their problem, however, was that she was still in contempt of court, and had no intention of purging her contempt. The government conjured a solution. The little-known Official Solicitor emerged from the shadows and applied for her release on health grounds. This public post is a 'solicitor of last resort', and that is certainly the use to which the government put it. The Home Office endorsed the application (but denied all knowledge of how it came about![465]) and the court agreed it. But then there was another obstacle: Nellie refused to leave prison. Harry Gosling recalled a conversation with Holloway's governor:

Gosling: 'Why do you keep this lady here in such circumstances?'
Governor: 'Good heavens, man, she won't go out! I have told her twice she can go!'
Gosling: 'But don't you see that her loyalty to her colleagues prevents her leaving of her own accord?'
Governor: 'What am I to do?'
Gosling: 'Put her out. She cannot stay here if you won't let her, can she?'[466]

George Lansbury wrote to Nellie that the councillors would support her whatever decision she took, but they were all concerned that their enemies would try to use her as a weak link and attempt to break their unity. Eventually, Nellie Cressall was 'put out by force' on the afternoon of Wednesday 21 September, having made it clear she would accept no conditions on her release. She checked with the governor that this was 'like an eviction'. 'Yes', he replied.[467]

Now free, Nellie blew the whistle on conditions in Holloway prison, including 'the dreadful screaming of the poor women in the padded cells'. She told how

'We women councillors were kept isolated, with as many wardresses to look after the five of us, as there were to look after the other thousand women in the prison. They were so afraid lest we should talk to those women, who were there for no fault of their own, but because of the rotten system.'[468]

Nellie's release showed that a government under pressure from working-class mobilisation will bend and break its own laws in order to get out of a tight spot. The Official Solicitor returned to the shadows[469]. Councillor Mrs Cressall gave birth to her baby on 31 October.

MOND BEGINS TO MOVE

Sir Alfred Mond knew he would have to make concessions. He hinted at a temporary Bill to ease the burden on the poor boroughs over the approaching winter.[470] He dropped his previous insistence that rates equalisation could not be discussed until after the royal commission reported, and asked Alderman Gentry to draft a detailed proposal. Gentry was keen to oblige with the help of other Labour mayors, but George Lansbury rightly insisted that this could not be done without Poplar's and Bethnal Green's involvement. And that would mean Poplar Borough Council being free.

According to Bethnal Green's Mayor Vaughan, Mond was by now 'in a frame of mind in which he wished the whole business over. He looked extremely fed up.'[471] Mond knew that Morrison and his allies had failed; he said so in a special memo to Cabinet.[472] So Mond approached Harry Gosling and 'told me all his difficulties, how these troublesome borough councillors had got put into jail, and now nobody seemed to know how to get them out, and could I possibly do anything?' Gosling went to both prisons and asked to see all the councillors. Brixton's governor read out a list of regulations showing why he could not, so Gosling told Mond to over-rule the governor. Mond did so, visiting hours were overlooked, and 'the lights, due to be put out, I believe, at eight o'clock, had to be kept burning'[473].

So came the plan. The councillors would apologise for offending the court, although not for refusing to collect the precepts. They would apply for release, and if the London County Council and the Metropolitan Asylum Board did not object, then they would be freed to attend a conference, which would discuss and resolve the issue.

By October, the inequalities between richer and poorer boroughs were starker than ever. The City of London charged a rate of 11s11d (59½p) and had no able-bodied poor to support. Hampstead's rate was 14s0d (70p), with only 76 able-bodied poor, just 0.009 per cent. Poplar by contrast, had to levy a rate of 27s0d (£1.35), supporting 4,000 able-bodied poor, 2.52 per cent. Shoreditch and Bethnal Green were not far behind Poplar, with around 1.5 per cent able-bodied poor.[474]

On 1 October, thousands of unemployed people gathered along Victoria Embankment, making their presence felt outside the MAB's offices, inside which the board debated the release plan.[475] Rev. Prichard, proposing to accept the plan, argued that Poplar's action had, 'established the essential justice of its cause'.[476] The seconder, Mr Winfield, noted Poplar's previous attempts to address the issue constitutionally and also Poplar people's huge support for their councillors.[477] Following the MAB's unanimous decision to support release, the *Daily Herald* confidently predicted that the 'Triumph of Poplar councillors is Certain'.[478]

But it would be more troublesome to prise a similarly conciliatory attitude from the LCC, which was more explicitly political than the MAB, had a sizeable anti-Labour majority, and was still smarting from Poplar's defiance. It was not keen on backing down without seeing any money.

At a special meeting on 4 October, A.A. Watts, a Poplar guardian but Battersea LCC representative, proposed a resolution calling for the councillors' release. However, Municipal Reform persuaded him to withdraw it and he replaced it with the softer: 'this council would welcome a conference between the Ministry of Health and the Poplar Borough Council with the object of overcoming the existing difficulties, and would further welcome any action by the Poplar Borough Council that would enable them freely to participate in such a conference.'[479] Harry Gosling recalled this as one of only two resolutions he had won unanimously in his 28 years as an opposition Labour LCC member, acknowledging that it was not 'a tribute to my own powers of persuasion, but rather to the tide of generous feeling that now and again for one brief moment sweeps even the London County Council off its feet'.[480]

That same day, around 40,000 people marched through London. Organisers the London District Council of the Unemployed (LDCU) reported that, 'To the casual observer passing, or rather attempting to pass along the Thames Embankment, it must have been obvious that here was a great cause, here was some underlying principle, that had brought this great mass out to demonstrate their poverty'.[481] One eyewitness described how 'Women with children, and elderly men, feeble through weeks of semi starvation, were unable to proceed and scores fell out and were compelled to rest by the roadside ... Pinched faces and halting gait told the tale of intense poverty'. *The Times* saw the march very differently, 'not composed of people in apparent distress ... The procession bore marks of exploitation by Communist agitators. The Red Flag was waved as well as sung about.'[482]

James Ramsay Macdonald – a prominent Labour figure though not at that time an MP[483] – held similar contempt towards the organised unemployed, writing that 'there is always enough of the flotsam and jetsam amongst unemployed demonstrators to make them something like a mob ... The pitiable vanity, ignorance and incompetence of some of the unemployed spokesmen ... may have created a few riots, but they have been precious contributions to the reaction'.[484] Macdonald welcomed the London Labour Party's circular against Poplar, and Morrison returned the compliment to his 'political hero'[485] by welcoming 'Straight Words from Mr. Ramsay Macdonald in support of London Labour Party Policy'.

The LDCU wanted the march to proceed to Spring Gardens, where the LCC was meeting. But the police diverted it to Hyde Park instead and banned a Trafalgar Square meeting. The LDCU felt that the leaders of the 2,000-strong Poplar contingent, which had 'insisted' on leading the march, went along with police plans, thus breaking the discipline of the unemployed movement.[486] A section of marchers went to Trafalgar Square anyway, where the police attacked them. 14 people were taken to hospital.[487] At the same time, Harry Gosling was telling the LCC that 'the luxury riot of the rich was creating a bitter feeling in the ranks of the starving'.[488] The LCDU's – and the rest of the unemployed movement's – support for Poplar's prisoners remained solid, their leader Wal Hannington later writing that 'the courageous stand of these councillors aroused the admiration of the whole working class'.[489]

Three days later, Mond sent a memo to the Cabinet suggesting that terms for settlement should include:

- a four-fold increase in the equalisation rate from 6d (2½p) to 2s (10p);
- a doubling of the allowance for workhouse inmates from 5d (2p) to 10d (4p), known as the Metropolitan Common Poor Fund (MCPF) capitation grant.

Mond argued that these measures were 'reasonable on their merits', and represented a 'temporary compromise between the claims of the poorer boroughs and the richer boroughs'.[490] The effect of the first measure would be that the eight richest authorities would pay £800,000 per year instead of £400,000, with the extra distributed amongst the other, poorer boroughs. Poplar would get £21,000.

Mond was looking for a way out, forced to do so by the councillors' determination, the mass mobilisations in their support, and the moves by other councils to follow their lead. The result of Poplar's choices was that the Minister of Health had no choice but to meet their demands.

RELEASE

October 9 was 'Unemployment Sunday', designated so by the TUC and Labour Party, and marked by big meetings across the country, attendances in some cases tens of thousands.[491] Many Poplar street corners hosted meetings, and in the evening over 5,000 people gathered at Bow Baths, with hundreds more accommodated by ad hoc overflow meetings. Jennie Mackay, temporarily paroled due to her father's death, told the meeting that she preferred to reserve her statement until she could 'be there with her imprisoned colleagues unconditionally'. Mentioning her bereavement, she broke down and resumed her seat.[492]

On Wednesday 12 October, the court heard the councillors' application to be freed, moved on the basis of two affidavits from Sam March.

The first apologised for upsetting the court, expressing 'profound regret that their action had involved them in disobedience to the Court'.[493] The affidavit's well-chosen words did not, though, apologise for refusing to collect the precepts – the very act that had placed them in contempt of court. It promised that the councillors would participate in a conference in good faith. The second affidavit detailed the worsening situation in Poplar, reminding the court of the real-life issue that had brought about this crisis, and giving the judges evidence that things had changed since legal proceedings had begun and that therefore they could change the court's decision. By the first week in October, the Poplar guardians were supporting 6,734 families, involving 19,091 men, women and children.

Mr. Macmorran KC presented the LCC's awkward lack of objection to the prisoners' application for release. Reading reports of the hearing nearly a century later,[494] you can imagine the LCC's representatives squirming as they tried to avoid admitting the scale of their climbdown, and the judges either mocking the LCC or expressing their indignation at their court being used as a rubber stamp for a political settlement made elsewhere. The key political players were not present, and without the Poplar councillors, there were none of the impassioned speeches of previous hearings. Delivering their verdict, the judges clearly saw through the verbal and political manoeuvring at work, citing significant obstacles to their granting release. But the judges, however irked, came to the rescue of their political masters and freed the councillors. For the first time in history, people imprisoned for contempt were released without first purging their contempt. Just a few weeks previously, the government had insisted that this was impossible.

No wonder that Keith-Lucas and Richards described Poplarism as 'the outstanding example of conflict between central and local government, which illustrates the thesis that when such conflicts do arise, the strictly legal

Victory! Released prisoners outside Brixton Prison.
Front row: J.J. Heales Goodway, W.H. Thompson (solicitor), C.E. Williams, B. Fleming, Mrs. Scurr, J.T. O'Callaghan, C.J. Cressall, J.H. Jones.. Standing: T.E. Kelly, J.A. Rugless, D. Adams, J.H. Banks, Walter Green, George Lansbury, Harry Gosling, Edgar Lansbury, Sam March, A. Baker, Mrs. M. Lansbury, John Scurr, Cr. Oakes, C.E. Petherick, R.J. Hopwood, C.E. Sumner, A.V. Farr.

relationship is soon submerged in the political'.[495] The judiciary is not a neutral arbiter above society but an institution which serves the existing order and its ruling class. Usually, it helps to restrain those who try to challenge that order, as it did when imprisoning Poplar's rebel councillors. But when the rebels get the upper hand, the judiciary can also help the ruling class to beat an orderly retreat. The Poplar councillors understood all along the class nature of the judiciary and the laws it administered. That is why they pursued a strategy of confronting them rather than deferring to them as Herbert Morrison and others advised. Poplar's strategy had won.

An order signed by Sheriff Algernon Miles instructed H.M. Prison Holloway to 'Discharge out of your custody the bodies of Julia Scurr, Jennie Mackay, Susan Lawrence, and Minnie Lansbury from all process now against them in my office.' The freed women councillors were taken to south London, where at 6.10 p.m., the men 'stepped through the gate of Brixton Prison, singing, laughing, and shouting, and free. They had made no compromise to get out, and they stood in resolve where they had stood six months before'.[496]

The councillors issued a statement:

We leave prison as free men and women, pledged only to attend a conference with all parties concerned in the dispute with us about rates

Three cheers for Poplar!

Victory celebration in Victoria Park.

... As to the bigger question of unemployment, we shall join with our comrades in the Labour and Socialist movement and with them continue to agitate for work or maintenance, always making it clear we want work rather than money for nothing ... To everybody, young and old, rich and poor, comrades in the movement or outside friends – including all those resident in every part of the country who kindly took care of our children – here's our thanks. We feel our imprisonment has been well worth while, and none of us would have done otherwise than we did. We have forced public attention on the question of London rates, and have materially assisted in forcing the Government to call Parliament to deal with unemployment.

They returned to Poplar as heroes, welcomed by a huge crowd, with brass band and red flags. They went first to Sam March's house, 'and from there the Irish band took them home, one by one, with pipes and drums playing Irish music.' The *Daily Herald* reported:

Joyful reunions inside their houses and joyful demonstrations without, the councillors must have felt a sense of triumph that compensated for the bitterness of the past few weeks. In the crowd that followed the band round the streets faces were smiling as they seldom smile ordinarily in that poor borough. Men took off their caps and waved them in the air, women shouted and laughed, and the children made sympathetic noises. The whole babel was a spontaneous outburst of working-class sympathy for its self-sacrificing champions.

A women's meeting was in progress at Poplar Town Hall, campaigning for the councillors' release; it was now transformed into a victory party when some of the freed councillors unexpectedly walked in. The following day saw a 'welcome home' meeting at Bow Baths, with 2,000 packed inside and more than that number outside on Roman Road. Sam March told one of the many celebrations: 'I want you to remember this occasion forever, and to remember the cause for which we took, and still take, our stand.'

Sam March's wish came true. More than fifty years later, Geoff Richman interviewed elderly Poplar residents, the twenty- and thirty-somethings of the rates rebellion year, and wrote of 'the glow which lights up the faces at the mention of Lansbury'[497]. Docker Charles Shed remembered that 'they went to prison cos they wanted the welfare improved and the government didn't want it.' Mrs. Langley said that everyone supported the rebels going to prison: 'I think the council was marvellous.' Mr. White thought that George Lansbury was 'the greatest man alive', but regretted that now, 'we've lost all our born leaders. There were other true men in those days ... mostly socialists ... follow Lansbury blind, we would. It was nice to be in his company. But now these people, they evade you like, they leave you to somebody else.' As well as capturing one of the qualities of working-class leadership, Mr. White reminds us of the anger that made so many respond to the councillors' struggle: 'people was getting browned off, always having to look for a job or getting help from somewhere.'

That was the issue that our freed councillors had to face as the party died down and the meetings began.

POPLAR'S VICTORY

The same day that the councillors walked free, a huge demonstration of unemployed people culminated in a deputation to the Ministers of Health and Labour.[498] The next day, George Lansbury, Charlie Sumner, John Scurr and Sam March met Sir Alfred Mond to prepare the ground for the all-important conference the following Monday. They had been out of prison for less than two days, and the speed with which the meeting was convened contrasts with the difficulty that local labour movement representatives usually find in getting an audience with the government.

The Ministry of Health was squeezed between competing pressures. The Geddes Committee[499] had recommended a severe cut in state spending. But resentment was growing amongst the jobless, and the minister knew he had to make serious concessions to Poplarism. The Cabinet's Home Affairs Committee had agreed to offer a rise in the equalisation rate, with the explicit intention of discouraging other councils from taking action similar to Poplar's.[500] Mond proposed to the conference the two measures he had previously proposed to the Cabinet: doubling the MCPF capitation grant; and a fourfold increase in the equalisation rate.

The London Labour councils concurred with the second of these, but wanted the package of measures also to include:

- the MCPF capitation grant to increase much more, to 1s8d (8p);
- the cost of supporting the unemployed to transfer from local government to national;
- or if that could not be agreed, pooling of outdoor relief spending across London.

Herbert Morrison acted as spokesperson for the Labour boroughs. He may have assumed this role as secretary of the London Labour Party, but it seems odd that the Poplar councillors allowed Morrison to speak for Labour when he had so consistently undermined their fight. Sam March or George Lansbury, without whose action this conference would not even be happening, might have been better spokespersons.

Mond refused to even discuss the notion of central government picking up the dole bill. The rich boroughs objected to equalisation because of the lack of control over how the poorer boroughs would spend the money. Rich boroughs were acting like rich people: unwilling to give up their wealth, and looking down on the poor as wasters who could not be trusted with cash. They proposed instead that the MCPF capitation grant increase to 1s3d (6p). Labour disagreed; Mond proposed a sub-committee; Morrison objected, saying it would achieve nothing because of the attitude of Westminster and the City.

Then Westminster's town clerk, John Hunt, proposed cross-London pooling of outdoor relief costs up to scales agreed by the Minister of Health. Labour agreed to discuss this in the sub-committee, which met the following day and agreed the proposal. Poplar would gain more than £250,000 per year. Other winners would be Bermondsey, Shoreditch, Southwark and Camberwell. However, Hackney and Fulham would lose out, so their mayors – Morrison and Gentry – proposed an increase in the equalisation rate as well. Hunt objected.

To some surprise, and to Morrison's and Gentry's anger, George Lansbury backed Hunt, saying that although he was not satisfied, the proposal was better than he had expected. Branson believes that 'It is possible that Lansbury feared that continued pressure for Morrison's demand might jeopardise the Hunt settlement',[501] but Lansbury himself said afterwards that as the richer boroughs were adamant about rates equalisation, he had felt there was no purpose in arguing further. Both these explanations seem at odds with George's approach up until that point, when no amount of fear, and no amount of stubbornness from rich boroughs or their friends in the LCC, the government or the courts, could deter him or cajole him into compromise. He also appears to have decided alone to support Hunt, breaking Poplar's crucial practice of deciding its choices and strategies collectively. Gentry was raging at Lansbury, accusing him of 'breaking solidarity' and 'parochial greed'.[502]

Morrison had attended the conference with the town clerk and borough treasurer, not even informing elected councillors. Indignant, Councillor Brown resigned his chairmanship of Hackney council's finance committee, and persuaded his fellow councillors to vote down its report by 29 votes to 26 – in effect, a censure of Morrison.[503]

The changes were put into legal form in the Local Authorities (Financial Provisions) Act 1921. As a result, the LCC estimated that the City of London's rate would rise by 7.5d (3.125p), Westminster's by 6.8d (2.833p), Fulham's by 4.3d (1.8p) and Hackney's by 0.5d (0.2p); while Bethnal Green's would fall by 1s7.8d (8.25p), Woolwich's by 2s4.4d (11.833p) and Poplar's by 2s9.2d (13.833p).[504] The Tories who led London's rich boroughs had lost, but they were determined to exact a price: no more Poplar rebellions. S. Marylebone[505] Board of Guardians passed resolutions asking the Ministry to withhold Poor Fund grants to guardians if their borough council refused to collect precepts, and to introduce 'effective central control of excessive local expenditure', and that it do so before equalising the rates.[506]

The act had two stings in its tail. It empowered the minister to install a commissioner to collect rates if a borough council refused to do so. And the Metropolitan Common Poor Fund would not pay the additional monies to councils upfront: instead, the Minister of Health would lend the money and the MCPF would refund it later. The government had quietly added two weapons to its arsenal.

Nevertheless, Poplar's victory was real. The council even got a reasonable deal enabling it to repay the precepts it had withheld via a five-year loan at 6½ per cent interest; the LCC loaning Poplar the money to pay its debts to the LCC itself and to the other bodies![507] Poplar's net gain over that five-year period was over a million pounds. George Lansbury later wrote that 'although our going to prison was a very inconvenient and not at all pleasant business for us, it resulted in a very great advantage to the people of Poplar'.[508] The LCC described the new policy of pooling out-relief costs as 'a reversal of the policy of parliament of the last fifty years'[509].

As one writer put it, 'Bad laws they changed by non-compliance and the unemployed of London they assisted by their courage and determination'.[510] Once again, central government had 'tried to pull up the Poplar weed and found it was a thistle'[511].

LONDON LABOUR: ON WHICH SIDE?

Beyond doubt, it had been the Poplar councillors' rate strike, and their determination to see it through even into jail that had won this huge victory for working-class people. Edgar Lansbury rightly stated that Poplarism had won in weeks what 'thirty years of constitutional action had failed to bring about'.[512] But while that was clear to almost everyone, Herbert Morrison was determined to claim credit. His report on the conference with Mond stated that the event had taken place 'arising from the requests made by the Labour Mayors to the Prime Minister at Gairloch', and did not mention Poplar's imprisoned councillors.[513]

In his later recollection of the conference on rates equalisation, Morrison accused George Lansbury of intransigence, jealousy and not understanding the technical details, and claimed that it was Morrison's own well-researched argument that was crucial in winning. Unable to completely deny the impact of

Poplar's actions, he asserts that, 'The credit for this had to be shared between the revolting Poplar councillors and the rest of us who had mastered the subject in considerable detail'.[514] But Poplar's councillors had been arguing their case in considerable detail for some time. They had produced popular pamphlets setting out figures, and had hammered out the technicalities in numerous meetings of the borough council, its finance committee and the local labour movement. It seems unlikely that they allowed themselves to be imprisoned over an issue whose finer points they could not be bothered with. Morrison's claims later found a supporter in Billington,[515] who argued that Morrison deserved credit because he 'raised perfectly valid arguments about the danger of government intervention in local affairs'. But it was plain that it had been action not persuasion that had forced the government's hand. Words played a supporting role to deeds. As Edgar Lansbury explained, 'governments will stand out till the crack of doom against reason and justice but will fall like ninepins before a loud hullaballoo or a parade of wooden soldiers'.[516] Morrison's claim for a share of the credit was like a word processor claiming joint authorship of a novel.

Morrison still worried about a backlash. Finally publishing the full text of his draft circular,[517] he repeated his concern that Poplar's action would set a precedent for Tory rebellions, claiming that 'some of the richer Boroughs are considering an organised refusal to pay the extra levy which the new demands upon the Metropolitan Common Poor Fund and the Equalisation Fund will entail.' Should Labour, in its moment of victory, run scared of threats like this? Had the richer Boroughs withheld their money, would thousands have demonstrated in their support?! Window bills in every house?! Massive crowds at the prison windows?! Not likely! The threat came to nothing. Edgar Lansbury replied in *The Communist* that 'The London Labour Party Executive and the Labour Mayors pulled all the wires to isolate Poplar'.[518] Despite having undermined and criticised Poplar, Morrison now made a pitch for unity: 'Let us fight capitalism with ability and efficiency; let us leave off fighting against ourselves.'[519]

Even Morrison's fellow Labour right-winger Jimmy Thomas, MP for Derby[520], admitted during the Parliamentary debate that the new Bill had arisen from Poplar's action. Declaring 'that is a bad thing for the constitution'[521], Thomas refused to endorse Poplar's fight even after it had proved itself successful and even though three members of his own National Union of Railwaymen – Albert Baker, Joe Banks and James Jones – were amongst the victorious jailed councillors.

The Webbs also both acknowledged and regretted Poplar's success, blaming the failure of successive ministers to address the genuine need to unite London's

Poor Law provision: 'The result was a revolt; an ignominious surrender, and what seems to us, as far as London is concerned, a calamitous further opening of the floodgates that the Poor Law Division had been vainly seeking to close.'[522] It was 'perhaps the nadir of weakness of the Government of these years'.[523]

Poplar's Conservative MP, Reginald Blair said, 'This is a great discouragement to those who believe in constitutional action and a great encouragement to those who believe in revolutionary methods'.[524]

The Poplarists and their critics lined up for the London Labour Party's annual conference, to be held on 26 November. A special executive meeting in late October[525] considered a draft from Morrison, chairman T.E.Naylor and treasurer Alfred Salter[526] defending the London Party's stand and criticising Poplar, and with only slight amendments, decided to include it in the executive's annual report[527]. John Scurr, Susan Lawrence and London Trades Council representative Duncan Carmichael registered their dissent. Scurr stood against Morrison for London Labour Party Secretary; Sam March stood against Naylor for chairman.[528] Resolutions from Stepney and from the Union of Post Office Workers London Telephonists condemned the Executive's refusal to support Poplar.[529]

Come the conference itself[530], delegates heard early on that Sam March had withdrawn from the election for Chairman. E. Fairchild of the ILP proposed the deletion of the parts of the Executive's report about Poplar, on the basis of the 'wide divergence of opinion in the London Labour Movement'. Poplar's supporters voted for the deletion, but it was lost on a card vote, 213 to 357. The two sides then struck a deal: the executive would withdraw the offending sections of the report, and Poplar's supporters would withdraw their resolutions. John Scurr then announced his withdrawal from the election for secretary. This left London Labour with no definite view on Poplarism and with its fierce critic Herbert Morrison still in charge. Perhaps Poplar's supporters should have seen the issue through to a definite conclusion. Even had they lost, they could have gone on to organise the Poplarist minority to spread their strategy across the capital.

The unemployed movement held its third national conference in Manchester in late November, with delegates from all around Britain wished on their way by local 'send-off' demonstrations.[531] With the unemployed and the Poplarists keen to build on their victory, and the government determined to recover lost ground, the battle between them was far from over.

4. THE YEARS AFTER

INTO 1922

On the very first day of 1922, Poplar's labour movement suffered a personal and political tragedy with the death of Minnie Lansbury from influenza and pneumonia. That evening, Charlie Sumner announced Minnie's death to a thousand-strong meeting at Bow Baths: 'The audience for a moment was stricken silent ... Then out of the silence came a woman's cry of grief, followed by the weeping of many women.' After a few minutes' standing tribute, the meeting was abandoned.[532]

Aged 32, Minnie was the youngest of the jailed councillors. Councillor Joe Banks wrote that 'The movement has lost a valuable member whose place it will be hard to fill'[533], Councillor Thomas Blacketer that 'Our loss is irreplaceable'. Minnie, he said, had 'died for the cause', arguing that imprisonment had weakened her physically, leaving her body unable to fight off the illness that killed her. [534]

On January 4, a crowd of thousands, mainly women, gathered outside Minnie's house to march to her funeral in tribute – the same house at which she had held a daily surgery at 9 a.m. during her years of involvement in the council and the community. Four of her fellow councillors bore her coffin on their shoulders[535], preceded by the Shenfield Boys' Band and followed by 500 local unemployed at the head of a vast procession and cars full of floral tributes from Labour Party, Communist Party and trade union branches.[536] At the crematorium[537], Reverend Kitcat told of Minnie Lansbury's three great qualities: 'her intellectual power ... her extraordinary liberal mind and generosity of disposition ... [and] her love of justice, and depth of her sympathy, for suffering and sorrow.'[538] Mourners wearing red flowers and badges sang The Red Flag. A local newspaper wrote, 'Cut off in the midst of her social and municipal activities, with only a few days warning, the tragic suddenness of Alderman Mrs Lansbury's death has made a profound impression on her many friends in Poplar'.[539]

George Lansbury paid tribute to his daughter-in-law:

Minnie, in her 32 years, crammed double that number of years' work compared with what many of us are able to accomplish. Her glory lies in the fact that with all her gifts and talents one thought dominated her whole being night and day: How shall we help the poor, the weak, the fallen, weary and heavy-laden, to help themselves?

When, 'a soldier like Minnie passes on, it only means their presence is withdrawn, their life and work remaining an inspiration and a call to us each to close the ranks and continue our march breast forward.'[540]

With Charlie Sumner as its new mayor, Poplar council published a leaflet for 1922, 'Poplar's Victory'. Its four pages concisely summarised what the council's actions had won, giving figures for how much rent tenants had saved through the moves to equalise rates and pool relief. It was typical of the publicity that was so crucial in keeping supporters informed and involved. Another pamphlet followed: 'The Rate Protest of Poplar' by John Scurr. Although it was rich in the detail of the campaign and the victory, Geoff Richman complains that 'there is no perspective in it for developing the popular enthusiasm through new political action'[541]. The government, licking its wounds from defeat, was determined to stop Poplar's defiance, making it all the more essential that the local labour movement had an effective strategy and all the more unfortunate if it did not.

But the council was not about to rest on its laurels or declare a truce with the government. On the contrary, it was heading straight into its next confrontation.

THE MOND CIRCULAR

As agreed by the post-prison conference, Sir Alfred Mond drafted scales for out-relief and arrangements for pooling costs, and sent them out on 4 January.[542] The Poor Fund (MCPF) would pay for relief up to this 'Mond scale'. If local boards of guardians chose to pay more, their borough council would have to raise the extra. The scale was 25s (£1.25) for a married couple; an extra 6s (30p) for their first child; 5s (25p) for the second and third; 4s (20p) for the fourth; and a fuel allowance of 3s (15p) in winter, 1s6d (7½p) in summer.

Eight responded to Mond's circular by raising their scales to match his, but fifteen London boards paid even less than Mond's meagre sums even now they saved nothing by doing so. Four boards paid higher than the Mond scale – including Poplar.[543]

Mond's scale came with two conditions that pushed relief levels down even further. Under 'less eligibility', relief had to be at least 10s (50p) less than a labourers' wage. The Poplar guardians described it as 'the damnable doctrine that because a sweated worker and his family starve slowly in the employ of a greedy profit-monger, they should as a matter of course be made to starve more quickly under the care of the Guardians of the Poor'.[544]

'Red Clydesider' John McLean argued that 'full maintenance must not be a penny less than the wages you are earning when at work ... Why? Because if the unemployed are getting less than the employed the tendency will be for the unemployed to 'scab' and reduce the wages of the employed'.[545] McLean recognised unemployment as a weapon of class struggle. He saw employers insisting that wage rates set by the labour market must dominate relief rates set by public authorities. Employers kept their own incomes high while driving workers into poverty and the unemployed into the hell that lies below poverty.

A labourer's wage was hardly enough to sustain one person, certainly not enough to keep a large family in the days before family allowances. Many families relied on income from their older children, but Mond's second rule meant that a claimant's children's earnings would be deducted from his relief. Guardians administered the 'resources' rule via the hated means test, which both invaded a family's privacy and spread poverty to every family member.

At the London Labour Party's municipal conference on January 14, guardian A.A.Watts successfully proposed a resolution that the Mond scale was inadequate and that Labour should demand extra monies for rent. Mond refused Herbert Morrison's request for a deputation to discuss this.

Jobless people were pressing their claims on Boards of Guardians, their confidence boosted by Poplar's victory, including in West Ham, a dockland area similar to Poplar. But marches and deputations of unemployed activists could not yet persuade their guardians, where the 'moderates' held a majority over Labour, to agree more generous relief. Hackney's Board of Guardians – which was not Labour-controlled – voted against adopting the relief scales that the borough's Unemployed Committee asked for. Hackney's Middle Classes Union had lobbied the guardians against the 'preposterous demands of the unemployed'.[546]

The Poplar guardians, though, were not willing to be dragged down to the level of the Mond scale. On January 18, they received a deputation of the unemployed, backed by several hundred supporters. A week later, the Board passed a resolution opposing taking into account any family earnings other than husband and wife. It also decided to pay 40s (£2) in relief – higher not only than the Mond scale, but even than the 36s (£1.80) demanded by the National Unemployed Workers' Committee.

Unlike 1921's acts of defiance, the Poplar labour movement had not debated and decided this in advance. Rather, it appeared as a spur-of-the-moment proposal from Charlie Sumner, which carried the vote 8 to 7 because the majority could not bring themselves to deny an unemployed couple £2 per week.

Wal Hannington recalled that the £2 scale 'almost sent the capitalist press mad. They screamed and raved about it in almost every edition of their papers.'[547] The right wing went to war against Poplar's 'extravagance', its decision to generate an 'army of wastrels'[548], to 'wreck local government', and to create 'communal ruin' and 'a privileged class of unemployed'.[549] Calling on the unemployed to 'Rally to Poplar', the newspaper *Out Of Work* reported that, 'Poplar has caused a flutter once more in the dovecots of Fat. Again the £9 per week prostitutes of the pen are busily engaged filling the dope Press with abuse of the unemployed and the Poplar guardians.'[550] On 25 January, 15,000 unemployed marched to the Poplar guardians' offices, Hannington writing that 'It was in no sense a hostile demonstration. On the contrary, it was a demonstration of support of the guardians who had come under the fire of the reactionaries from all quarters.'[551]

Local employer George Armstrong and Co. wrote to the guardians that 'as we have no wish to prevent [our employees] from getting as much as possible we propose to dismiss them so that they can take advantage of your relief'.[552] Since no worker from the firm claimed relief subsequent to this comment[553], we can assume that Armstrong did not carry out its threat: hardly surprising as the labours of its employees made its profits. If Armstrongs was really concerned for its employees to 'get as much as possible', it would raise their wages.

Poplar's guardians argued back against their critics. However, without preparation, strategy, or the resources to carry out their rushed decision, they reluctantly voted on 31 January to withdraw the relief scale. The Communist Party reported that, 'The reformist members of the Poplar council were very distressed about it, because they thought they would lose the votes of the small ratepaying class and may even go out at the next election.' The CP offered reassurance: 'Cheer up, old things! The Poplar guardians along with the rest of the guardians all over the country, would have gone bankrupt quite soon anyway. They might as well do so in paying decent relief, as to do so after half-starving the unemployed.'[554]

The press were delighted with 'Poplar's Climbdown'.[555] But a week later, hundreds of unemployed protested by occupying the building in which the guardians were meeting and Melvina Walker, an associate of Sylvia Pankhurst, denounced the guardians as 'merely a bulwark between us and the capitalist class to keep us in subjection'.[556]

There was further suggestion of a divide amongst the Poplarists later that year, a Ministry of Health official reporting that John Scurr had seen him informally and suggested a compromise involving the Poplar guardians making 'their sliding scale a good deal steeper', but with little prospect of success as Scurr was 'afraid of the extremists'.[557]

The guardians and the London County Council were up for election that Spring, so the voters would soon show what they thought of Poplarism – and of its opponents.

TO THE POLLS

Voters elected the LCC in March 1922, the guardians in April. For both elections, the Municipal Reformers (Conservatives) and the Progressives (Liberals) ran high-profile campaigns, and Poplarism was in their sights.

In Poplar itself, the Municipal Alliance got landlords and estate agents to raise local rents, then sent out canvassers blaming the council.[558] The PBMA accused the Labour councillors of 'poisonous maladministration', and of being 'intoxicated with unaccustomed power'. They appealed to women to 'not put a X against the names of those who have brought humiliation on the manhood of the Borough'.[559]

Herbert Morrison ran Labour's LCC campaign, concentrating on proving Labour's efficiency. His draft election address ignored London Labour's policy that the Mond scale was 'inadequate' and instead promised to 'adhere to it as a general rule'. Election leaflets declared that 'Labour candidates are the Ratepayers' REAL Friends'[560]. Under Morrison, London Labour promised to dutifully administer a system that it acknowledged was unfair. He even suggested that Labour should not stand in the guardians elections[561], but his Executive decided to go ahead.

Morrison wanted Labour to do more to impress the 'middle classes', writing a series of articles on this subject in the *London Labour Chronicle* in 1923. Left-wingers would advocate doing this by convincing better-off workers of the benefits of socialist policies, but for Morrison, as for many of his successors on the Labour right, winning over the middle class meant not fighting so hard for the working class.

Election night was not good for Labour in London. It gained only one seat on the LCC, far fewer than it had hoped. However, its share of the vote remained static at 33 per cent, and numbers voting Labour rose dramatically to 378,465 on a far higher turnout than three years earlier.[562] The next month, London Labour suffered a net loss of 18 guardians, falling to 125.[563] It now controlled only two boards – Shoreditch and Poplar – instead of three.

Jimmy Thomas blamed Labour's loss of seats on Poplarism: 'it is a revolt against the kind of Poplar methods of administration which certainly alarmed people.'[564] But against the grain, 'Poplarist' Labour candidates had triumphed.

Labour won all four LCC seats in Poplar with huge majorities: Sam March and Susan Lawrence polled over 10,000 votes each in South Poplar to Municipal Reform's 6,000. Charlie Sumner and Edward Cruse won Bow and Bromley with 8,000 votes to Municipal Reform's 4,500. In the guardians' election, the 43.2 per cent turnout in Poplar was the highest in London. The Municipal Alliance lost three seats as Labour's majority increased to a staggering 21 to 3. Edgar Lansbury romped home in Bow North, polling nearly four times his opponents' vote; Julia Scurr and Dave Adams took more than 2,000 votes each in Poplar North West.[565]

The *Evening News* and *The Nation* reported a 'Great Defeat of Poplarism'. *The Communist* mocked: 'We despair of satirizing such colossal absurdity.'[566] Noting that 'these results were secured at a time when the very name of Poplar was being used as a kind of bogey to frighten the London ratepayers', George Lansbury argued that, 'the setback to Labour may be due not to the misdeeds of Poplar, but to deficiencies in courage and ability on the part of the exponents of Labour policy in other parts of London.'[567] For in contrast to London Labour's accommodation to its opponents, Poplar Labour had stood staunchly against them, damning the Municipal Alliance as 'composed of the big slum owners, and profiteers of Poplar, whose only object is to grind out profit, rent and dividend. They don't live in Poplar, they won't die in Poplar, but they are the owners of Poplar. In order to increase their own profits, they want to starve the children, neglect the sick, abandon the aged, and drive the unemployed into the workhouse.'[568]

It was not, as Kenneth Morgan claims, that "Poplarism' cost Labour dear'[569]. Rather, Labour's defensive campaign outside Poplar had lost it votes. If opposition to or fear of Poplarism had been a factor, it was helped by Morrison's and Thomas' Labour echoing the opposition and spreading the fear. Inside Poplar, where working-class people had experience of the guardians and the council, and were themselves involved in the labour movement, they were less vulnerable to scaremongering and rallied round the socialist Labour candidates.

Later that year, Labour would have a chance to learn those lessons as borough councils went to the polls. But before then Poplar had to defend itself against a government on the offensive.

THE COOPER REPORT AND THE POPLAR ORDER

The Minister of Health considered his options against Poplar's impertinent and lavish guardians. Crossing items off his options list, Mond used the only two that remained, ordering an inquiry into the Poplar guardians and refusing them loans.

Mond appointed as his inquisitor Mr. H.I. Cooper, Clerk to the Bolton guardians and a stern defender of the Poor Law's oppressive principles. Cooper held his inquiry in private after the PBMA told him its opinion 'that at the moment no real good would arise from a Public Inquiry'[570]. The PBMA supplied Cooper with many examples of supposed undeserving relief recipients, Cooper having to refute some allegations as factually incorrect.[571] Cooper met frequently with the PBMA[572] but not (after an initial, acrimonious meeting) with the guardians. He did not interview anyone involved in assessing need and paying relief. The guardians denounced his method as 'a private and one-sided inquiry … to satisfy a discredited political organisation which has been repudiated repeatedly by the overwhelming majority of the people of Poplar'.[573] Herbert Morrison wrote that Cooper's report showed 'that he regarded himself as a servant of the Poplar Municipal Alliance rather than an impartial inquirer into the facts'.[574]

Poplar's opponents who anticipated an exposé of corruption were disappointed, as there was none to expose. Instead, Cooper's report, finished on 10 May, condemned the guardians' policies as 'foreign to the spirit and intention of the Poor Law Statutes'.[575] They did not discriminate between the deserving and undeserving poor! They thought that parents should not have to live off their kids! They served butter in the workhouse! And sent 140 poor children on a summer holiday! And handed out a couple of shillings extra at Christmas! Workhouse staff were in a trade union! These guardians even gave dole money to people who were not on the very edge of starvation!

Cooper complained that two-thirds of Poplar's rates were paid by business owners who lived outside Poplar and so did not have a vote. He did not consider that these employers chose to live elsewhere nor that they made their profits from the labours of Poplar's working class and so might owe a duty to their welfare.

Cooper claimed he could save £100,000 of Poplar's spending through 'careful administration', but Edgar Lansbury showed that £93,000 of this was cuts in relief and that 'The amount of the relief was a matter, not of "careful administration" but of principle.'[576] Even the *Poor Law Officers' Journal*'s editors admitted that Poplar's £100,000 - 'the measure of Poplar's sin' - 'certainly went into the stomachs and on the backs of the people'.[577]

The Poplar guardians responded to the Cooper Report with a pamphlet, 'Guilty And Proud Of It'. Their duty, they wrote, was 'to be Guardians of the POOR and not the Guardians of the interests of property … the poor are poor because they are robbed, and are robbed because they are poor'.[578]

The pamphlet, described by Raymond Postgate as 'among the more entertaining specimens of English political invective'[579], answered each of

Cooper's allegations without apology, and with no attempt to wriggle out of accusations, engage in special pleading, or quote examples of their harshness to balance claims of extravagance. It corrected Cooper's inaccuracies, and chastened him by pointing out that 'even the worst case in the world can not be improved by a lavish use of purely imaginary figures'.[580] The guardians expertly lampooned ruling-class hypocrisy, decrying Mond as 'one who considers one room enough for newly-married workers to live in, while his own daughter has three mansions'[581], and reporting that Poplar's unemployed claim their dole 'without shame or regret … in the same spirit as that in which ex-Cabinet Ministers, Royalties, and others accept their pensions and allowances'.[582] The Report was 'a record of Mr. Cooper's opinions, and a piece of impudent official anti-Labour propaganda', whose charges against Poplar were firstly, that it refused to treat paupers as criminals and secondly, that it had won the previous year's fight to pool relief costs. 'To that double charge and all that it involves Poplar, we repeat, is proud to plead guilty.'[583]

'Guilty And Proud Of It' did, however, tend to portray Poplar's poor only as benefit claimants and Labour voters, as objects rather than subjects of Poplar's policies. But it acknowledged that Poplar's victories thus far had been 'won by hard and keen fighting' and that more of the same was required. Quite right, since the Cooper Report now lay like a loaded gun on Sir Alfred Mond's desk.

Mond could not get Parliamentary time for a Bill allowing him to take control of Poor Law administration in Poplar, but his ongoing refusal of loans ratcheted up his conflict with the guardians, who were once more mobilising the local labour movement. On June 15, ten thousand people marched through the East End and rallied at Mile End Assembly Hall[584], where they unanimously agreed a resolution backing the guardians and their relief scales.

The following Tuesday, a Poplar delegation met Mond, to whom Edgar Lansbury complained that 'the [1921] Act did not give you power to withhold these loans arbitrarily'. Edgar threatened that Poplar council would again withhold the precepts from the cross-London bodies if the Department withheld the guardians' loans. Mond retorted, 'What I cannot understand is why Poplar has to operate on a basis of splendid isolation'.[585] The Minister of Health could see Poplar's weak spot. We might pose Mond's point the other way round: why did other Labour Boards of Guardians leave Poplar to fight alone?

Reaching no agreement with Poplar's guardians, Mond issued the Relief Regulations (Poplar) Order 1922,[586] declaring relief payments in excess of his scale illegal, and told the guardians that he would only deliver their loans if they obeyed the order. The guardians were furious at this attack on their work and bitter that while Mond sought to bring 'over-spenders' into line with his scale, he aimed no such action at those Boards which still paid out less. The order specified Poplar, even while there were other Boards of Guardians paying higher scales[587] and other councils charging higher rates.[588]

Poplar's response was swift and defiant. Meeting on 22 June, the council agreed to withhold the estimates for the following quarter, and stepped again onto the path it had taken in 1921. After another deputation on 28 June,[589] Mond backed down, agreeing to pay the loans with the sole proviso that the guardians report to his Ministry all cases granted payments in excess of his scale.

Edgar Lansbury had argued Poplar's case to the Minister with power, expertise and attention to detail, Charles Key writing to George Lansbury, 'I have never heard a case stated so well'.[590] But the guardians knew that their real strength lay outside the negotiating rooms. 'While Edgar Lansbury was able to out-argue the Ministry of Health officials on the details, *politically* the leaders sought only to "throw the voice" of the mass movement upward at the government.'[591] Key felt 'proud that in the tightest corner Poplar only fights the harder'[592].

In the first week of the new arrangement, Poplar reported 1,829 excess relief cases. The PBMA was crestfallen, especially when the Ministry of Health replied to one of its letters, admitting that most of the guardians' actions fell within their legal discretion. The PBMA retorted, 'after the efforts we have made to endeavour to assist the Ministry in the present unsatisfactory condition of affairs in Poplar, my Committee regard your reply as eminently unsatisfactory and they are reluctantly compelled to come to the conclusion that nothing is to be hoped for from your Department'.[593]

Poplar's labour movement celebrated its latest victory with a rally in Victoria Park attended by thousands and adorned with 25 trade union banners. Charlie Sumner addressed the crowds, appealing to other guardians to follow Poplar.

The authorities made a further attempt to restrain Poplar, District Auditor Twiss reporting on the guardians' 'enormous expenditure' of £229,690 on outdoor relief during the half-year ending 31 March 1922.[594] Twiss claimed that 'in numerous instances, relief had been granted without the slightest excuse. In others the relevant facts have been misconstrued and a fictitious set of circumstances set up with a view, presumably to justifying an order for relief.'

On behalf of the guardians, Chairman Edgar Lansbury replied that the Auditor's statements were 'personal and spiteful' and 'entirely outside the scope of his duties'. Where Twiss had argued that 'lavish' relief had 'the effect of destroying any desire on the part of the recipients to obtain work', Edgar replied that 'The actual fact is that whenever there is any work to do, there is the keenest competition to obtain it amongst those who are on relief.'[595]

Poplar's socialists reaffirmed their commitment to their policies, and faced the voters again. London Labour could now perhaps review its flawed approach to elections.

THE VOTERS JUDGE AGAIN

Running up to the borough council elections on 1 November, the Tories and Liberals ran a 'Down With Poplarism' campaign. The press told ever more outlandish tales of Poplar's excesses. The *Daily Telegraph* reported Poplar's quarterly rate of 5s10d (29p), but in its headline printed 7s10d (39p)![596] Herbert Morrison cried foul: 'I have had my differences with our Poplar friends … but … an indignant protest should be made against the wild exaggerations and unscrupulous methods of various people, from the Minister of Health and the leaders of the London Municipal Society to the poor souls who get a living by writing to order in the columns of the Evening News.'[597]

'What is the London Labour Party going to do about this attack?' asked Charlie Sumner[598]. 'If the London Labour Party would face the Moderates and Progressives on this issue of Poplar we should beat them to a frazzle … London Labour has nothing to be ashamed of in connection with Poplar. On the contrary, everything to be proud of.' But London Labour's leaders did as Sumner feared, and 'One half of the Labour movement join[ed] in the howl against the Poplar 'wastrels', as we were dubbed by the *Daily Mail*'[599].

Clement Attlee had warned that, 'There is nothing to be gained by not adopting a bold policy. Our opponents will not be conciliated by a show of moderation.'[600] Morrison's efforts to appear moderate did not spare his local party a right-wing assault. The electoral alliance of the Progressives and Municipal Reform in Hackney deplored the Labour council's 'extremist schemes', 'extravagance' and 'unadulterated Communism', and called on voters to 'Keep The Wasters Out'.[601] Perhaps Hackney Labour councillors' failure to emulate Poplar had made them more vulnerable to their opponents' propaganda: they all lost their seats.[602] The same fate befell Labour in Fulham, led by Morrison's ally Gentry.[603] Across London, Labour lost over 300 seats and seven of its eleven borough councils.

Labour's rout was country-wide. A triumphal *Glasgow Herald* described the night's results as 'the great wind of sanity that is sweeping over the country', but had to admit that 'curiously enough, Poplar, which has figured so conspicuously as the inebriated helot of socialism, is among the exceptions. It lies unrepentant among the pots.'[604] Along with Battersea, Bermondsey and Woolwich, Labour retained Poplar, disproving Morrison's belief that Poplar's policy 'would stand no chance of being endorsed by the electorate'[605]. Labour lost just one Poplar ward: Bow Central. Most of its candidates increased their vote, and the turnout of 51.5 per cent was well up on the London average of 36.4 per cent[606]. While politicians wring their hands over 'voter apathy', they could learn from Poplarism that involving local people in fighting for working-class interests is an effective way of increasing turnout.

John Scurr later described the PBMA's election campaign in a letter to the Alliance thus: 'an intensive publicity campaign against the policy of the Labour Party. The "poor" ratepayers whom you claim to represent found considerable sums of money to finance your campaign. You controlled the local press and you conducted a campaign of considered mis-representation and abuse of the Labour council. The result was that the people of Poplar accepted your association at its true value and treated your fulminations with the contempt that they merited.'[607]

One factor in Labour's losses was that the Tories and Liberals combined in a coalition against them. In post-election analyses, London borough Labour Parties also blamed: 'scurrilous lying literature circulated by our opponents'; poor Party organisation; working-class apathy; the wet weather on polling day; the opposition's greater resources, especially cars; and 'Property versus Poverty'. None blamed Poplar, whose relative electoral success Susan Lawrence attributed to 'the satisfaction of the electorate with the "Poplar policy".'[608]

John Scurr challenged the idea that Labour could win votes by promising to keep down the rates: 'Wherever such an attempt was made it ended in disaster. The electorate either frankly disbelieved them, or else felt that the opponents would do the job better. Labour lost because it allowed its opponents to choose the ground and the weapons of the battle.'[609] The Hackney result bears out this argument: prior to its across-the-board defeat, Labour had reduced Hackney's rate to the lowest in London[610], lower even than the rate levied by the previous Municipal Reform regime. Although Scurr does call for 'thorough radical reform of our rating system', it is not central to his argument, which could come across as defending high rates. The great victory of Poplarism in 1921 had both secured the council's services and cut the rates.

The Poplar imprisonments turned out to be the *Daily Herald*'s last major campaign before its perennial financial crisis forced it to surrender its independence and pass into official TUC control. George Lansbury had refused many offers from rich men to buy the paper, but would not let it pass out of the labour movement. Even its passage into official movement control – endorsed at the annual Trades Union Congress in September 1922 – left him with mixed feelings. The *Herald*'s financial footing was now secure, but 'Some of us regret the loss of freedom which this change of ownership and control involves ... all such movements as ours need the stimulus which independent thought and expression alone can give. Officialism always dries up initiative and expression.'[611] George resigned as Editor – 'it would be impossible for me to edit a paper acting under orders from a committee or congress'[612] – but stayed on as general manager, writing a Saturday column. Lansbury approved the appointment of Henry Hamilton Fyfe, a professional journalist who had converted to socialism, as the new editor.[613]

There was one more election in 1922. In October, the Tories left the coalition government. Andrew Bonar Law became prime minister, and Alfred Mond was out of office. His year-and-a-half at the Ministry of Health had confirmed Mond's virulent anti-socialism; he had 'a bitter anxiety over the growth of Socialism ... It had already touched him closely at Poplar ... when he was faced by Socialism, he was possessed with a passionate anger which shunned all compromise.'[614] His replacement, Sir Arthur Griffith-Boscawen, was Minister of Health for just a few weeks, losing his seat in the general election on 15 November.

As some of their enemies departed parliament, George Lansbury (Bow and Bromley) and Sam March (South Poplar) arrived. Poplar finally had socialist MPs as well as socialist councillors and guardians. Sitting nearby was Clement Attlee, newly-elected MP for Limehouse. Lansbury's election address denounced Bonar Law and Lloyd George: 'Tens of thousands of ex-servicemen, an equal number of women and men munitions workers, are now in workhouses, casual wards, and mental asylums, or dependant on the poor law, driven there by the callous, brutal indifference of the Government of which these two gentlemen were leading members ... a Government of dukes, marquises, earls and other persons who "Toil not nor do they spin".'[615] The Tories won, Labour more than doubled its seats to 142. Ramsay Macdonald, newly-elected MP for Aberavon, was 'the natural choice' as the new Labour leader, defeating J.R. Clynes[616]. 'He was, or had become, the voice of conscience, of the suffering millions still in vain pursuit of that promised land fit for heroes.'[617]

THE MINIMUM WAGE

In September 1922, the Labour Research Department hosted a conference giving Poplar a platform to explain its 'widely misunderstood' policy.[618] Susan Lawrence explained that 'Poplar council had always shown itself ready to stake its financial position for the sake of a principle', telling the story of how the Ministry of Health had tried to make Poplar charge 'exorbitant' rents for new homes built under a government scheme; the council refused; the Ministry threatened to withhold grants; the council stood firm; and arbitration reduced the rents. In contrast, other councils had accepted the high rents. If you choose to fight, you might win. If you choose not to, you have no chance.

Poplar's speakers also flagged up a simmering fight that was about to boil. Poplar believed that socialist councils should pay their employees a living wage. Other Labour councils, though, accepted that wages should fluctuate according to the market, which in the early 1920s meant that they should fall. It was a sharp political difference. Do you allow private employers a free hand to drive down not just their own employees' wages but council workers' too? Or do you use the power of public office to impose working-class needs in defiance of the market?

Several Labour councils, including Poplar, had introduced a minimum wage of £4 per week in 1920. The PBMA attacked the minimum wage from day one, and the further that industrial wages fell, the more hysterical the employers' demands that municipal wages should fall too. PBMA Secretary Alfred Warren badgered the Minister of Health, demanding that the government force the council and guardians to cut wages and 'economise' and even that relief claimants lose their right to vote.

The PBMA issued an extraordinary public statement, in which it argued that 'high' municipal wages were unfair on their own low-paid, private employees! 'This unequal and unfair treatment ... naturally breeds discontent amongst men engaged in similar occupations and trades under private control – not that the men employed by private undertakings are dissatisfied with their agreed scale of wages, but it is in the nature of things for them to make unfavourable comparison between themselves and the various artizans and workmen of the borough council and guardians.'[619]

The PBMA was scandalised that a council bricklayer earned two pence an hour more than a private brickie! A builder's labourer two-and-a-half pence more! A road labourer three pence more! And the greatest scandal? If a married couple were a Dustman and a Convenience Attendant, they would earn eight pounds a week between them. Perhaps the PBMA thought that people who worked with rubbish and effluent all day should not expect comfort at home. The PBMA seemed unconcerned that their employees might 'make unfavourable comparison' with employers' incomes. There is no evidence that Poplar's low-paid private-sector workers were demanding municipal pay cuts. Rather, their employers were demanding cuts and disingenuously using their own companies' low pay scales as a pretext.

Charles Key argued that 'wages must always present a difficult problem to a Labour borough council for the whole wage system is radically wrong. Under it rates of pay are fixed by no principle which Labour and Socialist members can justify. Remuneration bears no relation to the needs or responsibilities of the individual worker.'[620] Wages, he said, are not even genuinely related to the value of the work, 'for there are many in high positions doing work of less social value than that performed by the despised dustman or road-sweeper.'

But surely 'union rates' were fair? Not necessarily. A union agreeing a pay scale did not mean that it agreed that the workers deserved only that wage. Rather, it 'agreed' that this was the best it could achieve at that time. The union leaders proved too weak to effectively fight the wage cuts that swept Britain in the early 1920s. Having called members out for 85m strike days in 1921, they let this figure plummet to 19m in 1922 and 10m in 1923.[621] They needed to fight the wage cuts on the same three fronts that the employers fought – industrially, politically and ideologically. But they accepted the ideological justification for wage cuts, and industrially, restricted themselves to negotiating less painful cuts. Politically, a Labour council could refuse to cut wages. But some union leaders even set themselves against this! Herbert Morrison wrote that 'Ernest Bevin in particular did not like it. The increase had been simply bestowed on the members of his union, and the negotiating machinery had been ignored.'[622] Bevin, General Secretary of the Transport and General Workers' Union, was actually angry that Poplar council had not invited him to negotiate cuts in his members' pay! Focused on securing the role of officials, he saw negotiations as an end in themselves rather than a means to defend pay and conditions.

Communist J.R. Campbell argued that labour movement leaders' collaboration with wage cuts arose from a mistaken understanding of capitalism. Reformist leaders, he wrote, accepted the view that the slump was abnormal for capitalism, whereas communists recognised that economic crisis is a natural feature of the system. 'In the sphere of wages, the reformists stand for concessions to capitalism, in order to help capitalism get back to "normal", while the Communists stand for a resistance to the demands of the capitalists and the preparation for a decisive struggle against capitalism.'[623]

Hackney council cut wages to the JIC[624] rate plus 2s (10p). It showed, said Morrison, 'consideration to other grades of workpeople and the general working class community'.[625] There is evidence of some hypocrisy on Morrison's part. From February 1921, he was paid £420 per annum (£8+ per week) as London Labour Party Secretary, rising by annual increments of £20.[626] Further, his biographers argue that 'He was never as hard up as might appear from the salary he was paid, or as he often liked to make out, for on the side he was earning what must have been substantial sums from his journalism ... With his nominal salary he could portray himself as self-sacrificing and a humble earner.'[627] Moreover, Morrison took a different attitude to high-ranking council officers' pay than to ordinary council workers' wages, holding that 'higher salaries were essential for the borough to attract first-rate officials on whose efficiency depended the running of services'.[628]

Poplar council agreed to limited pay cuts in August 1922, when John Scurr argued that 'they had to face certain economic facts and compromise between their real views and the actual conditions prevailing'[629]. 'Compromise' was not the stance that had won them victory the previous year. Implementing only half the cuts already accepted by the unions and keeping the minimum wage, the council's small concession did not appease its opponents. Rather, it both infuriated them by its small scale and spurred them on by the fact that the council had conceded the principle.

Local employer and former mayor[630] Fred Thorne challenged the council by refusing to pay its full bill for relaying a drain and connecting to the sewer. Charged £30.0s.9d (£30.04), Thorne's building company offered £25, the sum it claimed the work would have cost had the council paid market-rate wages of 1s4d (6½p) per hour rather than its own rate of 1s10d (9p). The council sued Thorne. Metropolitan Magistrate John Cairns[631] asked rhetorically whether it would be reasonable for a business to pay the council's bill if it 'decided to embark upon a social experiment to pay its labourers and Carmen 20/- [£1] or some such fanciful figure per hour.' Cairns dismissed the summons and awarded Thorne 12 guineas costs.[632]

By 1923, the government felt helpless to restrain Poplar's guardians, a senior civil servant advising the Minister of Health that he had to 'consider the unpalatable policy of running away'.[633] However, the authorities did feel confident to move against Poplar on the issue of wages, and did so through the District Auditor.[634] Since their creation, District Auditors had steadily extended their reach beyond corruption cases into more political areas, auditing not just accounts but policies.

On 31 May 1923, District Auditor Carson Roberts – 'the doyen of district auditors during the first quarter of the twentieth century'[635] – summoned Poplar council to show cause why he should not surcharge them £17,000 for wages paid in excess of union rates for the year ending March 1922. This move was a shock, as the law[636] empowered a local authority 'to employ such servants as might be necessary and to pay them such salaries or wages as it might think fit'. Unlike in previous conflicts, the council wanted the hearing held in private so it could hear clear legal grounds. But a large crowd of supporters gathered outside singing The Red Flag and some came into the public gallery. The councillors allowed them in, and 'despite efforts by Lansbury and others to restrain them, they did not hesitate to applaud the councillors and shout rude remarks at their opponents.'[637] Mobilising support used to be key to Poplar's strategy: was it now embarrassing them?

The auditor explained that the legal issue was whether councils have complete discretion over wages. John Scurr, 1923's Mayor, submitted a statement outlining that by law they do, and also noting that Poplar's voters had endorsed the council's policy at the 1922 election. The Municipal Alliance had amalgamated with the Poplar Ratepayers' Association[638], and engaged top lawyer Edward Naldrett KC. He quoted the Thorne case and claimed great authority as a representative of 200 ratepayers. The auditor admitted that an 'association of ratepayers' had taken exception to the council's policy, a confession that he was acting on request of the employers.

The auditor ruled that the councillors must pay a surcharge, but of £5,000 rather than £17,000. Poplar council called a special meeting on 12 June and this time had no problem with large, singing crowds. The council decided to appeal. Although defying the auditor by continuing to pay its 'excessive' wages, the council was relying on the courts much more than two years previously. Why? Perhaps the councillors felt isolated. Or perhaps despite their certain knowledge of the law's bias against the working class, they were convinced that it was so explicit on this issue that they must win. If so, the court was about to remind them just how class-biased it was.

On 21 September, the court ruled in favour of the Auditor, on the grounds that the law did not actually mean what it said, stating that, 'We cannot think that the words "as they think fit" entitled a council to pay any sum that they like to any of their employees'.[639] What would they have made of the £150,000-plus salaries that councils pay to their chief executives now?! Poplar council decided to appeal again, but before the appeal was heard, Britain would have its first Labour government, and before that, Poplar would be at the heart of a major unofficial dock strike.

DOCKERS ON STRIKE

In 1922, dock employers had demanded pay cuts. The Transport and General Workers' Union (TGWU) had formed through amalgamation of 14 unions on 1 January that year, and General Secretary Ernest Bevin, keen to avoid a fight, agreed a three-stage reduction. But the union's leader had misjudged his members' mood: they were furious at cuts in their already-awful pay and ready to fight back. Hopes that the third shilling cut might not go ahead proved forlorn, and dockers' anger boiled over. They walked out of Hull docks on 2 July 1923, and most of the country's within days.

A week later, TGWU conference rejected strikers' requests to make the action official and urged them to return to work. London's delegates voted to continue and endorse the strike,[640] knowing that London dockers wanted to battle on. A smaller union, the Stevedores' Labour Protection League, now made the strike official, and its local membership shot up from 6,000 to 17,000.[641] Its head office was in Poplar, and the strike had strong local support, particularly in South Poplar's Irish community.[642] The socialist councillors were in the eye of the storm; several worked on the docks. John Hegarty and Henry Sloman were active in the stevedores' union and so fully part of the strike. Joe O'Callaghan was a former stevedores' union member and now assistant relieving officer. But Charles Petherick was in the TGWU, worked throughout the strike and temporarily moved to Tottenham to escape local hostility.[643] TGWU full-timer Dave Adams found his office occupied by the unofficial strike committee, accepted the situation and worked alongside them. The *Daily Herald* was showing signs of a rightward pull exerted by its new owners: 'If its heart was with the workers, its head and leading articles increasingly followed the officials.'[644]

Destitute strikers came to the Poplar guardians. It was illegal to pay relief to strikers[645], and London boards responded differently. Bethnal Green and Stepney paid relief to strikers' families; many boards refused even that. Poplar paid relief to strikers on the basis of need, as Chairman Edgar Lansbury argued that the guardians should not stand aside and see strikers starved back to work.[646] Without strike pay, poor relief helped the strikers get by, and Edgar proudly claimed that for the first time he could recall, workers 'had been able to stand up to the employers with a full belly', but bemoaned 'that the press had been filled with blackguardly comments concerning the humanity – or what was termed the evil-doing – of the Poplar Board.'[647] This was not the first time that the Poplar Board had funded working-class struggles. A few months previously, it had provided lodging and clothing for campaigners who had marched from Poplar to London to protest against hunger.[648]

The PBMA wrote to Minister of Health Neville Chamberlain, complaining that 'This undoubtedly is an illegal action on their part, and is very likely the reason why the strike is being prolonged'.[649] It reported receiving protest letters from 'very important and highly assessed Firms in this Borough', as though their opinions should be considered in proportion to their rateable value.

The dockers' claims drained the guardians' resources, and Poplar's relief scale was now higher not just than the lowest wages but also than ordinary wages. The guardians cut relief for families with two or more children. Two hundred supporters of Sylvia Pankhurst's Unemployed Workers' Organisation (UWO) invaded the guardians' meeting and locked everyone in. An official called the police, and against Edgar's objection, the guardians allowed them in. The police smashed windows, broke down doors, and hospitalised twenty protesters. Sylvia's biographer describes the UWO's protest as 'an undignified and unworthy attempt to make herself heard'[650], but although the UWO was a fringe group, it could mobilise hundreds of people, and this terrible incident suggests that the relationship between Poplar's labour representatives and the local working-class movement was not what it used to be. Some of the unemployed were protesting against them rather than in support of them.

Since Mond's departure, several Tories had sat in the Minister of Health's seat – Sir Arthur Griffith-Boscawen, Neville Chamberlain and, from 27 August 1923, Sir William Joynson-Hicks, a man who would go on to be remembered for 'the maintenance of public order during the General Strike of 1926' when he was Home Secretary.[651] By then, the dock strike had collapsed[652], but the new minister promised to take firmer action against Poplar. This delighted Sir Alfred

Warren, now no longer an MP but still Poplar's leading right-wing agitator. 'Jix', as Sir William was known, got Cabinet agreement for a bill allowing him to take over the powers of councils and guardians which defied him. If he did not like their policies, he could abolish them! But Conservative Prime Minister Stanley Baldwin, who had replaced Bonar Law in August, sprung a surprise which scuppered Jix's plan. On 13 November, he dissolved parliament and sought a mandate from voters for his trade protection policy.

THE FIRST LABOUR GOVERNMENT

In the general election on 6 December 1923, Poplar councillors John Scurr and Susan Lawrence joined March and Lansbury in parliament, John representing Mile End and Susan becoming Labour's first woman MP when she won East Ham North. Herbert Morrison became MP for South Hackney.

Baldwin's electoral gambit failed. The Conservatives were the largest party with 258 seats, but no longer had an overall majority, as the Liberals slipped to 159 seats and Labour swept forward to 191. The Liberals refused to form a coalition with the Tories, so the door was open for Labour to form a government. Labour had three options. It could refuse to govern without a majority. It could form a minority government, introduce bold measures to improve working-class life then, when the Tories and Liberals voted them down, call a general election on these policies and hope to win. But Labour leader Ramsay Macdonald had a third option – form a Labour government but do nothing to upset the Liberals. Liberal leader Herbert Asquith thought this a great idea, which should have alerted Labour to its foolishness. As the *Liberal Magazine*'s editorial gushed, Labour would have to 'turn its back on socialism'.[653]

George Lansbury wrote that 'it would be for me a great honour and privilege to serve in the first British Labour Cabinet'[654], but Macdonald offered him only the non-Cabinet post of Transport Minister[655], which Lansbury refused.[656] Macdonald's rejection of Lansbury is no surprise, since he thought that 'public doles, Poplarism, strikes for increased wages, limitation of output, not only are not Socialism, but may mislead the spirit and policy of the Socialist movement'.[657] The new Cabinet's token left-winger was 'Red Clydesider' John Wheatley. The good news for Poplar was that he was Minister of Health.

On 5 February, the guardians met Wheatley, a man they trusted would 'understand and sympathise with them in the horrible problem of poverty, misery and distress which faces them'.[658] Wheatley agreed to rescind the Poplar Order.[659] It was a massive victory for Poplar, whose guardians had lived with the threat of legal action for two years and were finally vindicated. Poplar celebrated at a public meeting at Bow Baths, where Charles Key urged other boards to now follow Poplar's path.

The *Daily Express* denounced the 'Free Hand' restored to Poplar[660]; the *Morning Post* deplored the 'Surrender to Poplar', alarmed at the 'First Taste of Socialism'.[661] The Tories, Liberals and Poplar employers were furious. So was Ramsay Macdonald, whom Wheatley had not consulted about his decision. Macdonald got the Cabinet to instruct Wheatley to issue a statement that the reason for his decision was a technical one that the Order had proved unworkable rather than a decision of political principle: 'The truth is that my predecessors recognised that it was impractical to enforce the Order'[662]. Outside Parliament, Wheatley's Parliamentary Private Secretary, Arthur Greenwood, offered a better explanation: that 'the government of Poplar must be carried on with the consent of the people of Poplar'[663].

Edgar Lansbury wrote an article in the *New Leader*[664], knocking down allegations of wastefulness and spelling out Poplar's achievements. Edgar pointed out that several Poplar guardians were dock and rail workers, paid less than they would receive in relief had they been unemployed. They did not resent the jobless, and were angry at low pay rather than high dole. The *Westminster Gazette* took this not as proof of the integrity of board members, but as an 'admission that it is the policy of the Poplar guardians to make unemployment more remunerative than employment'.[665] Eric Hodgson, a former Poplar church minister, wrote to the *Gazette* defending the guardians and the 'patient work and skilful organisation on the part of men and women devoted to a most depressing and exacting neighbourhood'. Edgar scolded the Ratepayers' Association: 'It is true that much of the money for this work must be taken from those who would pass on the other side. But surely this will be good for their souls even if it lightens their pockets!'

The Tories and Liberals forced a parliamentary debate on Wheatley's cancellation of the Poplar Order. They hoped to hammer the government, but Herbert Morrison recalled that 'in John Wheatley they had met more than they bargained for. He ... demolished the Opposition's case and came through triumphantly.'[666] Morrison could praise Wheatley's speech because Macdonald had again compelled him to argue that the Poplar order was ineffective, not that it was wrong.[667] The Cabinet had agreed 'that the Minister of Health should make it clear that the rescission of the Order was never intended in any way to encourage or condone slack administration'.[668] Morrison even urged the Liberals to aim their fire at previous ministers for failing to enforce the order! But why was the order ineffective? Because, as Edgar Lansbury said, 'the workers are with us. It is because [the Ministers of Health] have all realised that they are powerless in the face of real united working-class effort.'[669] As a letter to George Lansbury pointed out, the parliamentary debate, 'while reflecting great credit on Wheatley was really a triumph for the Lansbury policy of past years'.[670]

Parliament did not vote to condemn the government,[671] and Labour might have learned from this episode that it could pursue socialist policies and get away with it. But it did not. It dashed working-class hopes, and left the unemployment crisis practically untouched.

The minority Labour government lasted only until October 1924, when it fell not for any great radical reform, but because Attorney General Patrick Hastings prosecuted the communist *Workers' Weekly* for incitement to mutiny then backed down under fire from Labour MPs led by John Scurr. Ramsay Macdonald resigned. The first Labour government had not brought great reforms or a shift in class power. Poplar's pushiness had extracted a few victories, but as George Lansbury wrote in his new journal, *Lansbury's Labour Weekly*, Macdonald's government 'has not challenged Capitalism at a single point. It has followed, in foreign affairs, in dealing with unemployment, indeed on every vital issue, a policy of "continuity" with its capitalist predecessors.'[672] Lansbury had resigned as General Manager of the *Daily Herald* in January 1925, and five of the *Herald*'s staff, plus its company secretary, followed him to his new publication.[673]

John Wheatley was the only Cabinet minister to give socialists reason to cheer. He introduced a Housing Act which led to the building of half-a-million council homes, a landmark in the history of social housing. The following year and no longer in government, Wheatley visited Poplar to open a new block of flats and declared his 'great joy and pride in being associated with Poplarism … the Poplar Borough Council in many respects was a great pioneer in the work of social emancipation.'[674]

Macdonald's government had failed so miserably that the Conservatives romped home in the ensuing general election, and the new Minister of Health, Neville Chamberlain, was out to finally defeat Poplarism.

BACK IN COURT

Before Chamberlain took his seat, Poplar sat in the dock twice more. If 'Poplarism' had been street theatre in 1921, it was now courtroom drama.

During the 1923 dock strike, seething local employers had started to organise businesses to refuse to pay rates, one arguing that 'a threat not to pay rates might have an effect in retarding the guardians' present lavish expenditure, and might also shorten the Dock Strike'[675]. For 'shorten', read 'defeat'. But Health Minister Joynson-Hicks wrote to the PBMA that this action would be counter-productive, and the PBMA backed down.[676]

Determined that the Poplar guardians would not 'get away with it', eight local firms persuaded Attorney General Sir Douglas Hogg to apply for a court ruling that the payments were illegal, and the writ was issued three days before the general election, on 3 December 1923.[677] By the time the case was heard, in June

1924, Labour was in government and Hogg no longer Attorney General. But with the watchword 'continuity', Macdonald's Attorney General pressed ahead. A Labour government prosecuted a Labour board of guardians.

The court declared the relief payments illegal. The auditor imposed a surcharge of £1,843, most falling on guardians Julia Scurr, Helen McKay and Dave Adams, who had personally handled the most cases. The Poplar socialists had no intention of paying these or any other surcharges.

Poplar's £4 minimum wage also came back to court while Labour was still in office, and again the government let the case go ahead. The council enjoyed wide support on this issue, because the law was crystal clear – a council could pay the wages it saw fit. People could see that the Auditor's attack on Poplar was a politically-motivated attempt to re-write the law on behalf of embittered local capitalists. The three Appeal Court judges decided by two to one to back the council and disallow the surcharge. The councillors held a celebration party, but they knew their victory was only partial and would be short-lived. Not only did the Auditor appeal to the House of Lords, he also began the legal process again with respect to 1922-23. It was like groundhog day, with the argument, the crowds and The Red Flag just like the previous year.

The Auditor's Appeal to the House of Lords[678] was eventually heard in 1925. Five Law Lords overturned the Appeal Court ruling and endorsed the Auditor's actions. Their reasons are ruling-class 'justice' laid bare, an extraordinary collection of quotes revealing the prejudices held by both themselves and the system they represented. The council's workforce accurately described it in a resolution as 'biassed and unconstitutional class rule'[679].

£4 per week, said the judges, was 'unreasonable'. A bitter George Lansbury pointed out afterwards that four of the five Lords received over £120 per week. The exception was 'poor Wrenbury who drags out a hungry existence on about £55 per week – often when I see a man shivering at a street corner, I say 'That may be poor Wrenbury' … It needed high moral courage to announce to the world your profound conviction that any one of you was worth thirty ordinary men. Except of course poor Wrenbury who is worth only fourteen ordinary men.'[680] Lord Atkinson reserved particular outrage for the suggestion that charwomen might deserve £4 per week, a sum so high that it could not be considered wages at all, but 'gifts and gratuities disguised as wages and therefore illegal'. Atkinson implied that Poplar council's workers had not earned their money, earning him and his colleagues a stinging description by Charles Key as 'Noble Lords who are so class-bigoted as to hold that the payment of £4 for a week of 47 hours' hard manual labour is an "indulgence in philanthropic enthusiasm".'[681]

Claiming justification from the Public Health Act 1875, which empowered him to disallow illegal expenditure, the Auditor had disallowed expenditure with which he politically disagreed, and the Law Lords had endorsed his actions. Lord Atkinson even stated that for something to be illegal, there does not actually have to be a law against it! From now on, argued Charles Key, 'an Auditor would get all the support he required in stopping a Labour council from making any radical alteration in the condition of the working classes who had returned it to office for the specific purpose of serving their interests'.[682]

The judicial system had supported Poplar a few times, both in the Appeal Court on this issue in 1924, and in releasing them from prison in 1921. Now it was decisively against them. What was the difference? The justice of their case? No – the letter of the law was with the councillors in 1925, whereas even they accepted that they were guilty in 1921! The difference was that the state did not feel the level of working-class pressure in 1925 that it had in 1921.

The judges repeatedly quoted trade union agreement to wage cuts, and Lord Sumner pointed out in his judgment that if Poplar intended to be a 'model' employer, then 'the council's resolution is vox clamantis in deserto [a voice crying in the wilderness], for other authorities, with rare exceptions, turn a deaf ear to it.' The 'rare exceptions', Woolwich and Bethnal Green, had both been surcharged at the same time as Poplar.[683]

The timidity of most Labour and trade union leaders had caused working-class militancy to drain away like a receding tide, leaving Poplar high and dry. The council would now have to face a lonely choice of how to respond to the Law Lords' ruling.

HOLDING BACK THE TIDE

In the same week that Poplar council lost in court, Poplar voters elected an 'all red' board of guardians. A minority until just six years previously, Labour now held all 24 seats. The loyalty and support of local people came from the stubborn determination of both the council and the guardians to fight for improvements in working-class living standards whatever their enemies threw at them. It also came from the material improvements that Labour administration had delivered, which the council itemised in a pamphlet, 'The Work of Six Years 1919-1925'. The PBMA complained to the Minister of Health about the pamphlet, asking him to arrange for the District Auditor to bar the council from paying for it from the rates.[684]

In those six years, Poplar Borough Council had: built nearly 400 homes; carried out over 70,000 housing inspections, serving thousands of improvement notices on landlords; opened new public baths and swimming pools; increased library membership by 53 per cent and book borrowing by 95 per cent; massively extended electricity supply; employed over 5,000 jobless people in public works; asphalt-paved 62 streets; planted 2,165 trees; increased street-sweeping and sewer cleansing; improved open spaces, playgrounds, tennis and netball courts; extended public toilet provision; and set up a Sunshine Clinic for 'backward and ailing children'.[685]

Eighty years ago, with a political commitment absent from many town halls today, Poplar council made strides forward for working-class residents in the face of opposition from capitalists and their political servants. The LCC and the Ministry of Health blocked the council's plan to set up a TB clinic for the south of the borough.[686] When the council planned to introduce washing machines to public wash-houses, the laundry industry held special conferences to oppose the plan, even asking Laundry Engineers to refuse to supply machines![687] The council established four 'mechanical wash-houses' anyway, boasting that they were 'the most up-to-date in the Country, the mechanical process obviating the hard laborious work usually associated with wash-day'. The council expressly designed the policy to lift some burden from working-class women's shoulders.

The council's pamphlet concluded that it 'will only have served its purpose if it results in increased interest and activity on the part of the men and women of the Borough, for without their active co-operation no social evils can be wholly or permanently removed'. But while still calling on paper for activity, Poplar was no longer mobilising its supporters with gusto, and Poplarism was nearing its final days.

The £4 minimum, just declared illegal, was now 40 per cent above the pay of labourers in other councils, 78 per cent above female wages. George Lansbury argued against defying the court, as ratepayers could get an injunction against the council.[688] While true, this had not stopped them fighting earlier battles. More likely, the fading of working-class militancy across Britain under weak leadership was draining the combativity even of Poplar. Councillor Joe O'Callaghan 'thought the council would have put up a better fight before knuckling under',[689] but on 9 April the council passed a resolution from Charles Key: 'under protest and with great reluctance … to consider the whole question of wages with a view to bringing them into conformity with the decision of the House of Lords.' The council attempted to soften the blow by delaying and minimising the cuts. Their new lowest rate was £3.12s.6d (£3.62½), which was still more than 20 per cent above the usual rate for men, 50 per cent above that for women, and could buy more in the shops than the £4 rate when the council had first introduced it.

The PBMA raged to Health Minister Neville Chamberlain that 'the modification can only be described as ludicrous … flouting the decision of the Courts'[690]. Chamberlain was confident, bullish, and obviously felt that the Law Lords having rewritten the law in his favour, he could now set municipal wages in Poplar instead of the council. So he told them he wanted further wage cuts before he would remit the surcharges. The council entered into lengthy talks without retreating further. In December 1925, the court granted summonses against 39 councillors to recover the £5,000 surcharge plus £1,198 costs. The councillors remained defiant, but may have pondered that had they stuck to the £4 minimum they would be no worse off.

Realising that persecuting Poplar further would be unpopular, Chamberlain offered a deal. He would cancel the surcharges, safe in the knowledge that the Auditor could intervene again in future. Poplar council would keep its wage levels but vary them in future as JIC wage scales varied. Municipal wages would remain higher than in other councils, but the market was now in charge. The council accepted the deal and a mass meeting of 700 council workers endorsed it with just two votes against.[691]

But the PBMA would not let matters rest there. It decided to no longer contest elections,[692] and instead to 'devote some effort to set out the evils that have arisen in Local Government affairs, and especially with reference to the Poor Law and suggest remedies'. One such remedy would be to reverse the 1918 legislation allowing paupers to vote for guardians, since it was 'entirely unsafe to allow recipients of relief to vote on the levying of funds for that Relief or upon its administration. It is no use allowing sentiment to intervene in this matter'.[693] Chamberlain considered reversing pauper enfranchisement, but he was 'not deeply committed' to it and dropped it when officials 'got cold feet'.[694]

Another of the PBMA's 'remedies' would be to end the Minister of Health's practice of waiving surcharges. When the Auditor surcharged the council £23,000 for 1925-26, the PBMA mounted a legal challenge to the minister's right to waive surcharges and won, overturning half a century of custom and practice.[695] The PBMA was determined to bring down the heaviest penalties on the heads of these socialists who had dared to give workers hope, dignity and leadership.

The PBMA accused Poplar Labour of the crime of 'a communal responsibility debased to class self-seeking'[696] and bemoaned that in Poplar, 'The masters have there become the servants and the servants have become the masters'.[697] The PBMA still feared Poplarism and warned fellow capitalists: 'As Poplar is to-day so any community of a similar character may be in the near future ... The disease which has assumed such grave form in Poplar may spread.'[698]

Their fear was well-founded. Better late than never, some guardians were taking faltering steps along Poplar's road. West Ham's defiance of the Poor Law ran several years behind Poplar's: covering neighbouring, less urbanised districts as well as West Ham itself, the poor law union had elected a majority Labour board of guardians only in 1924. The new board brought year-round coal allowances,

May Day holiday and compulsory trade union membership.[699] The Ministry of Health tried to force the guardians to cut relief by imposing conditions on loans. Chamberlain fancied six months at West Ham's helm himself, confident that he 'could show a saving of something like £300,000 or £400,000 a year without inflicting any hardship on the deserving cases. The undeserving would no doubt speedily make tracks for one of the neighbouring Bolshie Paradises and it would be a glorious lesson for the country'.[700] *Lansbury's Labour Weekly* editorialised that his aggressive attitude 'stamps Mr. Chamberlain as the meanest and most despicable Minister ever put in control of local administration'.[701]

Union branches, local Labour Parties and unemployed groups formed the Active Resistance Committee in June 1925. It convened a conference, attended by Poplar delegates along with others, which pledged support to the West Ham guardians in their refusal to make cuts. But a government ultimatum in October 1925 persuaded the board to back down, although a minority of Labour guardians voted to resist. Local unemployed people protested against the surrender.

The government introduced its Unemployment Bill 1925, described by George Lansbury as 'contemptible ... a direct and cowardly attack on the most helpless section of the working class'[702]. It did not address unemployment itself, but instead cut benefit entitlement. As Lansbury wrote, 'Baldwin and his backers do not know how to decrease unemployment. But they do know how to make it look and cost less'. The new law drove even more unemployed people to the guardians, especially in areas dominated by casual labour. Lansbury told a public meeting that Chamberlain was 'doing his best to make his Ministry a Ministry of death'.[703]

The 1926 General Strike was a huge drain on guardians' resources and the Ministry of Health demanded West Ham make drastic cuts. This time, the Board refused. Chamberlain armed himself with the Guardians (Default) Act, empowering him to appoint commissioners to take over from Boards of guardians which were 'not discharging their functions'. It was a hammer blow at local democracy and against resistance to Poor Law degradation. As J.R. Campbell explained, 'The boards of guardians in this country were appointed by law to look after the interests of the poor. So long as those Boards were in capitalist hands and the poor, whether infirm or able-bodied, were treated with the utmost callousness and contempt, those boards of guardians were allowed to continue their democratic ways undisturbed. Immediately, however, Labour majorities began to appear on those Boards and began to utilise them in the interests of the working class, the capitalist government immediately restricted their powers.'[704]

Alfred Mond's biographer Hector Bolitho argues that Mond had advocated this measure since 1921: 'The practical man of affairs saw immediately what was needed, yet it took everyone else four years to come to the conclusion that he was right.'[705] Bolitho does not consider that it may have been the 1921 rate strike, or the troubles over the Poplar Order, that it may have been working-class resistance that made his 'reform' impossible to impose.

Immediately the Act came into force, in summer 1926[706], Chamberlain unseated the elected boards of guardians in West Ham and in Chester-le-Street, a move which the PBMA 'view[ed] with satisfaction'[707]. Six months later, he acted against the Bedwelty guardians. Ironically, a law aimed against Poplar's guardians was never used against them. Three appointed commissioners took over Poor Law administration in West Ham and immediately cut relief by one-third, mainly by kicking unskilled, long-term unemployed people off the books.[708] Attempted protests did not come off, perhaps because the West Ham Board had faltered the previous year; or perhaps because the working class was cowering in the shadows of the General Strike's defeat. Chamberlain's appointed Commissioner Sir Alfred Woodgate was ruthless in his opinions as well as his actions, saying that, 'If the people in great hardship let their children die because they have not enough to eat then the blame must be theirs for not bringing their cases forward'.[709] Ratepayers gave Woodgate gifts in gratitude for his work.[710]

Over the next three years, Chamberlain introduced new legislation to: disqualify rebel councillors from office; place the Metropolitan Common Poor Fund under the control of Ministry of Health nominees; and abolish boards of guardians. For Chamberlain's admirers, it was a 'significant legislative achievement'[711] which helped mark him as 'a committed believer in social progress and in the power of government, at both the national and local level, to do good'.[712] One of his biographers recognised that the 'roots of Chamberlain's battle for control of the Poor Law can be traced back to the 'Revolt of Poplar' in the autumn of 1921'[713]. He had completed a long and ultimately successful counter-offensive.

After decades of campaigning by socialists, the government had accepted that relief should be funded centrally. Charles Key, the last Chair of the Poplar Board of Guardians, wrote that, 'we are seeing the direct and inevitable result of Poplarism when we see the end of the Poplar Guardians'[714]. But the price was the abolition of democratic control over care for the poor. On 1 April 1930, local Boards of Guardians ceased to exist, their responsibilities in London transferred to the LCC's new Public Assistance Committee (PAC). Edgar Lansbury argued that abolition destroyed a democratic institution to which working people had secured increasing representation.[715] As the PAC had the same political make-up as the LCC, relief in Poplar was now administered by a Tory-majority body, and the new law ensured that neither PAC members nor relieving officers in Poplar could be Poplar people.[716] There had been local administration of poor relief for three centuries, but just a decade of participation by the people who depended on that relief was enough to prompt the government to scrap local control.

George Lansbury approved, believing that only central government could afford to fund unemployment relief and distribute it fairly. He also 'rightly foresaw that these new developments signalled the death throes of the Poor Law'.[717] The Act had not abolished the Poor Law, only its democratic administration. Democracy was scrapped before inhumanity was.

It also signalled the end of Poplarism.

5. OUTCOMES AND CONCLUSIONS

WHATEVER HAPPENED TO THE HEROES?

Neville Chamberlain had legislated away the main battleground between Poplar and the government. The guardians were gone, but Poplar Borough Council remained, and it stayed Labour. 1927's Official Guide recorded the council's continuing work in electricity supply, tree planting, Unemployed Relief Works, and particularly housing. Moreover, 'for a densely populated area its health records are an excellent testimonial to the efficiency of its administration.'[718] Poplar council could achieve so much because of the enduring jackpot of its 1921 victory, giving it 10s (50p) in the pound in rates relief.

Many of 1921's prisoners continued to be re-elected to the council, several serving as mayor, including Thomas Goodway, Albert Baker, Dave Adams and James Jones. Charles Key became the only person to be Poplar's mayor three times. But others had departed. During the 1920s, Poplar's labour movement mourned the deaths of Charlie Sumner, Joe O'Callaghan, James Rugless and Julia Scurr. George Lansbury believed that imprisonment contributed to their early death. Joe Banks resigned due to ill-health in 1922. Susan Lawrence was not reappointed as Alderman in 1924 as she was now an MP outside Poplar.

At the end of his mayoral year (1924/5), Edgar Lansbury left both the council and the board of guardians. He had married Moyna McGill in September 1924, and the first of their three children, Angela, was born in 1925. The family moved to St. John's Wood where Edgar ran a sawmill but, along with his brother William, was declared bankrupt in 1927. Edgar died of cancer in 1935, aged 48, and Moyna and the children moved to the USA, where Angela Lansbury became a highly successful actor. She still 'remembers her father with great affection as a gentle and placid man who worshipped, but was never intimidated by, his more famous parent George'.[719] G.L., as his family called him, would be a source of 'lifelong pride and inspiration'[720] to his granddaughter, whose first ambition was to enter politics rather than acting. She remembers him as a 'mesmerizing public speaker … He had tremendous physical energy, and she thrilled to the strides of this huge (to her though not in actuality) and 'enveloping', ruddy-faced man with muttonchop whiskers and 'an incredible beard' that brushed her face when he kissed her'.[721]

Many of those who had departed were on the left of Poplar Labour, and Rose argues that Poplar council's politics shifted from participation to elitism as the decade progressed, referring to 'jobbery', 'nepotism', 'snobbery', even 'racism' and 'corruption'.[722] Rose claims that councillors got council housing when others could not, and began refusing to see deputations from trade unions. Councillor John Hegarty was prosecuted for embezzling funds from the Amalgamated Stevedores' and Dockers' Union, of which he was secretary.[723] By 1929, the PBMA felt confident enough to launch an ultimately unsuccessful campaign to unseat George Lansbury from Parliament, having won back three seats on the board of guardians and increased its representation on the borough council to six.[724] As well as the usual tirade against heavy rates, high wages and poor relief, a PBMA leaflet claimed that 'Relatives and friends of the Socialist councillors and guardians are given jobs for which they have no obvious qualifications'.[725] At the end of the 1920s, the Communist Party and the ILP stood candidates against Labour in Poplar's local elections, 'accusing the Labour Party of selling out and of class collaboration ... When the revolutionary ardour of the Party began to fail, so too did its attempts at participatory politics'.[726]

Nationally, Labour again formed a minority government in 1929. Ramsay Macdonald left John Wheatley on the back benches, but could not leave 70-year-old Lansbury out of his Cabinet. Harold Wilson wrote that Lansbury got the post where he would cause the least damage: 'It was all done by agreement, [Philip] Snowden recording that, as George Lansbury had to be found a job, despite his 'Poplarist' reputation, it was he who suggested Lansbury for the Office of Works.'[727] Commissioner of Works Lansbury had a lido built at the Serpentine in Hyde Park.

Susan Lawrence was Parliamentary Secretary to the Ministry of Health in the 1929 government and the following year became the first woman to chair Labour Party conference.

Also in 1929, the TUC put the publication of the *Daily Herald* into a 'partnership' with Odham's Press, 'for practical purposes a commercial privatisation'[728]. Hamilton Fyfe had resigned as editor in 1926, finding increasing TUC and Labour Party control at odds with his view of the *Herald* 'as the property of the movement as a whole, and not just of its current leadership'[729]. Huw Richards argues that the paper's political journey had paralleled that of its former writer John Scurr, quoting Scurr's biographers: 'In 1921 he was an imprisoned Poplar councillor, in 1924 an MP so disillusioned by the first Labour government that he questioned the value of the exercise, and by 1929 a backbencher so conformist that he was described as one of the most loyal of the 'loyalist' MPs.'[730] The *Daily Herald* continued until 1964, when the International Publishing Corporation bought its remains and from them launched *The Sun*.

In 1931, Ramsay Macdonald, who so detested Poplarism, deserted the Labour Party to lead a 'National Government' dominated by Tories. It was the greatest betrayal in Labour's history, and the labour movement has spoken Macdonald's name with contempt ever since. J.H.Thomas, also a fierce opponent of Poplarism, went with Macdonald.[731] The Poplarists all stayed with Labour, for John Scurr and Susan Lawrence at the cost of their parliamentary seats.

The 1931 general election was a triumph for Macdonald's coalition, Labour plummeting from 300-odd MPs to barely 50. While Labour lost seats across the country, in Poplar it did not, a tribute to the political consciousness of working-class residents and the trust that their representatives had earned. Dave Adams replaced Sam March as MP for South Poplar. George Lansbury was the only Labour Cabinet minister to survive the rout, and so became Party leader, remaining so until 1935, when his pacifist views made his leadership untenable. In those four desperate years, Lansbury's leadership kept Labour's head up and laid the basis for its revival. He died in 1940, still MP for Bow and Bromley.

Lansbury's replacement as Labour leader was his deputy, Clement Attlee, who defeated Herbert Morrison in the leadership election. Attlee led Labour to its first majority government in 1945, introducing many of the measures that Poplar's Labour council had advocated a quarter of a century earlier – free school milk, family allowances, prison reform, public ownership of industry, and free state-provided healthcare.

Attlee's deputy prime minister was Morrison. He had become leader of the LCC in 1934, and came to 'personify Labour local politics in London and from 1934 London local government itself ... His was a distinctively "new" Labour, consciously distanced from the adversarial politics of Lansbury in Poplar and communist-influenced parties in Bethnal Green and elsewhere.'[732]

And Alfred Mond? In 1926, he became Chair of the newly-formed Imperial Chemical Industries (ICI) Ltd, and joined the Conservative Party. From 1928, Mond represented the employers at the Mond-Turner talks[733], which saw trade union leaders collaborate with the employers in disarming their own movement in the wake of the General Strike's defeat. The same year, he became the first Baron Melchett; he died in 1930.

Poplar Borough Council ended in 1965, merged with Stepney and Bethnal Green to form Tower Hamlets, one of 12 new inner London boroughs which were joined by 20 new outer London boroughs in response to urban London's expansion. The Greater London Council (GLC) replaced the obsolete London County Council. The Poplar Borough Municipal Alliance never regained any significant power, but persisted for as long as the borough council itself did, 'still raking over the old controversies, and proving once more that socialism means extravagance and waste'.[734]

The last of Poplar's 1921 prisoners died in 1973: Nellie Cressall, who had
served as a councillor until the council was scrapped, and delivered a speech at
the 1951 Labour Party conference which Aneurin Bevan called the finest address
he had heard on any platform.[735]

The legend of the 1921 Rates Dispute lived on. In 1939, the *East End News*
announced 'Guilty And Proud Of It – Poplarism will be enacted at Poplar
Civic Theatre, and at a pageant in West Ham on October 7'. In 1966, a mural
appeared on Hale Street dedicated to 'George Lansbury and the Poplar Rate
Rebels – Jailed For Supporting The People' and listing all their names.[736] In
the mid-1980s, Stratford's Theatre Royal staged Barry Keeffe's new play, 'Better
Times'. Why did Keeffe write about the Poplar rates rebellion? Because it was
'a great celebratory event in depressing times. It seemed right in 1984 to have a
blast at that.'[737]

Poplar today contains many physical dedications to its battling councillors,
from the Minnie Lansbury clock on Bow Road to children's home Dave Adams
House and Charles Key Lodge for disabled people. Susan Lawrence and John
Scurr have primary schools bearing their names. There is a Lansbury Gardens, a
Lansbury Lodge, a Susan Lawrence House and a Sam March House. A housing
development named after John Scurr has since been privatised and redeveloped,
and the Lansbury Estate, built in 1951, has now also transferred out of public
hands by the decision of Tower Hamlets Labour council.

1920s Poplar residents remembered and admired their socialist representatives.
One recalled decades later that: 'George Lansbury used to travel on the District
underground line to Westminster from Bow to carry out his duties as an M.P.
… He was always reading the morning news in the *Daily Herald*, but he was
always ready for a chat should you approach him. His wonderful work for the
poorer people of Poplar will never be forgotten.'[738]

POPLAR'S GREAT ACHIEVEMENTS

1927's Official Guide lamented that 'the name of Poplar has been known widely
as that of a place where rather daring experiments have been made by one of
the local governing bodies, and that it has in consequence gained a by no means
desirable publicity'. Perhaps the council and the guardians had become less
confident, but it is unlikely that they considered their struggles 'experiments'
nor the publicity they attracted undesirable. They had plenty to be proud of.

The 1921 Rates Rebellion had forced a fundamental shift in the rating system
in favour of working-class areas, had defended both workers and the jobless,
and had raised the living standards, political consciousness, aspirations and
confidence of its people. Harold Laski[739] rightly described Poplarism as 'the most

effective protest of our time against the theory that the poor must be humble, contrite and respectful.'[740]

Poplarism also dealt a death blow to the Poor Law, the hated system which humiliated and battered the poor, under which charities and guardians worked together to sift out 'deserving' and 'undeserving' paupers, and whose hell-on-earth workhouses had featured in Dickens' bleakest scenes. The Poplar socialists would have gladly accepted the Ministry of Health's description of them as 'would-be wreckers of the Poor Law system'.[741] A Ministry memo condemned Poplarism as 'a series of offensives directed by a certain political clique against various of the more vulnerable points of the system of local government'. The Poplar councillors and guardians were no 'clique' but representatives of a broad and democratic labour movement; and if points of the local government system were 'vulnerable', it was because they were plainly unfair!

The word 'Poplarism' had entered the political vocabulary and even the Oxford English Dictionary, sitting somewhere between 'politics' and 'poverty'. Term of abuse or badge of honour? The meaning of 'Poplarism' depended on your political stance: 'to some sections of the community it stands as a term of reproach and it is interpreted as meaning municipal extravagance; to others and especially to those who experienced it and knew it best, it meant humane treatment as opposed to semi-starvation.'[742] Poplarism's meaning was political as well as charitable, as A.J.P. Taylor described how it had become 'the name for any defiance by local (Labour) councils of the central government'.[743] When Allen and Unwin published its *History of Local Government in the 20 Century*,[744] Poplar was the only council to get a chapter to itself, Poplarism the only movement.

WHY POPLAR?

Why was this battle fought in the impoverished, dockland area of Poplar, East London? Because it suffered so harshly it had little choice but to fight; but also because it had the makings of an army to wage that fight. For forty years or more before the clash of 1921, socialists had promoted their politics on street corners, in workplaces and in homes. They educated themselves and those around them despite illiteracy, exhaustion and hostility. They had built up an experience and tradition of struggle, from the matchwomen's and dockers' strikes to the suffrage movement and support for anti-colonial struggles. Their leaders were able, experienced and popular. They could not allow that political investment to crash in the face of recession and crisis.

The East End of London has a deserved reputation as a centre of left-wing political activism. One London historian notes that 'A radically egalitarian and anti-authoritarian spirit has always been rising from the area'[745], citing examples from the London Corresponding Society in the 1790s through the nineteenth-century Chartists, to visits by leading Russian revolutionaries including Lenin and Trotsky. But East End radicalism is not simply something in the local water: rather, it is the result of the conscious efforts of the people and movements that lived, settled and grew there. The Poplarists did not simply inherit a left-wing tradition, they contributed to it. They took the torch and ran with it.

Rose[746] argues that there were four specific local factors which ignited this struggle in Poplar: class, neighbourliness, melodrama and religion. George Lansbury was a committed Christian, as were several of his fellow councillors and guardians: their churchgoing was greater than that of the local population, among whom it was less than 10 per cent[747]. There was a Christian flavour to some of the council's publications – for example, 'Guilty And Proud Of It' opens with a Biblical quote. But the vast bulk of leaflets, pamphlets, articles and speeches delivered by Poplar's Labour council to its audience appealed to their class interests not to their religious beliefs.

Labour MP Stephen Timms claims both George Lansbury and Tony Blair for one Christian socialism.[748] But Blair is surely the continuation not of Lansbury but of his bitter critics Morrison and Macdonald. Moreover, several of Poplar Labour's leading local opponents, such as Reverends Lax and Kitcat, were fervent Christians. Lax associated Poplarism, which he considered 'foolish nonsense', not with religion but with its rejection. He described how poverty and overcrowding 'introduced a new spirit into the district – first, indifference to the claims of religion, then second, a positive and definite estrangement, which ended in opposition'[749], bemoaned that 'blatant irreligion is not uncommon in Poplar'[750] and blamed, in part, 'the influence of anti-Christian Communism'[751]. If Lansbury's God was telling him to defy the law in defence of working-class interests, then Kitcat's God was telling him the opposite. In truth, it was not God telling the Labour councillors what to do, it was the labour movement. Even if religious conviction provided personal inspiration for some socialist councillors, even if Christianity flavoured Poplarism, it did not create or define it. Poplarism was not a holy war but a labour movement fight.

Class is only one of Rose's four factors because 'the workplace was of very little importance to local people and politicians' and rather, 'the industrial unrest which did occur in Poplar was caused by impulses with their roots firmly in family and neighbourhood life'.[752] This argument perhaps plays down the importance of workplace struggles, for example on Poplar's docks and railways, and seems to disregard the trade union background of many Poplar Labour leaders, such as Dave Adams and Sam March. Moreover, it reduces 'class' solely to the workplace. The working class does not just work – it plays, lives, uses services, raises children, helps each other, socialises and struggles in these arenas too. If Poplar had a particular neighbourliness and a love of melodrama that easily transposed from the music hall to the protest march, then that was part of its working-class culture, not separate from it.

Writing in the 1980s, James Gillespie argues that Labour politics in Poplar and other East End boroughs was not simply the product of 'a pre-existing class consciousness', and berates other writers, such as Noreen Branson and Morrison's biographers, for implying that it was.[753] Indeed, he bluntly states that 'in no sense' did such a consciousness even exist in the early 1920s, with the partial exception of among the dockers.[754] This seems rather a sweeping statement given the trade union growth in the area detailed by Bush[755], the wave of strikes across various industries, the significant involvement of NUR activists amongst others in Poplar Labour, and Gillespie's own admission that municipal union branches were active in local Labour Parties.[756] But while Gillespie later admits trade input, especially of money and leaders, he argues that any analysis of Labour's success in the East End around this time must also 'explain the solid penetration of areas which, although solidly working class in composition, were as recalcitrant to trade union organisation as before the war.'[757] We must assess 'the development of political Labourism in conditions which many have viewed as inimical to its survival'.[758]

Sweatshops, homeworking and casual labour persisted in Poplar and nearby boroughs. But, as Morgan argues, Labour's 1919 borough council victories 'showed how Labour could make new inroads into urban communities more complex than unreconstructed mining or textile villages'.[759] Having won those elections, Labour set about encouraging de-casualisation: improving municipal wages, carrying out its work with direct labour rather than contractors, providing resources to support industrial action that would further improve wages and conditions. Rather than de-casualisation propelling Labour to power, Labour in power propelled de-casualisation.[760] But casual labour still had a firm grip, albeit in a political context that Gillespie argues was 'radically transformed' by the extension of voting rights, consequent political intervention and wartime full employment that undermined the Poor Law.[761] Poplar's socialists had to take account of this reality, and build their local politics around 'the defence of immediate working class interests, particularly of the unemployed'.[762] The Poplarists, and other East End socialists, 'developed their strength out of novel political answers to the specific problems of their local economies'.[763]

Such 'novel answers' included using boards of guardians to pursue political goals. The Webbs saw this in many boards, including those dominated by capitalists, right-wingers and clerics, and complained that, 'The[ir] diverse policies seem to arise, partly from the relative wealth or poverty of the area concerned, but mainly from the particular social or religious creed, the profession, the interest or the impulse of the men and women who happen to be chosen from time to time as guardians in the several Unions by the habitually tiny fraction of electors who take the trouble to vote'.[764] Disturbing as it may have been to the Webbs, it was crucial to Poplar's fight: in a poor, working-class borough, the particular social creed of socialism meant an assertive, political fight for working-class interests. The success of this is shown in the fact that unlike elsewhere, far more than a 'tiny fraction' of Poplar's electors took the trouble to vote.

Gillespie concludes that 'The use of borough councils and boards of guardians to advance the interests of Labour's constituency provided the basis of political unity, not any sense of class unity engendered by the workplace'.[765] In truth, though, the Poplar socialists built a class unity that included the workplace, but embraced the community and the dole queue too. The simple reason is that 'working class' does not equate to 'big factory'. Rose and Gillespie are right to point out that Poplarism was not workplace-based – although workplace issues such as casualisation, low pay and unemployment were a significant element of it – but I would argue that it was no less a working-class struggle for that. Working-class battles can take place in communities and councils as well as in workplaces.

The heart of Poplar Labour was that at a time when Lloyd George proclaimed consensus but presided over inequality, when 'the reality of social division and conflict made a mockery of a governmental system [ie. coalition] which paid obeisance to national unity',[766] it fought for the working class in the workshop, the home, the pawnbrokers and the streets, as well as in the factory and the dock.

Listing reasons why this struggle did happen in Poplar does not mean that it could only happen in Poplar – nor that you cannot fight without intense poverty or four decades of preparation under your belt. The extent to which this fight did, did not, or might have happened elsewhere is crucial to the story of the rise and demise of Poplarism. And crucial to that is the politics of the Poplar socialists.

WHY DID POPLAR WIN IN 1921?

I suggest five key reasons: it was a labour movement fight; based on popular mobilisation; acting in unity and solidarity; with a clear understanding of the political issues; and prepared to defy unjust laws.

Poplar's struggle was no pressure group or single-issue campaign raised above class divisions. It was a socialist local labour movement in battle. Some modern writers[767] play down its essential labour movement nature, preferring instead terms such as 'radicals' rather than 'socialists'. They miss a key lesson of

Poplarism: the centrality of conscious working-class struggle based on labour movement democracy. As George Lansbury wrote, 'Our going to prison is an incident in the working-class movement – in the only fight that matters'.[768]

There were 70 trade union branches in Poplar, most of them affiliated to the trades council and the borough Labour Party. Together, these bodies decided to defy the law, and the council remained accountable to them during the struggle. In upholding this principle, Poplar Labour took the opposite view to that of Herbert Morrison, who wrote that, 'Such a policy is fatal. I decline to admit that it is democratic, for a democracy which is based upon the practice of those with inside knowledge receiving instructions from those without such knowledge is an insult to democracy'.[769] We can assume that Morrison meant 'inside knowledge' of local government affairs, not of unemployment, poverty or working-class struggle.

Poplar's labour movement was big and lively: the local Labour Party 'a model organization' with many individual members and one of the country's largest women's sections.[770] By 1923, South Poplar Constituency Labour Party had 2,800 members, the highest in London's constituencies. Party activists collected weekly subscription money from 20 members each, passing on news, hearing opinions and inviting people to meetings. Morrison, the supreme organiser, should have been impressed. However, beyond a common commitment to effective organising, Morrison and the Poplarists diverged. Gillespie argues that for Morrison, 'socialism was about building electoral majorities to legislate social reform, not about making socialists, nor about extra-Parliamentary class confrontations'[771], and that his approach that all Labour needed was an efficient machine to turn newly-enfranchised working-class people into Labour voters excluded consideration of political or ideological debates with the labour movement. An adequate understanding 'must account for the motivation of the mass of men and women who were drawn into the Party as activists, and the greater numbers who voted for it'[772]. In Poplar, cog turned cog – elected representatives reported to activists, who recruited members, who explained the issues to neighbours and workmates, who showed their support and some of whom got more involved. This was no 'focus group' or flat consultation exercise, but a living, breathing, growing movement, motivated and impassioned, and learning its socialist politics in the makeshift classroom and on the streets. Local Labour supporters were not a 'stage army' to be summoned just for this march or that election, but rank-and-file organisers and leaders of their own campaign.

The councillors themselves were an integral part of a battling community, not touchline coaches directing from the outside. As Poplar Labour's 1922 election leaflet stated, 'We all live in your midst. If rates and rents are high, we suffer with you, we are part of the life you lead.' Rose sees a Poplar trait of hostility to 'outsiders'.[773] However, George Lansbury, the best-loved of all the councillors, was from Suffolk via Australia, suggesting that Poplar residents had no problem with people coming from outside, rather with those – such as their employers, government ministers or judges – who remained outside while claiming the right to rule them. Theirs was a democratic expression of resentment at those who sought to control policy without having to live with its consequences.

Most of Poplar's male councillors were local workers, so were in daily contact with thousands of others. Charlie Sumner's son recalls that 'nearly everyone he passed by 'e knew 'em by their christian name, 'cause 'e either worked with 'em ... [or] 'e'd been to school at the school opposite.'[774] The women councillors were active in community initiatives such as Maternity and Child Welfare Committees, and in the Women's Co-operative Guild, organising education and campaigns. They lived their lives and struggles amongst Poplar's thousands-strong army of working-class women.

Local government politics had become an arena for socialist women, and Sheila Rowbotham argues that 'Labour women's organizations still retained a commitment not only to gaining access to the resources controlled by the state, but to the community-based democracy advocated by Sylvia Pankhurst'.[775] Poplar's socialist women were among many across the country who had moved from suffrage activism to campaigning for better poor relief and services.

By modern standards, the Poplarists were not perfect feminists. Poplar Labour stood only four women for the borough council in 1919[776], but these were four of only nine Labour women candidates across all the East London boroughs[777], and Poplar's new Labour administration added two female Aldermen[778]. Bessie Lansbury, a committed socialist and former suffragette activist, remained confined to her role as housewife and mother while husband George pursued his political career – a fact that Sylvia Pankhurst castigated him for[779], and about which Edgar expressed concern.[780] But George Lansbury was the highest-profile male supporter of feminism in Britain. He was close to Sylvia for the first two decades of the century, and in 1912 resigned his seat in parliament when his fellow Labour MPs refused his proposal that they vote against all government measures until the Liberals conceded votes for women.[781] His subsequent by-election campaign, although unsuccessful, brought women into socialist political struggle in a way which would stay strong throughout the campaigns of the 1920s, Lansbury claiming that, 'In our ranks today are many thousands of women who would never have heard of Trade Unionism and Socialism but for the suffrage agitation and the Daily Herald'[782], and that 'Nobody who knows the history of the struggle [for women's suffrage] can deny the great part taken by the Daily Herald and its League in winning that victory.'[783] In involving working-class women, introducing equal pay, and having women prominent in its leadership, Poplar Labour was ahead of its time.

Crucial to Poplar's mobilisation was the steady flow of information by word-of-mouth and in print. A stream of leaflets and booklets kept people informed of developments, refuted right-wing attacks, lampooned opponents, and tied the issue to the general case for socialism. A bona fide working-class voice with a mass circulation, the *Daily Herald* reported and cheered every step of Poplar's struggle. Even conservative historian Maurice Cowling acknowledged that direct action 'would have left little mark without the part played by the Daily Herald in systematising its insights and publicising its intentions'[784].

Poplar's campaign was both militant and sustained, showing that 'the modern working class has the capacity to mount not just periodic "outbursts of desperation and vengeance" but to sustain self-controlling organized "political struggle", to use the contrasting terms with which Lenin discussion the question'.[785]

Poplar's rebel councillors practised unity and solidarity. Politically, they came from varied backgrounds – some from the SDF, some the ILP, some were pacifists, some had fought in the war. Edgar Lansbury described the councillors and guardians as 'Labour, Socialist or Communist. In local affairs these three terms amount in practice to the same thing, for there is a united front in Poplar.'[786] The councillors were no sheep to George Lansbury's shepherd. Edgar insisted that 'The council was no 'one-man' show … there were forty-two Labour members, all eager and belligerent.'[787] Raymond Postgate, while acknowledging that George Lansbury was 'the most influential member of the borough council', attributes leadership of the rates rebellion as much to John Scurr, Charlie Sumner, Charles Key and Edgar Lansbury.[788] Poplar's supporters see it as 'an example of a radical movement apparently capable of transcending the barriers of ethnic, occupational, and gender conflicts which had long served to stultify the London socialist movement'.[789]

In Poplar's labour movement, people argued, resolved and then united in action. They marched together and took responsibility for each other's welfare even while demanding that the state should do so. The councillors won the trust of Poplar's working class 'because they have always been triers and stickers, and they are all class-conscious. They have never fallen down at the sound of the Capitalist trumpet … They are secure because their people know that they are sincere.'[790]

The Poplar socialists strove particularly hard to keep workers and jobless united. Right-wing politicians and newspapers encouraged those in work to despise and resent those out of work, aiming to turn the heat off the government's failings and onto the generous socialist guardians. While the organised unemployed saw themselves as part of the labour movement, some trade union leaders would not accept this, and the London Labour Party 'saw the unemployed as damaged individuals needing treatment, rather than active members of the labour movement'.[791] In contrast, Poplar Labour worked to a simple strategy: to 'bind the rebels together to fight for the things that matter'.[792]

Gillespie recognises the success of Poplar in uniting those in and out of work, and argues that, 'The otherwise contradictory interests of ratepayers, both working-class tenants and small business owners, and the recipients of (rate-financed) unemployment relief could be reconciled in a politics which focused its demands on the transfer of rate revenues from the wealthier boroughs of West London'.[793] The Poplar socialists, though, did not view the interests of working-class tenants and relief claimants as contradictory. Rather, they had common class interests: better relief would help stop wages falling; a working-class tenant and relief claimant may be one and the same person; or a working tenant one day could become a jobless claimant the next.

For Gillespie, 'The class struggle of Labour rhetoric was displaced into a demand for a redistribution of financial resources between urban areas'.[794] However, the fact that the existing rating system benefited rich areas at the expense of poor was not an invention of floundering socialists trying to avoid hard questions of social differences within their borough. Poplar's working class actively struggled for rates equalisation, and benefited from its gains. Gillespie further argues that 'Political unity was constructed, not at the level of class or position in (or out) of the work-force, but on the level of local government finance',[795] wrongly implying that 'local government finance' is a technical, classless issue. Poplar's rebellion was a genuine, united, working-class struggle, not a 'displacement' from it.

The Communist Party later asked rhetorically, 'Has it [Poplar's struggle] not demonstrated that when the movement enters a battle, united in its determination to advance the interests of the working class, clear in its mind that its enemy is the capitalist class, it is indeed a powerful and unconquerable force? George Lansbury knew who the enemy was in 1921.'[796]

Lansbury also acknowledged that Poplar's plans would cost money; he and his comrades understood that they were on a collision course with the vested interests of the rich and the capitalists, and with the whole Poor Law system. They understood that the law was not a neutral arbiter but an instrument of class rule. 'The law and justice', observed Edgar Lansbury, are 'two different things'.[797] They refused to delude themselves or their supporters.

Having identified the system and the laws as unfair, the Poplar councillors chose to defy them, but not before going through the entire menu of 'legitimate' options. Countless delegations, public meetings, petitions, resolutions, appeals and speeches failed to move a government stubbornly serving the ruling class. Back in 1911, before Poplar council was even Labour, it had presented a petition to King Edward when he opened Aldwych and Kingsway, calling for something to be done to ease the burden on poor boroughs.[798] Through 1920 and the first quarter of 1921, Poplar's Labour guardians circularised every MP and sent deputations to the prime minister, the Unemployed Grants Committee, the Local Government Board, and the Ministries of Health, Labour and Transport. On the day of her arrest,[799] a letter from Minnie Lansbury appeared in *The Times*: 'We have taken every course open to us in the processes of the law, and not a few extraordinary; we have employed the most skilful legal aid; and we have appeared in Court after Court precisely to have our action vindicated and to avoid going to gaol. The only step we have not taken, and will not take, is to leave 12,000 unemployed people to starve – for that is the alternative.'

Against the pessimistic predictions of opposition councillors and the Labour right, Poplar's defiance won. David Lloyd George and Alfred Mond proved that George Lansbury had been right when he wrote that, 'governments only concede just demands when they are no longer able to resist'.[800]

A NON-INFECTIOUS DISEASE

Poplar's 1921 victory became certain when two other east London councils voted to follow it in refusing to levy the precepts. However, they were the only two to do so, and they left it rather late. Stepney and Bethnal Green only voted to follow Poplar once the councillors were behind bars. Their action seemed like a protest at the imprisonment rather than at the unfair rating system itself. Had they acted earlier, victory may have come without prison, and a momentum may have built which could have drawn in more councils and gathered a mighty movement for redistribution of wealth and power. When the Poplar councillors stood in court on 29 July 1921, one of the judges asked, 'Suppose every other council did as you do, what would be the result?' The councillors answered, 'Why, of course, we should get our way.'[801]

Sylvia Pankhurst urged people to press councils into action. 'The rank and file should attend the council meetings of the Boroughs where the Labour Party is in power, and should make themselves felt. These meetings are open to the public, and it is possible for all of us to hold meetings outside the council halls, to visit the councillors and to bring all sorts of influences to bear upon them.'[802] Supporters of defiance packed the public galleries and made their feelings known, but while they won over some, the majority of councillors in the majority of councils dared not cross the line into illegality. While the labour movement offered the Poplar councillors its support, this took the form of sympathy rather than solidarity. Dozens of messages of support arrived with each day's prison post, many accompanied by a cheque. But the senders were helping a campaign confined to part of east London rather than resolving to spread it across the land.

After losing round one in 1921, the ruling class fought back and took its revenge against Poplar, helped by the failure of much of the labour movement's leadership to fight as hard for its class as the Tories did for theirs. Joynson-Hicks warned that, 'Poplarism is an infectious disease'.[803] The failure of the wider labour movement to take up Poplar's battling strategy and thus to realise Jix's fears was not simply due to cowardice or slowness by other Labour councils. Just as Tory-dominated governments fought to isolate and defeat Poplarism, so Labour's own right wing helped them with its own concerted effort against Poplar. Led by Herbert Morrison, vocally supported by Jimmy Thomas, the Labour right apologised for Poplar in public and attacked it within the labour movement. Edgar Lansbury defended Poplarism against both. 'Let nobody make the mistake of apologising for Poplar. Such apologies are an insult. Poplar challenges both open enemies and false friends. Lord Jessel[804] on the one hand, and Mr. Thomas on the other, talk of Poplarism and Poplar methods and finance as though the bare words conveyed their own condemnation.'[805]

Poplar's supporters could perhaps have fought harder against their opponents within Labour. John Scurr's decision to withdraw from the contest for London Labour Party Secretary and agree a non-committal compromise in the policy debate, left Herbert Morrison in pole position to pursue his long game of isolating Poplarism and reasserting 'constitutionalism'. If Scurr had stuck to his guns, then even had he lost the vote, he would have clarified the political issues and perhaps rallied the Labour left to continue their fight.

We might have hoped that the young Communist Party would play a stronger role in spreading Poplar's methods. CP members, such as A.A. Watts and Minnie and Edgar Lansbury, were at the heart of Poplar's struggle. But CP member Joe Vaughan allowed the council of which he was mayor, Bethnal Green, to dally until September before following Poplar. The CP's own history of the Poplar Rates Rebellion[806] praises Vaughan but mentions neither Edgar Lansbury's CP membership nor A.A. Watts or Minnie Lansbury at all. By the time of its publication, the CP was notorious for 'airbrushing' its own history.

Failure of solidarity left Poplar isolated and in isolation its belligerence withered. Even so, it deservedly held its municipal head high, its 1927 Official Guide describing how, 'Sometimes it would appear as if it was a case of "*Poplar contra mundum*" [Poplar against the world], but the people do not mind. They may divide on political and other issues; they may give and take shrewd blows; but whatever their internal differences may be, those who live in one or other of the three Parishes stand for the honour of their Borough.'

OTHER TIMES, OTHER CHOICES

The end of the Poor Law did not end conflict between central and local authorities, and councils would over and again find themselves up against unfair laws and forced to make choices just as Poplar had done.

In 1972, the Tories' Housing Finance Act compelled councils to increase rents by £1 per week. Knowing that their working-class tenants could not afford the rent rise, Labour councils faced a choice similar to that which Poplar had faced half a century earlier – comply or defy. Several Labour councils refused to raise the rents, and around 400 councillors faced surcharge or disqualification. While other councils backed down, Clay Cross – a former mining village on the outskirts of Chesterfield – took the 'Poplarist' stance and continued to refuse to raise the rents. In January 1973, the auditor surcharged eleven Clay Cross councillors £635 each, finding them guilty of 'gross negligence and misconduct'. Clay Cross Urban District Council appealed to the High Court but lost, as the Court upheld the surcharges, added £2,000 legal costs and barred the councillors from public office for five years.

In 1974, the newly-elected Labour Government repealed the Housing Finance Act and introduced legislation to exonerate the rebel councillors.[807] However, the House of Lords insisted on an amendment to keep the Clay Cross councillors disqualified, and the Commons narrowly accepted it. Just as in Poplar, unelected law-makers had trumped elected councillors.[808]

At the end of that decade, Dennis Skinner MP hailed the Clay Cross councillors' stand as 'a glorious fight. It was mainly successful. We've got to repeat it.' Twenty Clay Cross councillors were still disqualified, ten were undischarged bankrupts, but 'they are not bowed down. They are still active, still fighting, they still think that what they did was right.' [809] Skinner attributed Labour's repeal of the Housing Finance Act to Clay Cross's stand, and called for 'not one Clay Cross, but countless Clay Crosses, up and down the country.'

As Skinner spoke, local councils were gearing up to defend themselves from a Thatcherite onslaught, and they naturally looked at earlier struggles in Clay Cross and Poplar for inspiration and guidance. In December 1979, a joint meeting of the Labour Party's National Executive and Shadow Cabinet discussed how Labour councils should respond to the newly-elected Tory government's plan to force them to sell council houses. Young Socialists representative Tony Saunois argued for defiance of the law and cited Poplar 1921 as an example, but Labour leader Jim Callaghan insisted that the Party would act only within the law.[810] Labour MP Stephen Timms remembers discussions in his local Labour Party in the early 1980s. 'When ... we were struggling with dealing with the cuts imposed on our budgets by the then Tory Government in rate-capping, it was the example of George Lansbury which many people pointed to.'[811] Labour Parties again faced the choice of whether to accept or defy the Tory attack, and arguments raged in Party meetings around the country. Martin Pilgrim argued in 1984 that both sides of the debate could cite Poplar. While rebels could quote Poplar as a 'precedent in the struggle for municipal socialism', opponents of illegal action could argue that it was a 'warning to councillors to act within the law'.[812]

Several Labour Parties chose to follow the same defiant road that Poplar had, including Lothian, Lambeth and Ken Livingstone's GLC. However, none followed their chosen road to its destination, all backing down when the pressure intensified.[813] Liverpool City Council, led by Militant, went further than others in confronting the Tories, but it too eventually backed down and agreed a compromise which included attacks on workers and communities.[814]

In many of these councils, there were socialists prepared to see the fight through, including John McDonnell in the GLC, and Hilda Kean and Eddie Barns in Hackney council. But Labour's right wing and soft left defeated them, and the ultimate victor was Margaret Thatcher's Tory government. *Socialist Organiser* regretted that, 'Instead of mobilising, councils have gone for doing the best they can within the Tories' limits. In the one area where the new left's words can be translated into direct action, they have been administrators, not fighters. A few councils have gone to the brink – and then retreated, keeping their powder dry for better days.'[815]

MUNICIPAL SOCIALISM?

The Poplar story shows that the structure of local government sets limits around what socialists can do. *The Communist* described how, 'A thousand checks and counter-checks have been devised by the governing class to prevent the workers obtaining control over local governing bodies. Parliament bars the way, and working-class councillors are threatened with expensive lawsuits when any municipal council is audacious enough to overstep the bounds carefully set by the vested interests.'[816] Sue Goss argues that the period from 1919 onwards was one in which 'Labour local authorities were testing their strength, and the early years especially were characterised by important struggles between Labour authorities and the government – testing the limits of local authorities' powers'.[817]

Limits demand choices. They can be an excuse not to take effective action, or they can galvanise principled councillors into defiance. Labour councils must choose whether to pursue socialist policies, or to allow the law to stop them doing so; to challenge the system or to slot into it. In the arena of local government, these are the two souls of socialism. Many Labour councils have chosen to administer rather than fight. Many have clung on to office even while central government and their own capitulation have stripped most of their power away. Many rested on the council bureaucracy and vested interests.

Labour administrations, whether in town halls or in parliament, face a choice: which class do you serve? A few times, Labour in power has acted for the working class, for example building council housing or setting up the National Health Service. These are the achievements for which people admire and appreciate Labour. More often, though, Labour administrations have sought to administer capitalism and prove themselves no threat to the employers' interests, even to undo the progress of their predecessors.

During the 1980s, David Blunkett outlined a vision of municipal socialism[818], urging Labour councils to be 'model employers' and arguing that 'local socialist initiatives can establish in a community setting an alternative set of values to those of the Thatcher Government.' So far, so Poplarist. But as leader of Sheffield council, Blunkett did not follow Poplar's path the full distance. He argued that 'we must improve our services before we defend them', whereas Poplar had done both together. In practice, Blunkett's council was far from a 'model employer' and, unwilling to fight effectively to defend services, found it hard to improve them. Benevolent municipal administration became a substitute for genuine working-class socialism, and then became less benevolent.

Poplar's stance was more principled and confrontational, but some would dispute that sticking to principle is a practical option. Poplar's victory suggests that refusing to back down can be the most effective way to win. Sticking to a principle inspires those around you: people rarely take to the streets in their thousands to demand that their representatives compromise with their attackers. It is also inescapably logical that you will not win a demand by dropping it. Susan Lawrence argued that Poplar's distinguishing mark was 'a certain fierceness of attitude', which came from taking its power seriously: 'In Poplar Labour had tasted power, it had governed, and it had gained a self-assertiveness in defence of working-class rights.'[819]

A limited extension of the franchise had enabled George Lansbury and Will Crooks to win seats on Poplar's Board of Guardians in 1893.[820] In neighbouring West Ham, gas workers' trade union leader Will Thorne worked with the SDF, ILP and others to win the first Labour majority on a town council, improving local services from 1898 until a ratepayers' alliance unseated them in 1900.[821] The ruling class had worked hard to keep working-class representatives out of positions of power. When it could no longer resist the movement demanding their right to stand and vote, it then sought to restrict their ability to act. If it could not take their positions, it would take their power. The extension of voting rights meant that by the 1920s, more working-class people than ever were participating in their own local governance, which raised the question of what working-class representatives should do once in power.

George Lansbury had learned his approach to political office from SDF leader H.M. Hyndman, who 'pointed out to him that before long, there was no doubt, the working class would take over the control of the country, and it was the duty of himself and other workers to learn how to administer it. It was a revolutionary task to become a guardian, a councillor, and even in due course an M.P.; and in each case to become a complete master of the job.'[822] Lansbury – who had a 'very activist notion of the role of local authorities'[823] – argued that Labour councils must prove themselves different from the Tories and Liberals. If Poplar council had chosen not to defy the law, then it would have had to increase rates to an absurd level, cut relief payments, attack its employees' pay and conditions, abandon its many improvement schemes, and stop tackling private landlords' exploitation and abuse of tenants. And it would not have won a change in the law. It would have been hardly different from the previous Municipal Alliance regime. Sadly, many Labour councils have taken this path, closing facilities and attacking their workforce rather than attacking the unfair laws. No wonder that few people vote in local elections when restrictive structures, and councillors' acquiescence to them, allow so little difference between the competing parties.

After Labour's successes in the 1919 council elections, those socialists who recognised the limitations of municipal power disagreed as to their response. Theodore Rothstein, a BSP member who went on to become a founding member of the Communist Party, argued that, 'We must turn the local councils into so many forts from which to assail the Capitalist order.'[824] But the small Socialist Labour Party, a communist group that opposed affiliation to the Labour Party, argued that socialist councillors were 'working desperately hard and giving up their scanty leisure in order to help make the worn-out capitalist state machinery continue to resolve. By doing so they are immobilising themselves as active soldiers in the revolutionary ranks, and misleading the workers into expecting great results where none, or next to none, are possible.'[825] The SLP contended that socialists had three possible policies: stand for councils and try to improve working-class life; stand for councils purely on the basis of propaganda; or do not stand. The SLP sympathised with the third action, advocated the second, and opposed the first on principle. Writing before Poplar's Rates Rebellion, the SLP does not consider a further option: to stand, get elected, build a movement, improve things for the working class, and when capitalism's laws get in the way, defy them, win changes in the system, and thus build the movement further.

The Unemployed Workers' Organisation (UWO), set up from Sylvia Pankhurst's Workers' Socialist Federation (WSF) was 'anti-parliamentarian', arguing that socialists should not stand for public office as the result 'is that working-class representatives become responsible for maintaining capitalist law and order and for enforcing the regulations of the capitalist system itself'.[826] Sylvia's view would see pro-capitalist parties have a free run in elections, and would leave no room for Poplar's spectacular defiance and achievements. Ironically, Sylvia's argument let councillors and guardians off the hook by suggesting that the mere fact of holding office compelled them to retreat. Poplar's labour representatives had surely proved the opposite.

In "Left-Wing Communism': An Infantile Disorder',[827] Lenin polemicised against the SLP and WSF's opposition to standing in elections, arguing that 'revolution is impossible without a change in the views of the majority of the working class, and this change is brought about by the political experience of the masses, and never by propaganda alone'[828] and that 'the revolutionary class must be able to muster all forms, or aspects, of social activity without any exception'[829]. Lenin advocated that communists reach an electoral pact with Labour, and where there was no communist candidate, vote Labour.[830]

The Communist Party saw a more positive role for engagement in local authorities, seeing elections as 'a chance for the expression of workers' grievances and the workers' determination to take in hand the solution of their own class difficulties'.[831] Warning workers 'against placing their hopes upon the futile machinery of borough councils' and citing Poplar's clash with the law, it called on voters to 'Send working-class representatives to the municipal bodies; demand that they take every action possible to assist the workers; watch their actions after the election. But if they fail to achieve much, after having honestly tried, vent your wrath not upon them but upon the machinery of local government which was expressly designed to prevent them doing all those things that you would wish them to.'[832] An apparently battling strategy, this does, however, prepare to protect those councillors who choose not to fight, as if people cannot be simultaneously angry towards those who attack them and those who fail to resist.

POPLARISM, REFORM AND REVOLUTION

During the decade following Poplar council's 1921 victory, the ruling class exacted its revenge and clawed back the concessions that working-class defiance had forced from it. Unless the workers' movement replaces capitalism with socialism, it will always have to defend the gains it wins, and will not always succeed in doing so.

The fiercely anti-revolutionary Herbert Morrison was convinced that Communists were behind Poplarism, manipulating naïve 'soft left' councillors such as George Lansbury. Morrison felt that the Communists' 'purpose was to discredit the Labour Party and to encourage the growth of reaction so that they would be the only feasible opposition to the Tories'.[833] G.W. Jones praises Morrison's 'pursuit of a constitutional middle way, between the apparent drift and neglect of the government and the reckless illegality of the militant left'[834], as though the Tories' unemployment crisis and the Poplar councillors' resistance to it were two enemies to be fought with equal tenacity. Morrison, argues Jones, waged a successful campaign to stop the Labour Party 'falling for the superficially seductive, but constitutionally dangerous, attractions of Poplarism'. But Poplar's victory was not 'superficial'. And its councillors would undoubtedly have retorted that it was better to endanger the constitution than to endanger the poor.

The first two decades of Labour had seen a battle between Fabians and Marxists over the political shape of the new party, the Fabians gaining the upper hand. By 1922, the Communist Party argued that Labour Party leaders, 'in their overwhelming majority, were financially and otherwise no longer members of the working class, but of the middle class. They were Liberals, and might be conservatives, in all else but defence of their own unions, finances and privileges ... even before the war, the Labour Party had become quite distinctly a class organisation of the proletariat which was dominated by that section of the middle class whose profession it was to organise trade unions.'[835] So trade union leaders Ernest Bevin and Jimmy Thomas opposed Poplar's action. And Herbert Morrison, having left behind his youthful spell with the SDF, became a ferocious Party administrator, anti-communist and guardian of Labour respectability. Their position strengthened with the influx of Liberals into Labour's leadership when Labour began to run ahead of the Liberals in elections after working-class enfranchisement in 1918.

Some modern supporters of Poplarism seem to agree that it was not the Labour way of doing things, Lavalette, for example, arguing that 'Poplar council's stand was an aberration, though a magnificent one, in the history of Labour.'[836] However, the fact that few other Labour councils have taken action like Poplar's may not be because it is impossibly against the nature of Labour, but because the right wing won the battle within the party. When the Poplar labour movement took the course that it did, it was carrying out its vision of the purpose of Labour, not an aberration from it. Poplarism was a movement of the Labour Party, not – and never conceivably – of the Tories or Liberals.

There was a united front in Poplar – reformists and revolutionaries united in working-class interests. Against some who said that it should not work with Labour, the Communist Party asserted that, 'Against the Capitalist parties of all shades a united working class front is indispensable ... we work hand in hand with the Labour Party. We refuse to oppose them to the advantage of the

Capitalists'.[837] This was a time when the Communist Party was still non-sectarian, when it could still possibly have turned the Labour Party away from reformism and towards class-struggle socialism-from-below. Poplar's struggle was for reforms: revolutionaries supported it because, as the Communist Manifesto argued, they must fight 'for the enforcement of the momentary interests of the working class; but in the movement of the present they also represent and take care of the future of the movement'.[838] The same year as Poplar's Rates Rebellion, the Comintern's *Thesis on Tactics* urged a fight for reforms based on the needs of 'the broadest masses' for 'demands whose fulfilment is an immediate and urgent working class need'. That rich areas share some of their wealth with poor areas was one such demand.

A modern-day critic argues that, 'Poplarism was either a revolutionary doctrine – the town halls as soviets creating fiscal chaos as a prelude to uprising – or futility which ran the risk of damaging the lives of real people in real locations'.[839] Poplar's achievements proved its struggle to be far from 'futile', and real people's lives were so damaged by the existing system that the councillors probably considered any risk to be worthwhile. Not all the councillors saw their policy as a 'revolutionary doctrine', and none saw their aim as 'creating fiscal chaos'. But many did want the overthrow of capitalism and its replacement with socialism. How did their struggle link to this goal?

George Lansbury admitted that 'We are under no delusions about our day to day work. We are only patching up and making good some of the evils of Capitalism', whilst also writing that the councillors were 'using the whole machinery of local government and Parliament for the transformation of Capitalist Society into Socialism'.[840] Councillor Joe Banks said that 'Our fight will be a forerunner of a complete change in the social conditions of the people'.[841] However, these quotes offer little clarity as to *how* Poplarism leads to socialism, Gillespie remarking that, 'only rhetorical attempts were made to link policies, which Lansbury admitted offered little more than a 'bandage', to more general socialist objectives'.[842] The answer to this should lie with a conception of Poplarism as transitional politics, linking immediate demands with the ultimate goal. 'Transitional' can not simply mean fighting for small reforms under capitalism and making speeches about how the real answer is socialism. Rather, it has to link the two, seeing the bridge in the development of the working-class movement.

Sylvia Pankhurst supported Poplar's struggle, but also advised workers that 'The Poplar councillors in prison are doing what they can: they ask you to run forward a little step to capture a little post on the road: we ask you to keep your eyes fixed on the final goal; to make straight for it, and concentrate your energies not on palliatives, but on making your fellow workers into Communists.'[843] But the problem with staring straight ahead is that you might stumble into potholes in the road – and you might not take with you people who want to travel along the road but can not yet see the final destination. George Lansbury had himself cautioned against 'palliatives', ten years before the Rates Rebellion, writing that, 'the poor are being fleeced and robbed, and we are teaching them to be content with state palliation of the ills which accompany the fleecing and robbery … it is essential to arouse in the minds of the workers a detestation of their poverty and a determination to demand … a standard of life equal to that of the richest in the land.'[844] With more political clarity about these issues, and more effort to develop and organise Marxists, Poplarism might have spread further, lasted longer, and contributed to a more effective movement.

The essential difference between Poplar council and Hackney council in the 1920s was not simply between revolutionaries and reformists. Rather, it was between labour representatives who fought for the working class and those who capitulated to the ruling class. Between those who saw the working class as the active agent of its own liberation and those who saw it as a passive recipient of the few crumbs that its representatives could persuade the rich to drop.

IS POPLAR RELEVANT TODAY?

Reviewing Keeffe's play about Poplarism, Michael Billington complains that 'As in many left-wing plays, the past is used too simply as a model for the present'.[845] So why might Poplar council's actions not be a model for today?

Perhaps such extreme poverty no longer exists? There are still pawnbrokers, sweatshops and TB cases in Poplar.[846] In the 1920s, poor residents hid when the tallyman or the landlord knocked; today they worry about the electricity key and the credit card bill. In the 1920s, desperate people sold matches and razor blades on the pavement; today, they sell dodgy fags and DVDs in the supermarket car park. Today, 'overcrowding' is defined differently, but still in a manner described by housing charity Shelter as 'Dickensian'. In April 2001, 10,007 Tower Hamlets households and 431,482 English households lived in overcrowded accommodation, and more than one million children in England live in housing that is overcrowded, run-down, damp or dangerous.[847] Looking back, we can feel outrage at 1920s poverty and take comfort that our own is not so bad. Each era presents its own conditions as 'normal' and often only time and progress expose how outrageous they are. Maybe a century from now, people will look back on early 21st century Britain and ask why we did not fight poverty as hard as we might.

Perhaps local government funding is fair now, unlike in the 1920s? Councils no longer have to fund poor relief, and receive greater government grants. However, central funding still does not match working-class areas' needs, and councils still have to tax local people: the poor still keep the poor. Council Tax[848] for 2009/10 is £1,195 in Tower Hamlets, £1,308 in Hackney, but £687 in Wandsworth and £688 in Westminster. There is widespread anger against the unfair, regressive Council Tax, but it is now pensioners rather than councillors who go to prison for refusing to pay it!

Perhaps Poplar had to act because the government would not listen to lobbying, but now it will? As the current government coerces councils to transfer their housing to private companies, registered social landlords or arms-length management organisations (ALMOs), a broad coalition has lobbied intensely for a 'fourth option' – to fund councils to retain and improve homes. Yet, despite representations from trade unions, campaigns, residents' groups, its own MPs, and even after majority votes at three successive Labour Party annual conferences, the government does not move.

Perhaps the timing was good in 1921, but people just don't fight like that any more? In 1921, there was slump, poor health, illiteracy, and there had never even been a Labour government. Pessimistic yet rose-tinted views see past struggles as naturally militant in a way that they could never be today. But the factors that now persuade fainthearts that there is no will to fight also applied then. Mrs Smith told Richman[849] that 'I didn't go [to the prison demonstrations] cos I had the young babies. But politics really and truly I've never been involved in them much … them days you're only a youngster, you're only thinking of your own problems, of going out of a night.' Mrs Langley did not go to the meetings because her husband would not let her.

Perhaps local government has lost so many powers that it has no muscle to fight? Since 1921, it has lost poor relief and healthcare to national control, a positive change. However, it has also lost functions to quangos and private firms, such as contractors, housing associations and urban regeneration companies. White argues that local government is now 'little more than a fiction. It is "virtual reality", local democracy for the Gameboy Age' and alleges that 'fear plays a large part in the government's strategy: fear of dissent, fear of political opposition, fear of an alternative power-base that has won competing legitimacy through the ballot box.'[850] But local councils still provide significant services. Their cuts still hurt. They could still refuse to make them, refuse to go along with government schemes such as ALMOs and Academies, and could mobilise to demand adequate resources for their area.

But the law is different now: rebel councillors would not face prison, and instead, government appointees would take over. This should make rebellion an easier choice for councillors, with less at stake personally. But perhaps defiance would be ineffective? However, if a campaign of defiance also mobilised the local community and labour movement, as Poplar's did, the government may find it impossible to move in just as in August 1921. Time and again, the law has proved itself politically flexible. In the 1970s, Conservative-run Tameside council defied the Labour government and refused to make its schools comprehensive: the courts backed the council. In the 1950s, Birmingham Corporation introduced free travel passes for pensioners, only to see the policy ruled illegal despite the law empowering local authorities to charge such fares 'as they see fit'[851]. The courts have constantly reinterpreted the law, and while they usually do so in favour of the political right, mobilised labour movement pressure can force them to act in working-class interests.

Perhaps radically improving working-class life is a pipe-dream? In 1922, the anti-socialist *Glasgow Herald* warned that 'any dallying with Utopian schemes must lead inevitably to poverty and ruin ... The tragic example of Russia in national socialism may not prove so potent as that of Poplar in municipal socialism'.[852] Poplar's councillors knew that their people already suffered poverty and ruin, and the idea of abandoning them was fantasy of the horrific kind. Their choice was between two prisons: the literal one; and political imprisonment, caged by unfair laws.

Many Labour councils today choose to cut and privatise services. They may feel uncomfortable at first but soon move from apologetically justifying these policies on the basis of 'no choice' to positively advocating them. And some

Some of the people for whom the council fought.

choose policies that should be anathema to socialists – such as fat-cat salaries for Chief Executives – without any law or budget forcing them to.

Writer Jerome K. Jerome lived in Poplar as a youth in the late nineteenth century. He later wrote that 'There is a menace, a haunting terror that is to be found nowhere else', and believed that it instilled in him a melancholy that showed itself even in his humorous books such as *Three Men In A Boat*.[853] In Poplar's labour movement, the same experience produced not melancholy but a determination to fight back. They had decades' campaigning experience before the rates crisis, which had taught them that you only win through struggle.

In the 1920s, Poplar's councillors and guardians chose to fight. Had they chosen differently, we would not even remember them.

APPENDIX I – LEGAL ISSUES

Refusing the precepts

On 22 March 1921, Poplar Borough Council voted to delete the precepts for the cross-London bodies from its Finance Committee's report. On 31 March, it set the rate for the quarter ahead: 4s4d (22p) in the pound instead of 6s10d (34p).

On 3 June, the LCC applied to court for a provisional mandamus requiring the council to pay its instalment. On 10 June, the Metropolitan Asylum Board (MAB) obtained a similar mandamus. At the 'return' hearing on 20 June, Poplar council's solicitor, W.H. Thompson, instructed Henry Slesser KC. Alexander Macmorran KC represented the LCC. The judges - the Lord Chief Justice and Justices Sankey[854] and Branson[855] - awarded the mandamus, giving written judgment on 7 July.[856]

On 20 July, Slesser asked for a 'stay of proceeding' until after the council's Appeal. The court heard the Appeal two days later and dismissed it. Slesser asked for another stay to allow an appeal to the House of Lords; the court refused.

On 25 July, the LCC and MAB asked the court to issue writs against the councillors. The next day, the LCC agreed 'that all such further steps be taken as may be necessary to enforce payment.'[857]

On 29 July, opposition councillors got the writs against themselves dismissed. The Court served writs on the Labour councillors, ruling that, 'Unless the members of the Poplar Borough Council concerned obey the order of the Court and levy the necessary rates within 14 days they will go to prison.' The judges rejected the legal argument that the case had been taken against the council so could not be pursued against individual councillors, but awarded costs against the council as a body.

George Lansbury and W.H. Thompson asked Master of the Rolls[858] Lord Sterndale to convene the Appeal Court, which took place at 10am the next day. Poplar's barristers again argued that the mandamus was issued to the council not individual councillors. The 'argument lasted the whole day'[859], and Lord Justice Warrington admitted that there was enough substance to their argument to allow a full appeal. This should have delayed the case for weeks, as the bank holiday at the start of August marked the start of the courts' summer break[860]. But the judge scheduled the Appeal for Thursday 4 August, when the Appeal

Court heard and rejected the council's final appeal. The Master of the Rolls extended the 14-day deadline to one month. The Appeal did, however, reverse the earlier award of legal costs against the council.

Imprisonment

The councillors were to go to prison not for a fixed term, but until they 'purged' their contempt by agreeing to pay the precepts. George Lansbury later recalled, 'It was very amusing for us to be told that we were in prison *sine die*, which meant that we might be there for ever.'[861]

The 1898 Prison Rules established three divisions, according to the nature of the crime. Category 1, or first division, prisoners, were allowed their own food, some alcohol and clothes, did not have to work and could have some visitors. Categories 2 and 3 were tougher: prison dress and food, hard labour, often solitary confinement.

The Court Grants Release

On 12 October, the Lord Chief Justice and Justices Bray and Sankey heard the councillors' application for release. Mr. Disturnal KC, representing the councillors, moved that they be freed on the basis of two affidavits from Sam March. The first 'disdain[ed] any wish to treat the Court otherwise than with the respect due to it', and 'anxious to disavow any intention of contumacy [disobedience]'.[862] It promised that the councillors would participate in a conference in good faith. The second affidavit detailed the worsening situation in Poplar.

Mr. Macmorran KC, on behalf of the LCC, did not object to the prisoners' release. Justice Bray asked: 'What is to happen about levying the rate?' Macmorran replied: 'I don't know', so Bray countered: 'Don't the LCC want the money?'. The Lord Chief Justice's attempts to get Macmorran to state the LCC's position on the prisoners' release drew a series of evasive answers.

The judges cited obstacles to release. Poplar's affidavit may have assured no personal offence to the court, but the issue was not offence but contempt. The councillors were refusing to carry out their statutory duty. Poplar was still receiving the services of the LCC, the MAB and the other bodies, but was not paying for them. But the judges agreed to the release. They thought the LCC's statement that it would 'welcome any action by the Poplar Borough Council that would enable them freely to participate in such a conference' was 'an ingeniously framed sentence' which enabled them to free the prisoners. Trying to uphold the court's credibility, the judges stated that 'it would be wrong to encourage these borough councillors to think that they could disregard their statutory duties', but their ruling vindicated them for having done exactly that!

The 1921 Act and the Poplar Order

The Local Authorities (Financial Provisions) Act 1921 redistributed funding to the benefit of poorer boroughs. The Act empowered the Minister to install a Commissioner to collect rates if a borough council refused, but made no similar provision to replace a rebellious Board of Guardians.

Mond's memorandum in January 1922 attempted to define payments above his scale as 'unlawful' because guardians could legally only 'relieve destitution', and threatened that the District Auditor would disallow 'over-generous' scales and surcharge guardians. A surcharge is a charge on a public servant or body found to have unlawfully spent public funds through misconduct. But this was no use against guardians, like Poplar's, who were so poor that they had nothing to surcharge! A ratepayer could apply for an injunction restrain the guardians, but they would simply defy it.

Mond's alternative was the Relief Regulations (Poplar) Order 1922, declaring relief payments in excess of his scale illegal.

District Auditors and the Minimum Wage

In 1923, the Auditor ruled that the councillors must pay a surcharge of £5,000 for paying 'excessive' wages. At a special meeting on 12 June, Finance Committee member James Rugless outlined to the council its two legal options for appealing – to the courts, or to the Minister of Health. The councillors appealed to the court.

On 21 September, the court ruled in favour of the Auditor. Together with Justices Sankey and Salter, Lord Chief Justice Gordon Hewart presided. Hewart (1870-1943) was a Liberal MP from 1913 who served as Attorney General from 1919, then Lord Chief Justice from 1922 until 1940. Ironically, he coined the maxim that 'not only must justice be done; it must also be seen to be done'. The judges' ruling stated that, 'We cannot think that the words 'as they think fit' entitled a council to pay any sum that they like to any of their employees ... A councillor is not entitled to be unduly generous at the expense of those on whose behalf he is a trustee ... a payment to a servant ... may be of so excessive a character as to go beyond the limits of legality and become an illegal, or ultra vires payment.'[863]

In 1924, the Appeal judges decided by two to one to back the council and disallow the surcharge, but only one upheld the council's argument. One agreed with the Auditor. The third judge's decisive view was that the Auditor had a right to intervene, but should not have done so because £4 was reasonable in 1921/22. The Auditor appealed to the House of Lords, and began the legal process again for 1922/23.

The Auditor's Appeal to the House of Lords[864] was heard on 3 April 1925.

Five Law Lords – Atkinson, Buckmaster, Sumner, Carson and Wrenbury – overturned the Appeal Court ruling and endorsed the Auditor's actions. Their judgment was later labelled by one writer as 'The Rule Against Socialism'.[865]

Their Lordships were peeved at 'how little the respondents proposed to be guided by anything that could be called the market rate of wages'. Lord Sumner said he could find nothing in the law authorising councils 'to be guided by their personal opinions on political, economic or social questions' on spending matters. Describing borough councils as 'practical enterprises', Sumner disregarded the notion that voters elect councillors because of their opinions.

Lord Atkinson said that the councillors should not allow themselves 'to be guided ... by some eccentric principles of socialistic philanthropy, or by a feminist ambition to secure the equality of the sexes in the matter of wages.' Never mind that the councillors had been elected as socialists and were well-known feminists!

Laws To Kill Poplarism

Neville Chamberlain's Audit (Local Authorities) Bill 1927 created a new penalty of five years' disqualification from holding office. Labour dubbed the Bill the 'Political Opponents (Suppression) Bill'. Susan Lawrence, John Scurr and George Lansbury all spoke against it in Parliament.

The new law cancelled all previous surcharges, which by this time amounted to a small fortune. George Lansbury alone had £43,300 against his name for overpaid wages to council workers in 1924/25[866]. The PBMA complained that 'the penalties were not sufficient', and that when the law disqualified a rebel councillor, 'there was nothing to prevent another candidate with a like policy being elected.'[867]

The following year, the Local Authorities (Emergency Provisions) Act 1928 placed the Metropolitan Common Poor Fund under the control of Ministry of Health nominees. Chamberlain's Local Government Act 1929 abolished Boards of Guardians and transferred their functions to Public Assistance Committees of local authorities. The government centralised relief under a national Unemployment Assistance Board in 1934.

APPENDIX II: POPLAR'S COUNCILLORS

The 30 Jailed Councillors

Name, dates if known, ward represented, listed occupation and biographical notes, together with the quotes they gave to the Daily Herald at the time of their arrest.

David (Dave) Morgan Adams (1875-1942), Poplar North West ward, Trade Union Official. Born in Poplar; moved to Wales as a boy. Coal miner at age 12, then seaman at age 14, then soldier, then returned to Poplar as casual dock labourer. Secretary, Export branch of the Dock, Wharf and Riverside Workers' Union 1911-20; later, TGWU full-timer. Served on military conscription tribunal during 1914-18 war. Poplar councillor 1919-42; Poplar guardian 1913-30; LCC representative for Poplar 1930-31; MP for South Poplar 1931-42; Mayor of Poplar 1934-5.

Albert Baker (1887-1956?), Poplar Cubitt Town ward, Railwayman. Born in Poplar. Railway worker from age 14; worked at railway goods yard. Member, Amalgamated Society of Railway Servants (ASRS) 1901, then Poplar no.1 branch National Union of Railwaymen (NUR); Poplar Trades Council Executive 1911-13; Poplar councillor 1919-37; Poplar guardian 1919-30; Mayor of Poplar 1933-4.
'As I started, so I will continue to fight for the right of the poor of Poplar.'

Joseph (Joe) Henry Banks (1871-1938), Bromley South West ward, General Secretary. Born in Poplar. Railway worker. Member, ASRS 1894, then Poplar no.1 branch NUR. Secretary, Poplar Trades and Labour Representation Committee; later, Secretary of Poplar Trades Council until 1922. Sacked by Great Eastern Railway in 1910 for taking unauthorised leave to act as George Lansbury's election agent. Labour agent for Bow and Bromley until 1922. Served on military conscription tribunal during 1914-18 war. Treasurer of Trade Union Rights Committee 1915-17. Poplar councillor 1903-22 (resigned on health grounds); Poplar guardian 1911-22.
'Our fight will be the forerunner of a complete change in the social conditions of the people.'

George Joseph Cressall (1880-1951), Poplar Millwall ward, Secretary. Born in Stepney. General labourer at Hubbuck's Paint Works. Member, Bromley East branch, General Municipal Workers Union; delegate to Poplar Trades Council from 1912. First active politically in the Liberal Party from 1902, then left because of low wages of LCC workers and helped to form the Limehouse branch of the ILP in 1907. Married Nellie in 1904; they had eight children 1904-27. Moved to Poplar 1912. In 1918, became full-time agent and secretary of South Poplar Labour Party. Poplar councillor 1919-49; Poplar guardian 1922-25, 1928-30; Mayor of Poplar 1931-32.
'This stand is to bring about equalisation of rates which politicians have been talking about for 30 years.'

Nellie Frances Cressall (1882-1973), Poplar Millwall ward, Married Woman. Born in Stepney, née Wilson. Worked in laundry on Whitechapel Road. 1907, joined Limehouse ILP. 1912, became active in East London Federation of Suffragettes. Served on Food Control Committee during First World War. Poplar councillor 1919-65; Mayor of Poplar 1943-44. Appointed member of the Lord Chancellor's committee on divorce, 1946. 'Freeman of the Borough of Poplar', 1959.
'We expect the working women who are left behind to back us up by refusing to pay if the rates are levied.'

Albert Victor Farr (1872-1941), Bow North ward, Postman. Born in Bethnal Green. Member, Union of Post Office Workers. Poplar councillor 1919-22.

Benjamin (Ben) Fleming (1879-1965), Poplar East ward, Labourer. Later, hospital porter. Poplar councillor 1919-31; Poplar guardian 1919-30.
'Fighting to a finish. There can only be one end - a win for Poplar. But the people must back us up.'

Thomas John Goodway (1870-1947), Bromley North East ward, Postman. Born in Chelsea, moved to East London aged 10. Sacked in 1890 for taking part in strike; reinstated 1893. Secretary, Bow branch Postmen's Federation, later Union of Post Office Workers. Member of Bow & Bromley ILP. Poplar councillor 1912-47; Mayor of Poplar 1926-7. LCC member for Bow & Bromley from 1939.
'We don't want to leave you, but we think we ought to go!'

Walter Henry Green (1871-1957), Bow Central ward, Dock Labourer. Born in Bethnal Green. Poplar councillor 1919-22; Chair of the Libraries Committee.
'We are determined to carry on.'

James Joseph Heales (1873-1955), Bow North ward, Bootmaker. Born in Bethnal Green. Poplar councillor 1919-22.
'When Mayfair does its bit the people of Poplar will be able to do theirs.'

Robert John Hopwood (1877-1964?), Alderman, Toolmaker. Worked for Bryant & May matchmakers before 1914-18 war; secretary of Bow branch of the Amalgamated Society of Engineers; Secretary of Poplar Trades Council 1923-24. Poplar Alderman 1919-25.
'It's a goal through gaol we want!'

James Horatio Jones (1861-1946), Bromley South East ward, Checker. Born Portsea. Apprenticed to boat-builder. 1889, helped to found no.4 branch London Carmen's Union. Later railway worker (checker) with Midland railway; member of Poplar no.1 branch NUR. Churchwarden. Poplar councillor 1917-45 (aged 84); Mayor of Poplar 1939-40.
'I am proud to belong to a council which is doing a real Christian action.'

Thomas Edwin Kelly (1873-1941), Bromley North West ward, Grocer. 1902, Secretary of Bow & Bromley branch, National Amalgamated Union of Shop Assistants. ILP member 1906. Unsuccessful candidate for borough council 1906 & 1912. Poplar councillor 1919-28.
'We are determined to stand by our principle no matter how long we may be in gaol.'

Edgar Isaac Lansbury (1887-1935), Bow North ward, Timber Merchant. Son of George. Brought up in Poplar, trained for civil service, but went into business as timber merchant with brother Willie in 1910. Married Minnie Glassman 1914; Moyna McGill 1924. Member of Communist Party; May 1924, elected substitute member of Central Executive Committee. Poplar councillor 1912-25; Poplar guardian 1920-27; Chairman of Poplar Board of Guardians 1922-25; Mayor of Poplar 1924-25.
'Personal liberty is an important thing. So is justice. We will sacrifice liberty till justice is done.'

George Lansbury (1859-1940), Bow West ward, Editor. Born near Lowestoft, moved to London aged 7; married Elizabeth (Bessie) Brine 1880; emigrated to Australia 1884; returned 1886; became timber merchant. Active in Liberal Party from 1886; began to question Liberalism during 1889 dock strike; 1892 joined SDF; later joined ILP. 1889 joined Gasworkers' Union. Member of Royal Commission on Poor Law, signed Minority Report. Christian; pacifist. Founder and editor of the *Daily Herald*. Member and Trustee of National Union of General Workers. 1910, elected MP for Bow & Bromley, but resigned to unsuccessfully fight by-election on issue of votes for women in 1912. Author of many pamphlets and books. Poplar councillor 1903-40; Poplar guardian 1893-, 1904-30; Mayor of Poplar 1919-20, 1936-37. MP for Bow & Bromley 1910-12, 1922-40. Leader of Labour Party 1931-35.
'We are going to stand together, and we expect the movement to do likewise.'

Minnie Lansbury (1889-1922), Alderman, Married Woman. Born Minnie Glassman in Stepney to Jewish parents. School teacher. 1914, married Edgar Lansbury. 1915, committee member of East London Federation of Suffragettes; 1916, became Assistant Secretary. Served on War Pensions Committee 1914-18; elected Assistant Secretary of Workers' Socialist Federation 1918. Member of Communist Party from its inception in 1920. Poplar Alderman 1919-22. Died 1 January 1922 of pneumonia, probably made worse by effects of imprisonment. Commemorated by a memorial clock on Bow Road.
'I wish the Government joy in its effort to get this money from the people of Poplar. Poplar will pay its share of London's rates when Westminster, Kensington, and the City do the same!'

(Arabella) Susan Lawrence (1871-1947), Alderman, Spinster. After graduating from Cambridge University, elected as Conservative member of London School Board in 1900, and of LCC for West Marylebone 1910; joined Fabian Society 1911; joined ILP 1912. Met Mary Macarthur and joined Women's Trade Union League; became organiser for National Federation of Women Workers. Labour member of LCC for South Poplar 1913-1928; Poplar Alderman 1919-24. MP for East Ham North 1923-24, 1926-31; first woman to be elected MP and take up her seat in her own right. Parliamentary Secretary in first and second Labour Governments; 1928, first woman chair of Labour Party; sat on Labour Party National Executive until 1941.
'We go cheerfully determined to see this thing through. I hope our example will not be lost on all local authorities throughout the country.'

Jennie Mackay (1872-1955), Bromley Central ward, Married Woman. First woman member of union that became National Union of General Municipal Workers. Member of SDF. Active suffragette; arrested 1913. Served as school manager and on school care committee. Poplar councillor 1919-45.
'We want our sisters to stand by us, even it it comes to a "no rent" strike.'

Samuel (Sam) March (1861-1935), Bromley South West ward, Trade Union Secretary. Born Romford, one of 15 children. Farmworker as a child, then bakehouse worker. Moved to Poplar aged 18, became milk roundsman then carman (driver of horse-drawn vehicles). 1889 joined London Carmen's Union, became branch chairman; 1896, became full-time General Secretary of the union, in 1912 renamed National Union of Vehicle Workers. Member of Poplar Labour League. Unsuccessful candidate for borough council in 1900. Served on military conscription tribunal during 1914-18 War. Became national secretary of Commercial Road Transport section of newly-formed TGWU, 1922. Poplar councillor 1903-27; LCC member for South Poplar 1919-25; MP for South Poplar 1922-31; Mayor of Poplar 1920-21.
'We are as determined as ever to see the matter through. The workers must stick to the fight. They must follow it up while the council is away.'

John Edward Oakes (1876-1961), Bow Central ward, Toolmaker. Born Poplar. Poplar councillor 1919-25.

Joseph (Joe) Thomas O'Callaghan (1879-1926), Poplar Cubitt Town ward, Stevedore. Worked as assistant relieving officer from 1921. Poplar councillor 1919-25.
'It is criminal to expect a casual labour borough to pay heavy rates. All are willing to remain in prison till our aim is achieved.'

Alfred Partridge (1864-1940), Bow West ward, Farrier. Born Ely. Poplar councillor 1903-34; Poplar guardian 1919-22, 1925-30.

Charles Petherick (1883-1965), Poplar Millwall ward, Dock Labourer. Born Stepney. Registered dock labourer from 1908. Sacked following strike in 1912, returned later that year. Permanent labourer, 1914-45. Secretary, South Dock branch of the Dock, Wharf & Riverside Workers' Union; later member of TGWU. Poplar councillor 1919-31; Poplar guardian 1925-30.

James John Rugless (1873-1926), Poplar Cubitt Town ward, Leadworker. Born Bethnal Green. Poplar councillor 1919-26.
'All the prisons in the country will not alter our determination to win.'

Josiah Russell (1882-1943), Bromley South East ward, Railway Carman. Born Stepney. Poplar councillor 1919-31.

John Scurr (1876-1932), Alderman, Journalist. Born Australia, adopted by uncle and raised in Poplar when mother died. Of Irish descent. Office worker, then ran own shop. Married Julia O'Sullivan, 1900. Joined Poplar Labour League 1897, then became Secretary; active in SDF, ILP, later in British Socialist Party. Executive Committee member of United Irish League 1900-06. President of Poplar Trades and Labour Representation Committee 1911. Became *Daily Herald* writer 1912. President of the London district committee of the dockers' union during 1910-11 strikes. Unsuccessful candidate in Parliamentary by-elections in Bethnal Green, 1911 & 1914. Suffrage activist, arrested for pro-suffrage speech. Poplar Alderman 1919-25; Chair of Finance Committee, 1921; Mayor of Poplar 1922-23; Poplar guardian 1922-25; Alderman of LCC 1925-29. MP for Mile End 1923-31. LCC member for Mile End 1931-32.
'Glad to be in this fight. Poplar leads the way, and we are going to win. Our motto is "No surrender!"'

Julia Scurr (1871-1927), Poplar North West ward, Married Woman. Born Limehouse (née O'Sullivan), daughter of Irish immigrants. Active in Irish community and in East London Federation of Suffragettes. Organised feeding of 7,000 children during 1912 dock strike. 1914, led a deputation to Ministers against sweated labour. Poplar councillor 1919-25; Poplar guardian 1907-27; LCC member for Mile End 1925.
'We are happy about going to prison for a principle. We expect all working women to carry on the fight for rates equalisation while we are there.'

Henry William Sloman (1879-1957), Poplar West ward, Stevedore. Member of Stevedores' Labour Protection League, later Amalgamated Stevedores and Dockers. Branch secretary 1925, 1928. Poplar councillor 1919-31.
'I am quite prepared for anything that comes along so long as we can do the people some good; determined to win.'

Charles (Charlie) Edwin Sumner (1867-1925), Bromley South West ward, Labourer. Worked at Pearce's Chemical factory. Active in Bromley East branch of Gasworkers' Union in 1890s, later full-time organiser for National Union of General Municipal Workers. Served on military conscription tribunal during 1914-18 War. Poplar councillor 1900-25; Poplar guardian 1907-25; Chairman of Board of Guardians 1919-22. Member of LCC for Bow & Bromley 1919-25.
'Government departments have not carried out their pledges. Therefore, ours is the only method of maintaining the poor.'

Christopher (Chris) Edward Williams (1885-1966), Bromley Central ward, Labourer. Born Poplar. 1905, joined Gasworkers' and General Labourers' Union. 1912, unsuccessful candidate for borough council, backed by Poplar Trades and Labour Representation Committee. Served as solider during World War 1. Post-war, member of War Pensions Committee. Poplar councillor, 1919-31; Poplar guardian 1925-30.
'I should be a traitor to those left behind on the battlefields if I did not take my stand against the attempt to overburden soldiers' widows with heavy rates.'

Councillors who were not imprisoned:

Thomas John Blacketer (1881-1953), Bromley North West ward, Locomotive Engine Driver. Succeeded Joe Banks as Secretary of Bow & Bromley Labour Party. Poplar councillor 1919-34; Poplar guardian 1922-31; Mayor of Poplar 1930-31.

Albert Edward Easteal (1882-1956), Bow Central ward, Clerk. Before war, munitions worker. Served in the Army in World War I. Chairman of Poplar's Baths and Wash-houses Committee 1921-22. Mayor of Poplar 1935-36.

Joseph Arthur Hammond (1874-1938), Bromley South East ward, Railway Signalman. Member of NUR Poplar no.1 branch; branch secretary 1918; delegate to 1921 NUR AGM. Poplar councillor 1919-38; Mayor of Poplar 1925-26.

John Hegarty, Poplar West ward, Stevedore. Active member of Stevedores' Labour Protection League; later, Secretary of Amalgamated Stevedores' & Dockers' Union.

Peter Hubbart (1875-1956), Poplar West ward, Corn Porter. Joined Dockers' Union 1892. Executive member, later General Secretary, of Poplar Labour Protection League. Poplar councillor 1919-48; Poplar guardian 1919-31; Mayor of Poplar 1929-30.

Christopher (Chris) John Kelly, Bromley North East ward, Railway Carman. Poplar councillor; Poplar guardian. 1922, elected LCC member for Whitechapel.

Charles William Key (1883-1964), Bromley North West ward, Schoolmaster. Headmaster of Dingle Lane School. Poplar councillor 1919-40; Poplar guardian 1935-31. Chair of Poplar council's Public Health Committee; only person to be Poplar's Mayor three times (1923-24, 1928-29, 1932-33). MP for Bow & Bromley 1940-50; Parliamentary Secretary to Ministry of Health, then Ministry of Works, in 1945 Labour government; awarded Freedom of the Borough of Poplar 1953.

Henry Raymond Lewery, Poplar East ward, Railwayman.

William Lyons. Elected to council in by-election, 23 June 1921, Poplar East ward.

Mrs Jane Ann March, Poplar North West ward, Married Woman. Wife of Sam March. Mayoress of Poplar 1921.

Herbert Walter Rawlings, Bromley North East ward, Engineer.

John (Jack) Thomas Wooster (1862-1947), Bromley Central ward, Labourer. Left school at 11 and worked 12-hour days in Simpson & Payne's candle factory. Later, bricklayers' labourer. Joined SDF, later ILP, later Poplar Labour League. Poplar councillor 1919-47; Chairman of Works Committee; Mayor of Poplar 1927-28.

(Resigned: **John Clifford**, Bow West ward, Secretary; **John Suckling**, Poplar East ward, Boiler Maker.)

CHRONOLOGY

1919
6 March: LCC elections.
5 April: Boards of Guardians elections.
1 November: Borough council elections.

1920
17 February: Willows vs Poplar Borough Council; the council wins the right to award pay rises dependant on union membership.
10 May: Dockers refuse to load the 'Jolly George' with munitions for use against Russia.
27 May: Poplar council introduces minimum wage for employees of £4 per week.
October: Government announces funding for public works schemes.

1921
January: government refuses public works grant to Poplar council.
22 March: Poplar council votes to delete precepts for cross-London bodies from Finance Committee report.
31 March: Poplar council sets rates, not including precepts.
3 June: LCC applies to court for a rule of mandamus requiring Poplar Borough Council to pay its first instalment.
20 June: 'Return' hearing; mandamus granted.
29 June: Poplar council sets new rate, minus precepts.
8 July: King and Queen visit Poplar to open Royal Albert Dock extension. Poplar council displays a banner in support of its campaign.
25 July: LCC and MAB apply for writs to attach the councillors.
29 July: Court hearing; march.
2 August: Mond ends wartime 'stereotyping' of MCPF.
4 August: Poplar council sets next quarter's rate, minus precepts.
28 August: 4,000-strong march to Tower Hill.
31 August: Poplar council meets for the last time before prison.
1 September: Arrests begin.
5 September: Trades Union Congress begins.

11 September: First council meeting in Brixton prison.

11 September: Huge demonstration at the Obelisk in Bow and Poplar's Dock Gates.

21 September: Nellie Cressall released.

22 September: Bethnal Green votes to follow Poplar's course of action.

22 September: Labour Mayors meet Lloyd George in Gairloch.

24 September: Special conference to protest against the London Labour Party circular which had advised local Labour Parties not to follow Poplar's example.

27 September: Women councillors come from Holloway to join council meeting.

4 October: LCC votes to support conference that facilitates councillors' release; 20,000+ people march through London against unemployment.

5 October: Stepney council votes to disregard the precepts.

12 October: councillors' application for release heard in court.

13 October: councillors released.

17 October: Conference on equalisation of rates.

10 November: Local Authorities (Financial Provisions) Act.

26 November: London Labour Party Conference.

1922

1 January: Minnie Lansbury dies.

5 January: Metropolitan Common Poor Fund (Outdoor Relief) Regulations 1922.

25 January: Poplar guardians decide to pay 40s in relief.

31 January: Poplar guardians withdraw the relief scale.

March: LCC elections.

April: Boards of Guardians elections.

10 May: Cooper Report completed.

20 June: Relief Regulations (Poplar) Order.

22 June: Poplar council votes to withhold the estimates for the following quarter.

28 June: Mond backs down.

August: Poplar council agrees limited pay cuts.

1 November: Borough council elections.

15 November: general election. Tories win, Labour increases seats, George Lansbury and Sam March elected.

1923

31 May: District Auditor summons Poplar council to discuss wages.

12 June: Poplar council decides to appeal Auditor's decision.

2 July: Dock strike begins.

27 August: Sir William Joynson-Hicks becomes Minister of Health.

21 September: Court rules in favour of the Auditor.

6 December: general election.

1924

January: Formation of first (minority) Labour Government.

5 February: Poplar guardians meet Health Minister John Wheatley, who agrees to cancel Poplar Order.

June: Poplar guardians prosecuted for paying relief to striking dockers.

October: Labour government falls.

1925

3 April: Auditor's Appeal to the House of Lords regarding £4 minimum wage succeeds.

April: Guardians' election - Labour wins every seat in Poplar.

9 April: Poplar council agrees to abide by Lords' ruling and cut wages.

1926

May: General Strike.

15 July: Boards of Guardians (Default) Act receives Royal Assent.

July and August: Chamberlain unseats West Ham and Chester-le-Street Boards of Guardians.

1927: Audit (Local Authorities) Bill.

1928: Local Authorities (Emergency Provisions) Act.

1929: Local Government Act.

1 April 1930: local Boards of Guardians cease to exist.

BIBLIOGRAPHY

Noreen Branson, *Poplarism 1919-25: George Lansbury and the Councillors'
Revolt*, Lawrence & Wishart, 1979

1. PRINTED PRIMARY SOURCES

a. Contemporary Newspapers

The Call
The Communist
The Councillor (pub. London Labour Party)
Daily Express
Daily Herald
Daily News
East End News & Chronicle
East London Advertiser
East London Observer
The Evening News
Glasgow Herald
Hackney and Kingsland Gazette
Hackney Spectator
Illustrated London News
Lansbury's Labour Weekly
London Evening Standard
London Labour Chronicle (pub. London Labour Party)
Labour Monthly
London Municipal Notes
Morning Post
Municipal Journal
The Nation
New Leader
Out Of Work (pub. London District Council of the Unemployed)
Poor Law Officers' Journal
The Socialist (pub. Socialist Labour Party, 1920s)

The Times
Votes For Women
Westminster Gazette
The Worker (pub. Poplar Trades and Labour Representation Committee)
Workers' Dreadnought

b. Contemporary pamphlets and articles

J. Burrow & co, *Official Guide to the Metropolitan Borough of Poplar*, 1927 - issued by authority of Poplar Borough Council

J.R. Campbell, *Communism and Industrial Peace*, The Dorritt Press, January 1928

Editors of the Poor Law Officers' Journal, *The Poplar Case Examined*, 1924

Charles Key, *Red Poplar*, 1925

Labour Research Department, *Poplar Finance and Poplar Policy*, 1922

Edgar Lansbury, 'Poplar Leads: Warning to Labour Government', *Workers' Weekly*, 15 February 1924

George Lansbury, *Smash Up The Workhouse*, ILP, 1911

George Lansbury and others, *War Against Poverty*, 1911

George Lansbury, *What I Saw In Russia*, 1920

George Lansbury, 'Poplar and the Labour Party: a Defence of Poplarism', *Labour Monthly*, June 1922

George Lansbury and others, *Guilty And Proud Of It*, 1923

V.I. Lenin, *'Left-Wing Communism': an infantile disorder*, Bookmarks, 1920:93

Poplar Borough Council, *Poplar's Case*, 1921

Poplar Borough Council, *Poplar's Victory*, 1922

Poplar Borough Council, *The Work of Six Years 1919-1925*, 1925

Poplar Borough Municipal Alliance, *The Breakdown of Local Government: The Story of Poplar*, 1925

John Scurr, *The Rate Protest of Poplar*, 1922

John Scurr, *Labour and the Rates*, Labour Research Department, 1923

c. Archived material

Verbatim record of Trades Union Congress 1921

Held at Tower Hamlets Local History Library and Archives:

Minutes of Poplar Borough Council

Minutes of Poplar Board of Guardians

Minutes of Poplar Borough Council Baths and Wash-houses Committee

Orders of Library books by councillors in Brixton and Holloway prisons

Poplar Baths: weekly returns showing numbers of users of wash-houses and amounts of money received, Oct 1918 - Mar 1923.
Scrapbook, 1932-1956, mostly re baths and wash-houses but some general material re Poplar municipal affairs.
Poplar Borough Municipal Alliance correspondence file.
Rates Dispute: Judgments.

Held at London Metropolitan Archives:

Minutes, Metropolitan Asylum Board

Minutes, Metropolitan Water Board – ACC/2558/MW
Minutes, London County Council
Minutes, London Labour Party Executive meetings – ACC/2417/A/001
London Labour Party folios – ACC/2417/A/006, 007, 008
London Labour Party Conference Papers – ACC/2417/G
Letters between Ministry of Health and Poplar guardians – PO/BG/119
Poplar Board of Guardians – miscellaneous – PO/BG/152

Held at Hackney Archives:
Election material

Held at the National Archives:

MH 79/305 Report on the Poplar Board of Guardians: Boards of Guardians (Default) Bill 1923
MEPO 5/97 Police Rate Warrants: Poplar Borough Council's refusal to pay covering dates 1921-1922
MH 68/234 Poplar Parish: appeal against auditor's decision in respect of School bands' expenses for playing outside Brixton and Holloway Prisons where some guardians were imprisoned
WO 32/5719 Case against George Lansbury for attempted conversion of British prisoners in Moscow to Socialism; statements by Lansbury and prisoners
HO 144/5992 DISTURBANCES: Activities of Mr. George Lansbury MP
FS12/135, Yearly Returns of the National Amalgamated Stevedores' and Dockers' Union to the Registrar of Friendly Societies, 1922 & 1923.
Cabinet papers, referenced as C.P./number

Held at the British Library of Political and Economic Science:

The Lansbury Collection, referenced as LSE/LANSBURY/series number/piece number

Held at the Museum in Docklands:

Port of London Authority employment record cards

d. Photographs

Album of photographs presented to W.H. Thompson, Solicitor for the Defence of the Poplar Borough Council during the period of the Rate Strike 1921 – held by Thompson's Solicitors.

2. SECONDARY SOURCES

a. Biographies

Steve Allen and Laurie Flynn, *The Search for Harry Thompson*, Thompson's Solicitors: London, 2007

Hector Bolitho, *Alfred Mond, First Lord Melchett*, Martin Secker: London, 1933

Tony Benn, *Conflicts of Interest: Diaries 1977-80*, Arrow edition, 1991 (first published 1990)

Alan Bullock, *Ernest Bevin: a biography*, Politico's 2002

Bernard Donoughue and G.W. Jones, *Herbert Morrison: Portrait of a Politician*, Weidenfeld and Nicolson: London, 1973

David Dutton, *Reputations: Neville Chamberlain*, Arnold: London, 2001

Harold Finch, *The Tower Hamlets Connection: a biographical guide*, Tower Hamlets Library Service, 1996

Harry Gosling, *Up and Down Stream* (autobiography), Methuen, 1927

Martin Gottfried, *Balancing Act: The Authorised Biography of Angela Lansbury*, Little Brown, 1999

Shirley Harrison, *Sylvia Pankhurst: A Maverick Life 1882-1960*, Aurum, 2003

Bob Holman, *Good Old George*, Lion Hudson, 1990

Edgar Lansbury, *George Lansbury: My Father*, Sampson Law, 1934

George Lansbury, *My Life* (autobiography), Constable & co, 1928

George Lansbury, *Looking Backwards – and Forwards* (autobiography), Blackie, 1935

William Lax, *Lax Of Poplar: By Himself* (autobiography), The Epworth Press, 1927

Keith Laybourn (ed), *British Political Leaders: A Biographical Dictionary*, ABC-CLIO, 2001

Kenneth O. Morgan, *Labour People: Hardie to Kinnock*, Oxford University Press: Oxford, 1987:1992

Lord Morrison of Lambeth, *Herbert Morrison: an autobiography*, Odhams, 1960

Emmeline Pankhurst, *My Own Story* (autobiography), Eveleigh Nash, London,

1914

Harry Pollitt, *Serving My Time: An Apprenticeship In Politics* (autobiography), Lawrence & Wishart, London, 1940

Raymond Postgate, *The Life of George Lansbury*, Green & co, 1951

Jonathan Schneer, *George Lansbury*, Manchester University Press, 1990

Robert C. Self, *Neville Chamberlain: A Biography*, Ashgate Publishing, 2006

John Shepherd, *George Lansbury: At the Heart of Old Labour*, Oxford University Press, 2004

Harry Wicks, *Keeping My Head: The Memoirs of a British Bolshevik* (autobiography), Socialist Platform, 1992

b. Modern articles and pamphlets

Michael Billington, 'Better Times' (review), *The Guardian*, 6 February 1985

David Blunkett and Geoff Green, *Building From The Bottom: The Sheffield Experience*, Fabian Society, 1983

John Cunningham, 'Old Poplar yields up the roots of revolt', *The Guardian*, 1 February 1985

Phil Fennel, 'Roberts vs Hopwood: The Rule Against Socialism', *Journal of Law and Society*, volume 13, no.3, Autumn 1986, pp.401-422

James Gillespie, *Economic and political change in the East End of London during the 1920s*, University of Cambridge PhD dissertation, 1984

James Gillespie, 'Poplarism and proletarianiam: Unemployment and Labour politics in London 1918-34' in David Feldman & Gareth Stedman Jones, *Metropolis London: Histories and Representations since 1800*, Routledge, 1989

Historians' Group of the Communist Party, *The Poplar Story 1921*, 1953

Alan Johnson, 'The making of a poor people's movement: a study of the political leadership of Poplarism 1919-25', in Lavalette and Mooney (eds), *Class Struggle and Social Welfare*, Routledge, 2000

G.W. Jones, 'Herbert Morrison and Poplarism', *Public Law*, Spring 1973

Brian Keith-Lucas and Peter G. Richards, Chapter 4 - 'Poplarism', *A History of Local Government in the Twentieth Century*, George Allen & Unwin, 1978

Michael Lavalette, *George Lansbury and the Poplar Councillors' Revolt*, 2006

'Poplar 1921: When the Council Defied the Courts and Won', *Militant*, 14 March 1980

John O'Mahony, 'The Labour Party in perspective', *Workers' Liberty*, no.28, February 1996

William Pike, 'Guilty and Proud of it', *Public Service and Local Government*, 1980

Martin Pilgrim, 'Learning from the lessons of the Poplar Uprising', *Municipal Journal*, 14 September 1984

Gillian Rose, 'Identity, politics and culture: Poplar in the 1920s', *Environment and Planning D: Society and Space*, 1988, volume 6, pp.151-168

Gillian Rose, 'Locality-studies and waged labour: an historical critique', *Transactions of the Institute of British Geographers*, NS 14, 1989

Gillian Rose, 'Imagining Poplar in the 1920s: Contested concepts of community', *Journal of Historical Geography*, 16, 4 (1990) pp.425-437

Mordechai Ryan, 'Britain's biggest left party 1893-1945, and what became of it - the history of the ILP', *Solidarity 3/85*, 8 December 2005

P.A. Ryan, 'Poplarism', in P. Thane (ed), *Origins of British Social Policy*, Croom Helm, 1978

John Shepherd, 'George Lansbury and the Bow & Bromley By-Election of 1912', *East London Record* no.19, 1998

Socialist Organiser, *Illusions of Power*, 1985

Socialist Organiser, *Liverpool: What Went Wrong?*, 1988

O.Tapper, 'Poplar On Trial' in *East London Papers vol.3.2.57*, 1960 (contained in collected East London Papers vols. 1-5, 1958-62, University House)

David Walker, 'In Praise of Centralism: A critique of the new localism', *Catalyst*, November 2002

Jerry White, 'From Herbert Morrison to Command and Control: the decline of local democracy', *History and Policy*, April 2004

c. Local and general history books

Peter Ackroyd, *London: The Biography*, Chatto & Windus, 2000

Philip S. Bagwell, *The Railwaymen*, George Allen and Unwin, 1963

Julia Bush, *Behind the Lines: East London Labour 1914-1919*, Merlin Press, 1984

Hugh M. Coombs, *Accounting Innovation: Municipal Corporations 1835-1935*, Routledge New Works in Accounting History, 1996

M.A. Crowther, *The workhouse system, 1834-1929: The History of an English Social Institution*, Routledge, 1983

Sue Goss, *Local Labour and Local Government: A study of changing interests, politics and policy in Southwark, 1919 to 1982*, Edinburgh University Press, 1988

Wal Hannington, *Unemployed Struggles 1919-1936*, Lawrence & Wishart, 1977 (first published 1936)

Stephen Inwood, *A History Of London*, Macmillan, 1998

George Lansbury, *The Miracle of Fleet Street: The Story of the Daily Herald*, Victoria House, 1925

John Marriott, *The Culture of Labourism: The East End Between The Wars*, Edinburgh University Press, 1991

Kenneth O. Morgan, *Consensus and Disunity: The Lloyd George Coalition Government 1918-1922*, Clarendon Press, 1986 (first published 1979)

Winston G. Ramsey, *The East End Then And Now*, After The Battle, 1997

Huw Richards, *The Bloody Circus: The Daily Herald and the Left*, Pluto Press, 1997

Geoff Richman, *Fly A Flag For Poplar*, 1974

Peter Taaffe and Tony Mulhearn, *Liverpool: A City That Dared To Fight*, Fortress Books, 1988

Sheila Rowbotham, *A Century of Women*, Penguin, 1999

David Skinner and Julia Langdon, *The Story Of Clay Cross*, Spokesman Books, 1974

A.J.P. Taylor, *English History 1914-1945*, Oxford University Press, 1992 (first published 1965)

D. Vincent, *Poor Citizens. The State and the Poor in Twentieth Century Britain*, Longman, 1991

Sidney and Beatrice Webb, *English Poor Law History: Part II: The Last Hundred Years, Volume II*, private subscription edition, 1929

d. Websites

Stephen Timms MP – www.stephentimms.org.uk

TB Alert – www.tbalert.org

Shelter – www.shelter.org.uk

Compendium of Communist Biography By Surname – http://graham.thewebtailor.co.uk/

e. Modern newspapers

The Guardian
Hackney Gazette
Socialist Organiser
Socialist Review
Solidarity (pub. Workers' Liberty)
Workers' Action

3. REFERENCE WORKS

Who's Who
Oxford English Dictionary
Dictionary of Labour Biography
Dictionary of National Biography

OTHER BOOKS

Karl Marx and Frederick Engels, *Manifesto of the Communist Party*, 1848
J. Ramsay Macdonald, *Socialism: Critical and Constructive*, Cassell & co, 1924
Harold Wilson, *Governance of Britain*, Joseph, 1976
Robert McKee, *Story*, HarperEnterntainment, 1997

Notes

1   *Hackney Gazette*, 13 September 2001.
2   Gillespie, 1989, p. 163.
3   1928, p. 287.
4   *The Guardian*, 11th November, 2000.
5   Advertisement in *East London Advertiser*, election day, 1 November 1919.
6   *News & Chronicle*, 4 November 1919.
7   *New Leader*, 15 February 1924.
8   For a description of the Lansburys' time in Australia, see Shepherd, 2004, p. 11-17.
9   In 1913-14, 14.7 per cent of Poplar residents were registered to vote in local elections; in 1919, 36.1 per cent - Gillespie, 1984, table 8.1, p. 377.
10 Minister of Poplar Methodist Church 1902-37; Poplar Alderman 1906-1919; Mayor of Poplar 1918-19.
11 Speech to inaugural meeting of Poplar Chamber of Commerce, 4 November 1919, reported in *East London Advertiser*, 8 November 1919.
12 PBMA manifesto, *East London Advertiser*, 16 August 1919.
13 Municipal Reform leaflet to women voters, Hackney Borough Council election 1919.
14 London Labour Party folios, ACC/2417/A/006/139.
15 Richards, 1997, p. 2.
16 G.Lansbury, 1925, p. 44-7.
17 G.Lansbury, 1925, p. 7-8.
18 Richards, 1997, p. 17; G.Lansbury, 1925, p. 89-90.
19 Richards, 1997, p. 19.
20 Postgate, 1951, p. 155.
21 From 31 March 1919.
22 G.Lansbury, 1925, p. 121-2.
23 G.Lansbury, 1925, p. 67.
24 G.Lansbury, 1925, p. 22.
25 G.Lansbury, 1925, p. 39.
26 G.Lansbury, 1925, p. 34.
27 Taylor, 1965:92, p. 142.
28 G.Lansbury, 1925.
29 Richards, 1997, p. 27.
30 *Who's Who*, 1918.
31 This famous quote is from Lloyd George's speech at Wolverhampton, 23 November 1918.
32 Broadcast, 28 July 1940, quoted in Morgan, 1979:86, p. 7.
33 Bush, 1984, p. 206.
34 Bush, 1984, Ch.6 and p. 207-8.
35 *London Labour Chronicle*, March 1919.
36 London Labour Party folios, ACC/2417/A/008/984.
37 corresponding to today's London Boroughs of Camden, Greenwich, Hackney, Hammersmith & Fulham, Islington, Kensington & Chelsea, Lambeth, Lewisham,

Southwark, Tower Hamlets, Wandsworth and Westminster.

38 Created in 1889 by the previous year's Local Government Act, the LCC replaced the unelected, scandal-ridden Metropolitan Board of Works.

39 From 1904, following the abolition of the London School Board.

40 Donoghue & Jones, 1973, p. 82.

41 Municipal Reform election advert in *East London Advertiser*, 1 March 1919.

42 Manifesto for guardians election, *London Labour Chronicle*, April 1919, p1.

43 The Poor Law Amendment Act followed the previous year's Poor Law Commission, set up by Whig Prime Minister Earl Grey (after whom the tea was named). Ratepayers elected Boards of Guardians, and the government appointed a 3-man Central Poor Law Commission.

44 Manifesto for guardians election, *London Labour Chronicle*, April 1919, p1.

45 London Labour Party folios, ACC/2417/A/006/25.

46 The Representation Of The People Act 1918, which followed the steady widening of the franchise for electing guardians during the nineteenth and early twentieth centuries.

47 Joe Banks in *The Worker*, no.18, October 1910, LSE/LANSBURY/30/11.c.2.

48 *News and Chronicle*, 31 October 1919.

49 Bush, 1984, p. 234.

50 Cross-London organisation of the Conservative Party in local government.

51 *London Municipal Notes*, December 1919.

52 Founded in 1883. Britain's first socialist party. Took part in conference to establish Labour Representation Committee, but did not affiliate to Labour Party. Led by H.M. Hyndman. Marxist, but had a reputation for sectarianism towards the labour movement.

53 Formed in 1912 by merger of SDF with many ILP branches, believing the Labour Party to be too timid and moderate. Formed the core of the Communist Party when it formed in 1920.

54 Formed in 1893; founding Chairman James Keir Hardie. Argued for direct working-class political representation, and was instrumental in setting up Labour Representation Committee in 1900; affiliated to the Labour Party when it formed in 1906. Was a major force in British working-class politics. Continued to organise after Labour admitted individual members and formed branches in 1918, but disaffiliated from Labour in 1932.

55 A group within the labour movement, named after Fabius Maximus, a Roman general whose military successes were attributed to cautious, patient tactics.

56 G.Lansbury, 1925, p. 34.

57 G.Lansbury, 1925, p. 88-89.

58 Bush, 1984, p. 27-8.

59 Bush, 1984, p. 28, quoting *East London Observer*, 30 October 1915.

60 Bush, 1984, p. 23.

61 Poplar was one of only seven London Boroughs in which Labour contested every seat, the others being Camberwell, Greenwich, Islington, Lewisham, Stepney and Woolwich – London Labour Party folios, ACC/2417/A/006/139.

62 Foreword to Key, 1925.

63 *Daily Herald*, 4 November 1919.

64   Morrison, 1960, p. 80.
65   Postgate, 1951, p. 217.
66   In fact, Sumner was first elected to a local council seat in 1897, but neither Poplar Borough Council nor the Labour Party existed at the time!
67   Biographical sketch by Junius Junior, *East London Advertiser*, 7 February 1920.
68   Joe Banks in *The Worker*, no.18, October 1918 – LSE/LANSBURY/30/11.c.2.
69   George Lansbury resigned the seat in 1912 in protest at government opposition to votes for women, but lost the resultant by-election.
70   Bush, 1984, p. 49.
71   Bush, 1984, p. 39.
72   Bush, 1984, p. 45.
73   Bush, 1984, p. 54.
74   PBMA, 1925.
75   Metropolitan Borough of Poplar, Members of the council 1919-22, November 1919, attached to legal papers held at Tower Hamlets Local History Library and Archive.
76   Postgate, 1951, p. 152.
77   Quoted by John Groser in Richman, 1974, p. 80.
78   Postgate, 1951, p. 104.
79   Morgan 1987:1992, p. 61.
80   A civic post second only to the Mayor. Created by the 1835 Municipal Reform Act, the 'aldermanic bench' was part of the English borough council system until the 1972 Local Government Act scrapped it.
81   Formed in 1913, to mobilise for the vote amongst East London's working-class communities.
82   Told to me by Chris Sumner, who recalled his parents – Charlie Sumner's son and daughter-in-law – often saying so.
83   The 1869 Municipal Franchise Act allowed unmarried and widowed ratepaying women (ie. those who did not have a husband to vote on their behalf) to vote in some municipal elections; the 1888 Local Government Act extended this; and in 1907, women became eligible to become members of county and borough councils.
84   Pankhurst, 1914.
85   *East London Advertiser*, 14 November 1919.
86   *East London Advertiser*, 14 November 1919.
87   The term is Johnson's, 1990.
88   Taylor 1965:92, p. 122.
89   Taylor 1965:92, p. 121.
90   quoted in Bagwell, 1963, p. 375.
91   Bush, 1984, p. 195.
92   Bush, 1984, p. 103.
93   Bush, 1984, p. 84.
94   *Daily Herald*, 22 February 1919.
95   Morgan 1979:86, p. 74.
96   Ministry of Labour report, May 1919.
97   A cross-union rank-and-file organisation, involving stewards from most

shipbuilding and repairing trades in yards from London docks to Tilbury; Bush, 1984, p. 197.

98 Forerunner of the present-day RMT.

99 Bagwell, 1963, Chapter XV.

100 Morgan 1979:86, p. 77.

101 Postgate, 1951, p. 217.

102 Key, 1925.

103 *Daily Herald*, 13 December 1919.

104 G. Lansbury, 1922, p. 388.

105 13 December 1919.

106 Marx, Inaugural Address of the International Working Men's Association 'The First International', Written: October 21-27, 1864; online version at Marx & Engels Internet Archive www.marxists.org

107 G. Lansbury, 1922, p. 389.

108 Survey of London Life and Labour, 1928.

109 Speaking at public rally, 15 June 1922.

110 Key, 1925, p. 6.

111 Holman, 1990, p. 101.

112 Lax, 1927, p. 55.

113 Key, 1925, p. 6.

114 Ramsey, 1997, p. 103 (photograph).

115 Report of the Sub-Committee to Poplar Borough Council Baths and Wash-houses Committee, 21 November 1919.

116 George Lansbury gave a report of the council's work during his year as Mayor, reported in *East London Advertiser*, 6 November 1920.

117 *Socialist Review*, September 1924.

118 G. Lansbury, 1928, p. 2.

119 Founder of the Salvation Army.

120 Editors of the Poor Law Officers' Journal, 1924, p. 7.

121 LSE/LANSBURY/8/87.

122 Britain would have to wait for the last of these demands until Labour's 1946 School Milk Act. Thereafter, it nourished generations of kids until scrapped for secondary school pupils by Harold Wilson's Labour government in 1968 and for all over-sevens by Education Secretary Margaret Thatcher 'Milk Snatcher' in 1971.

123 LSE/LANSBURY/92.

124 LSE/LANSBURY/87 – record of Deputation to Prime Minister of Local Authorities of Greater London on the Question of the Supply, Price and Distribution of Milk and Coal, 23 December 1919.

125 The Milk and Dairies Act.

126 Gillespie, 1984, table 1.4.

127 Gillespie, 1984, chapter 4.

128 Rose, 1989, p. 320, quoting 1921 Census.

129 Bullock, 2002, p. 38.

130 Gillespie, 1984, p. 127.

131 quoted in Key, 1925, p. 13-14.

132 Bullock, 2002, p. 39.

133 Gillespie, 1984, chapter 2.

134 Gillespie, 1984, p. 47-8.

135 Gillespie, 1984, p. 78.

136 At Poplar Borough Council meeting on 27 November 1919, quoted in *News & Chronicle*, 2 December 1919.

137 *East London Advertiser*, 21 February 1920.

138 *East London Advertiser*, 27 December, 1919.

139 *East London Advertiser*, 27 December, 1919.

140 Finch, 1996, p. 58.

141 G. Lansbury, 'My Life', 1928, quoted in Postgate, 1951, p. 63.

142 G. Lansbury, 1911, p. 7.

143 Elizabeth Robins, article in *Votes For Women*, December 1909.

144 Postgate, 1951, p. 86.

145 Postgate, 1951, p. 87.

146 G.Lansbury, 1922, p. 386.

147 G.Lansbury, 1928, p. 133.

148 Postgate, 1951, p. 92.93.

149 To £40,000 more than the previous year; Bush, 1984, p. 217.

150 Bush, 1984, p. 217, quoting *East London Advertiser*, 27 September 1919.

151 Gillespie, 1984, p. 382.

152 S. & B. Webb, 1929, p. 897.

153 It continued for ex-service personnel until March 1921; Hannington 1936:77, p. 13.

154 *East London Advertiser*, 21 February 1920.

155 Richman, 1974, p. 128.

156 *East London Advertiser*, 17 January 1920.

157 Postgate, 1951, p. 166.

158 2002:2004, p. 184.

159 G.Lansbury, 1920, p. 28.

160 Letter, Churchill (War Office) to Secretary, Department of Military Intelligence, 5 August 1920, WO 32/5719/53317.

161 *Daily Herald*, August 1920, quoted in G.Lansbury, 1925, p. 146.

162 G. Lansbury, 1925, p. 109.

163 *East London Advertiser*, 20 March 1920.

164 Rose, 1988, p. 156, referencing Pollitt, 1940.

165 On 8 August 1920, a joint meeting of the Labour Party National Executive, the Parliamentary Labour Party and the TUC agreed to threaten a general strike to prevent war against Russia – Postgate, 1951, p. 209.

166 Quoted in Taylor, 1965:92, p. 146.

167 Bullock, 2002, p. 52.

168 The tonnage of goods carried on Britain's railways fell by 15.28 per cent and passenger journeys by 38.09 per cent, excluding those made on season tickets: Bagwell, 1963, p. 419.

169 Bagwell, 1963, p. 420.

170 People receiving relief payments without being admitted to the workhouse.

171 Ramsey, 1997, p. 103.

172 Taylor 1965:92, p. 146.
173 Morgan 1979:86, p. 106.
174 Morgan, 1979:86, p. 6.
175 Letter, Herbert Morrison to Party whips, Metropolitan Borough Council Labour Parties, 2 October 1920; London Labour Party folios, ACC/2417/A/006/404.
176 *East London Advertiser*, 15 October 1920.
177 *East London Advertiser*, 15 October 1920.
178 Hannington, 1936:77, p. 17-18.
179 Hannington, 1936:77, p. 28-29. Established 15 April 1921 at the International Socialists' Club, Hoxton, the NUWM became a national organisation with 3-400 branches, including in Poplar. Existed until 1939.
180 Gillespie, 1984, p. 416, referencing LLP Executive minutes, 7 September 1921, folio 714.
181 1914, describing her experience when elected a guardian in Manchester in 1894.
182 Postgate, 1951, p. 62.
183 Holman, 1990, p. 102.
184 Donoughue and Jones, 1973, p. 47, referencing *Hackney Spectator*, 26 November 1920.
185 Donoughue and Jones, 1973, p. 47, referencing letter from Morrison to Lloyd George, 4 December 1920, quoted in *Hackney and Kingsland Gazette*, 8 December 1920.
186 *The Councillor*, January 1921.
187 *Out Of Work*, 4 April 1920.
188 Hannington describes the factory raids on p. 26-7 and p. 45-50 of his book, *Unemployed Struggles 1919-1936*.
189 *East London Advertiser*, 6 November 1920.
190 *East London Advertiser*, 5 June 1920.
191 Gillespie, 1989, p. 171.
192 Liberal MP for Camberwell North West.
193 Poplar Borough Council, *Poplar's Case*, 1921, p. 2.
194 Branson, 1979, p. 24-5.
195 Poplar Borough Council, *Poplar's Case*, 1921, p. 2.
196 Gillespie, 1984, p. 74.
197 Poplar Borough Council, *Poplar's Case*, 1921, p. 2.
198 27 January 1921.
199 Local taxes levied on property.
200 St.Marylebone, Hampstead, Kensington, Westminster, Chelsea.
201 Bethnal Green, Bermondsey, Limehouse, Poplar, Greenwich.
202 Key, 1925.
203 Cited in Key, 1925, p. 14.
204 *Westminster Gazette*, 1 October 1920.
205 Deptford Borough Council meeting, 27 October 1920.
206 *Stratford Express*, 25 December 1920.
207 The Metropolitan Asylum Board existed from 1867 to 1930, was responsible for the care of London's sick poor, and was largely made up of guardians of the Poor, independents, charitable types and Ministry of Health nominees.

208 The Metropolitan Water Board took over all London water supply at the end of the
    19 century, bringing water supply into public ownership.
209 G.Lansbury, 1922.
210 According to Edgar Lansbury (1934, p. 72), the original suggestion had been
    Charlie Sumner's.
211 Key, 1925, p. 17.
212 Branson, 1979, p. 29-30.
213 *Daily News*, 23 March 1921.
214 11 March 1921, contained in MEPO 5/97.
215 Letter, George Lansbury to J. Buteaux Skeggs, 15 March 1921, contained in MEPO
    5/97.
216 Branson, 1979, p. 30.
217 Branson, 1979, p. 34.
218 Statement of council's resolutions, contained in MEPO 5/97.
219 E. Lansbury, 1934, p. 72.
220 *East End News*, 26 April 1921.
221 *East End News*, 26 April 1921.
222 *Daily Herald*, 16 April 1921.
223 *Workers' Dreadnought*, 10 September 1921.
224 *Daily Herald*, 30 September 1921.
225 Rose, 1988, p. 159.
226 Wicks, 1992, p. 64.
227 Rose, 1988.
228 1913-18.
229 *East End News*, 17 May 1921; Bedlam was the popular name for the Bethlem Royal
    Hospital, an institution for people with mental health problems.
230 *East End News*, 8 April 1921.
231 Received and noted at borough council meeting, 26 June 1921.
232 *East London Observer*, 26 March 1921.
233 *Daily Herald*, 30 July 1921.
234 *Daily Herald*, 30 July 1921.
235 Gosling, 1927, p. 99.
236 Allen & Flynn, 2007, p. 21-25.
237 Gary Slapper, Professor of Law, Open University, quoted in Allen & Flynn, 2007,
    p. 2.
238 Gary Slapper, Professor of Law at the Open University, on why he included
    Thompson in his list of the ten greatest lawyers of all time for The Times Online,
    2004 – quoted in Allen & Flynn, 2007, p. 1.
239 A mandamus is rarely used, a device of last resort where no other legal remedy is
    available. It is an instruction from the court, ordering a named body or person to
    carry out a particular action that is their legal duty.
240 Instructing the council to pay two instalments each of £7,000 towards its half-year
    precept of £28,143.
241 Letter, Receiver of Metropolitan Police to Under-Secretary of State, Home Office
    – MEPO 5/97/27857/39.
242 ACC/2558/MW/1/54/1/559-60.

243 An affidavit is a sworn statement of fact.

244 Slesser was Standing Counsel to the Labour Party, going on to become an MP and serve in the first Labour government.

245 KC stands for 'King's Counsel', a senior rank of lawyer appointed by the Crown.

246 The second highest judge in England & Wales, after the Lord Chancellor.

247 Wilful disobedience to, or disregard for, a court order.

248 *Daily News*, 21 June 1921.

249 *East London Advertiser*, 25 June 1921.

250 *East London Observer*, 11 June 1921.

251 Shepherd, 2002:2004, p. 213.

252 Lansbury topped the NEC election poll with 2,112,000 in 1920 and 3,012,000 in 1922 – Donoghue & Jones, 1973, p. 95.

253 Richman, 1974, p. 132.

254 *Daily News*, 30 June 1921.

255 *East End News*, 28 June 1921.

256 Branson, 1979, p. 40.

257 J. Hannington, 1936:77, p. 29-30.

258 A writ is a formal written command, issued by a court – in this case a demand that the councillors show cause why they should not be committed for contempt of court.

259 *Daily Herald*, 26 July 1921.

260 letter to *Daily Herald*, 30 July 1921.

261 At the hearing on 29 July.

262 Judgment, Supreme Court of Judicature, Court of Appeal, 27 July 1921.

263 *Daily News*, 25 July 1921.

264 Labour member of LCC 1919-25; Labour MP for Woolwich East 1922-31.

265 *Daily News*, 27 July 1921.

266 *Daily News*, 27 July 1921.

267 Morgan 1979:86, p. 107.

268 *Who's Who*, 1918.

269 E.T. Raymond in *Everyman*, 9 November 1918, quoted in Bolitho, 1933, p. 206-7.

270 Morgan 1979:86, p. 98.

271 *Dictionary of National Biography*, 1922-30.

272 Home Affairs Committee 95, meeting Thursday 28 July 1921, CAB 26/3 – Minutes.

273 *Daily Herald*, 30 July 1921.

274 In Greek legend, a sword hung over the head of Damocles while he feasted; used to denote a precarious situation, imminent peril.

275 E. Lansbury, 1934, p. 71.

276 McKee, 1997, p. 101.

277 *Daily Herald*, 29 July 1921.

278 *East End News*, 2 August 1921.

279 Photograph, album presented to W.H. Thompson.

280 *Daily Herald*, 30 July 1921.

281 *Daily Herald*, 30 July 1921.

282 *Daily Herald*, 30 July 1921.

283 Judgment, Supreme Court of Judicature, Court of Appeal, 4 August 1921.

284 *Daily Herald*, 30 July 1921.

285 *Daily Herald*, 30 July 1921.

286 £28,143.12s (£28,143.60).

287 Quoted in *Daily News*, 31 July 1921.

288 Branson, 1979, p. 51.

289 *East London Observer*, 13 August 1921.

290 Judgment, Supreme Court of Judicature, Court of Appeal, 4 August 1921.

291 *Daily Herald*, 2 September 1921.

292 Draft London Labour Party Municipal Circular, 5 August 1921, ACC/2417/A/007/685.

293 Morrison, 1960, p. 86.

294 *Daily Herald*, 30 July 1921.

295 PO/BG/119/90.

296 They represented what American Marxist Hal Draper would call in 1966 'The Two Souls of Socialism'.

297 *London Labour Chronicle*, March 1923; italics original.

298 E. Lansbury 1934, p. 68.

299 Hackney Borough Council minutes, 6 January 1921.

300 Minutes of Joint Meeting of the Executive Committee of the London Labour Party and the Metropolitan Mayors, 4 August 1921, ACC/2417/A/001/691.

301 5 August 1921, London Labour Party folios, ACC/2417/A/007/688.

302 According to the *Daily Herald*.

303 *East London Advertiser*, 13 August 1921.

304 In Section 168 of the Metropolis Management Act 1855.

305 It was not re-enacted for the new Metropolitan borough councils established by the Local Government Act 1899.

306 *East London Observer*, 30 July 1921.

307 *East London Observer*, 13 August 1921.

308 CAB 23/27, 17 August 1921, Home Affairs Committee of Cabinet.

309 Poplar Borough Council minutes, 18 August 1921.

310 CAB 23/27, 17 August 1921, Home Affairs Committee of Cabinet.

311 CAB 23/27, 17 August 1921, Home Affairs Committee of Cabinet.

312 *East London Observer*, 3 September 1921.

313 *East London Observer*, 3 September 1921.

314 *Daily Herald*, 1 September 1921.

315 *Daily Herald*, 1 September 1921.

316 Branson, 1979, p. 62.

317 Quoted in Historians' Group of the Communist Party, 1953, p. 3.

318 *The Times*, 1 September 1921.

319 *Daily Worker*, 7 May 1951.

320 *Daily Herald*, 2 January 1922.

321 *East London Advertiser*, 3 September 1921.

322 *Daily Herald*, 1 September 1921.

323 *Daily Herald*, 2 September 1921.

324 *Daily Herald*, 2 September 1921.

325 *Daily Herald*, 2 September 1921.

326 *Daily News*, 3 September 1921.

327 *Daily Herald*, 3 September 1921.

328 *Daily Herald*, 5 September 1921.

329 *Daily Herald*, 2 September 1921.

330 This film survives, and is held by the British Film Institute.

331 A Christian peace charity founded in 1914.

332 Told to me by Charlie's grandson, Chris Sumner.

333 When I was Chair of my ward Labour Party in the 1990s, one of our Labour councillors told me why he had buckled under and agreed to cuts during the 1980s. He knew that Labour could win the battle against the Tory government's rate-capping policy if they were ready to go to prison, but, having a young family, he was not prepared to do so.

334 *Daily Herald*, 6 September 1921.

335 *Daily Herald*, 6 September 1921.

336 PBMA Secretary to Home Secretary, 6 September 1921, PRO, HO45/112, 33/423 652.

337 Pike, 1980, says 10,000; Richman, 1974, says 15,000.

338 *Daily Herald*, 7 September 1921.

339 *Daily Herald*, 7 September 1921.

340 G.Lansbury, 1925, p. 32.

341 *Daily Herald*, 9 September 1921.

342 This, and all other quotes from proceedings at the Trades Union Congress 1921, are taken from the official verbatim record.

343 Letter, Herbert Morrison to London Labour Party Executive and Mayors, 7 September 1921; London Labour Party folios, ACC/2417/A/007/715.

344 By the *Daily Herald*.

345 The 1914 Prison Rules superceded the 1898 Rules.

346 *Daily Herald*, 3 September 1921.

347 *Daily Herald*, 3 September 1921.

348 letter to *The Times*.

349 George Lansbury in petition, HO 144/5992.

350 G.Lansbury, 1928, p. 158.

351 Historians' Group of the Communist Party, 1953, p. 9.

352 *Daily Herald*, 10 October 1921.

353 Tapper, 1960, p. 63.

354 *Daily Herald*, 9 September 1921.

355 It did not take place.

356 E.Lansbury, 1934, p. 74-5.

357 Tapper, 1960, p. 63.

358 Subjects of petitions are recorded in the minutes of Poplar Borough Council meetings.

359 The councillors were not allowed to have the apples, so resolved that they be given instead to children in Lambeth schools.

360 These petitions, handwritten on official forms, are contained in HO 144/5992.

361 *Daily Herald*, 3 September 1921.

362 Letter, George Lansbury to Prison Commission, 13 October 1921, contained in HO 144/5992.

363 With comments dated 14 September 1921, contained in HOI 144/5992.

364 *Daily Herald*, 7 September 1921.

365 G.Lansbury, 1925, p. 41.

366 Poplar Borough Council minutes, 12 September 1921.

367 Held at Tower Hamlets Local History Library and Archives.

368 Minutes of Poplar Borough Council Baths and Wash-houses Committee, 6 September 1921.

369 Handwritten letter from Cllr J.H.Banks to Mr Jefferson Hope, in Scrapbook 1932-1956, held at Tower Hamlets Local History Library and Archives.

370 Poplar Borough Council minutes, 22 September 1921.

371 Their handwritten orders are preserved in a file at the Tower Hamlets Local History Library and Archives.

372 *Daily Herald*, 8 September 1921.

373 G.Lansbury, 1925, p. 41.

374 Vincent, 1991, p. 60.

375 Letter, Daisy Lansbury to Bishop of Chelmsford, 5 September 1921, LSE/LANSBURY/28/125.

376 Headline, *Daily Herald*, 3 September 1921.

377 *Daily Herald*, 3 September 1921.

378 Postgate, 1951, p. 218.

379 *Daily Herald*, 10 September 1921.

380 Verbatim record, Trades Union Congress, 1921.

381 *Daily Herald*, 5 September 1921.

382 *Daily Herald*, 9 September 1921.

383 Vincent, 1991.

384 S.&B. Webb, 1929, p. 898.

385 Shepherd, 2004, p. 134.

386 Verbatim record, Trades Union Congress, 1921.

387 E.Lansbury, 1934, p. 75.

388 *Daily Herald*, 8 September 1921.

389 *Daily Herald*, 5 September 1921.

390 Donoghue & Jones, 1973, p. 73.

391 According to Minnie Lansbury's sister, *Daily Herald*, 10 September 1921.

392 MH 68/234.

393 Branson, 1979, p. 70-1 and footnote 16.

394 The Women's Co-operative Guild was founded in 1883, with the purpose of spreading the co-operative movement; later, broadened its political scope, and campaigned for women's suffrage, minimum wages and maternity benefits.

395 People and organisations sending support are recorded in the minutes of the council meetings held in Brixton prison.

396 *Out Of Work*, vol.1, no.17.

397 Minutes of Metropolitan Asylum Board meeting, 10 September 1921.

398 *Daily Herald*, 5 September 1921.

399 *Daily Herald*, 12 September 1921.

400 PO/BG/152/6/1639.
401 20 September 1921, LSE/LANSBURY/30.a.8.
402 *Daily Herald*, 3 September 1921.
403 *Daily Herald*, 12 September 1921.
404 *Daily Herald*, 5 September 1921.
405 *Daily Herald*.
406 *Daily Herald*, 12 September 1921.
407 For example, on 1 October 1921.
408 *Daily Herald*, 10 September 1921.
409 *Daily Herald*, 10 September 1921.
410 Minutes of Poplar Borough Council, 21 September 1921.
411 Quoted in Richman, 1974.
412 Morrison, 1960, p. 87.
413 *Daily Herald*, 1 September 1921; his metaphor came from the ancient Greek story of Cadmus, who scattered on the ground the teeth of a dragon he had slain.
414 *Daily Herald*, 21 September 1921.
415 *Daily News*, 3 September 1921.
416 Founded in March 1919 in response to working-class enfranchisement. Strike-breaking body designed to encourage business owners and professionals to organise to protect their interests.
417 Special Weekly Report, CP 3361 (CB 24/128), reference in Morgan 1979:86.
418 Editorial, 17 September 1921.
419 *Daily Herald*, 30 July 1921.
420 10 September 1921.
421 A person appointed by the court to receive property or monies in dispute.
422 Delegate J.H. Hayes' speech to the Trades Union Congress 1921.
423 *Workers' Dreadnought*, 10 September 1921.
424 Letter to *The Times*, 26 September 1921.
425 Morrison, 1960, p. 86.
426 Morgan, 1979:86, p. 285, referencing CAB 27/114.
427 No.240, September 1921.
428 E.Lansbury, 1934, p. 73-4.
429 *Daily Herald*, 15 September 1921.
430 *East London Observer*, 17 September 1921.
431 Attlee had been Mayor of Stepney the previous year, 1919-20.
432 *Daily Herald*, 26 September 1921.
433 Gillespie, 1984, p. 420.
434 *Daily Herald*, 21 September 1921.
435 *Daily Herald*, 7 October 1921.
436 Stated by Jack Jones, West Ham MP, in his speech to the Trades Union Congress 1921.
437 Recorded in Shoreditch Borough Council minutes, October 1921.
438 At conference convened by Labour Research Department, 23 September 1922.
439 This and subsequent quotes from *Hackney and Kingsland Gazette*, 16 September 1921.
440 Donoughue and Jones, 1973, p. 48.

441 Branson, 1979, p. 84, 85.
442 Morgan 1979:86, p. 285.
443 *Hackney and Kingsland Gazette*, 16 September 1921.
444 Branson, 1979, p. 85.
445 *Hackney and Kingsland Gazette*, 16 September 1921.
446 In the *Woolwich Pioneer*, 30 September 1921, reprinted in *London Labour Chronicle*, October 1921.
447 Morrison, 1960, p. 84-5.
448 Morgan 1979:86, p. 287.
449 *The Times*, 3 September 1921.
450 London Labour Party folios 2839-48, quoted in Branson, 1979, p. 86.
451 MP for Newcastle-upon-Tyne, Western Division, Home Secretary 1919-22.
452 Morgan 1979:86, p. 55.
453 *Daily Herald*, 24 September 1921.
454 *Daily Herald*, 24 September 1921.
455 *Daily Herald*, 24 September 1921.
456 Minutes of Poplar Borough Council meeting held in Brixton prison, 23 September 1921.
457 24 September 1921.
458 *Daily Herald*, 26 September 1921.
459 *Daily Herald*, 26 September 1921.
460 *Daily Herald*, 27 September 1921.
461 *The Communist*, 12 November 1921.
462 Branson, 1979, p. 75.
463 At Stepney council's meeting on 13 September.
464 Eliza Henman, quoted in Richman, 1974, p. 53.
465 *Daily Herald*, 23 September 1921.
466 Gosling, 1927, p. 98-9.
467 *Daily Herald*, 22 September 1921.
468 *Daily Herald*, 30 September 1921.
469 The Official Solicitor came back into the spotlight more than fifty years later to release the Pentonville Five, dockers imprisoned for defying anti-union legislation.
470 *Daily Herald*, 1 October 1921.
471 *Daily Herald*, 29 September 1921.
472 7 October 1921.
473 Gosling, 1927, p. 98.
474 Recorded in Shoreditch Borough Council minutes.
475 Minutes of Extraordinary Meeting of the Metropolitan Asylum Board, 1 October 1921.
476 *Daily Herald*, 3 October 1921.
477 *Daily Herald*, 3 October 1921.
478 *Daily Herald*, 3 October 1921.
479 Minutes of special London County council meeting, 4 October 1921.
480 Gosling, 1927, p. 94.
481 *Out Of Work*, vol.1 no.18.

482 Historians' Group of the Communist Party, 1953, p. 18.

483 He lost his Leicester seat in the 1918 general election, going on to be elected for Aberavon in 1922.

484 *London Labour Chronicle*, October 1921, p. 3, summary of article in Scottish '*Forward*', 24 September 1921.

485 Donoughue and Jones, 1973, p. 94-5.

486 *Out of Work*, vol.1, no.18.

487 *Daily Herald*, 5 October 1921.

488 *Daily Herald*, 5 October 1921.

489 Hannington, 1936:77, p. 35-6.

490 PRO, Cab 24/128, CP 3371..

491 *Daily Herald*, 10 October 1921.

492 *Daily Herald*, 10 October 1921.

493 This and subsequent quoted descriptions of the court hearing are from the *East London Observer*, 15 October 1921.

494 See legal appendix.

495 1978, p. 65.

496 This and other quotes from the *Daily Herald*, 13 October 1921.

497 This and subsequent quotes from Richman, 1974, p. 79.

498 Hannington, 1936:77, p. 40-1.

499 Set up in August 1921, and chaired by Tory MP Sir Eric Campbell Geddes, the Committee produced a report into National Expenditure which became known as the 'Geddes axe'.

500 PRO, Cab 23/27. C.H.A. 17/10/21.

501 Branson, 1979, p. 109.

502 Letter to the *Daily Herald*, 21 October 1921.

503 Donoughue and Jones, 1973, p. 50.

504 LCC Minutes of Proceedings, 1 November 1921.

505 The abbreviation used at the time for Saint Marylebone.

506 Letter from S. Marylebone guardians, acknowledged in Metropolitan Asylum Board minutes, 6 December 1921, Finance Committee report.

507 London County Council minutes, 1 November 1921, Report of the Local Government, Records and Museums Committee.

508 G.Lansbury, 1928, p. 161.

509 London County Council minutes, 6 December 1921, Finance Committee report.

510 Tapper, 1960, p. 65

511 Postagte, 1951, p. 223.

512 E.Lansbury, 1934, p. 76.

513 Hackney Borough Council minutes; *London Labour Chronicle*, November 1921.

514 Morrison, 1960, p. 88.

515 1985.

516 1934, p. 69.

517 *London Labour Chronicle*, November 1921.

518 *The Communist*, 12 November 1921.

519 *London Labour Chronicle*, November 1921.

520 And General Secretary, National Union of Railwaymen.

521 *House of Commons Hansard*, 2 November 1921.

522 S.&B. Webb, 1929, p. 901.

523 S.&B. Webb, 1929, p. 900.

524 *House of Commons Hansard*, 3 November 1921.

525 Minutes of London Labour Party Executive, 25 October 1921, ACC/2417/A/001/750.

526 London Labour Party folios, ACC/2417/A/007/754.

527 London Labour Party Conference papers, ACC/2417/G/001.

528 Election ballot papers, London Labour Party folios, ACC/2417/A/007/797.

529 London Labour Party Conference Papers, ACC/2417/G/001/105-152.

530 London Labour Party Annual Conferences, Summary of Proceedings, ACC/2417/G/010/811.

531 Hannington, 1936:77, p. 43.

532 *Daily Herald*, 2 January 1922.

533 Letter, J.H. Banks to George Lansbury, 1 January 1922, LSE/LANSBURY/8/141.

534 This underlines the courage of Poplar's councillors in the 1920s. Later councillors in similar situations backed down from fighting the government for fear of losing their liberty, but they had no need to fear for their lives. Modern prisons are not holiday camps as tabloid newspapers often make out, but jail conditions have improved massively. The major turning point was Labour's 1948 Criminal Justice Act, which abolished penal servitude, hard labour and flogging, and promoted rehabilitation.

535 Hubbart, Hegarty, Adams and Blacketer.

536 *Daily Herald*, 5 January 1922.

537 City of London Crematorium, Ilford. Minnie's ashes were later interred at the Jewish Cemetery in East Ham.

538 Quoted in *East London Advertiser*, 7 January 1922.

539 *East London Advertiser*, 7 January 1922.

540 *Daily Herald*, 7 January 1922.

541 Richman, 1974.

542 Metropolitan Common Poor Fund (Outdoor Relief) Regulations 1922; Statutory Rules and Orders, 1922, no.3.

543 Branson, 1979, p. 117.

544 *Guilty and Proud of It*, 1922.

545 Speech as part of unemployed deputation to Trades Union Congress, September 1921.

546 *Hackney and Kingsland Gazette*, 16 September 1921.

547 Hannington, 1936:77, p. 53.

548 *The Times*, 28 January, 1 February 1922.

549 *Municipal Journal*, 3 February 1922.

550 *Out Of Work*, vol.1, no.25.

551 Hannington, 1926:77, p. 53.

552 Quoted in the Cooper Report.

553 Edgar Lansbury, quoted in Editors of the Poor Law Officers' Journal, 1924, p,17.

554 *The Communist*, 4 February 1922.

555 Branson, 1979, p. 127.

556 *Daily Herald*, 8 February 1922.

557 Memorandum, W.A. Robinson to the Minister of Health, 17 October 1922, MH 79/305

558 G.Lansbury, 1922, p. 384.

559 Quoted in Key, 1925, p. 23.

560 LCC election 2/3/22, London LP point no.3.

561 Gillespie, 1984, p. 423, citing London Labour Party Executive minutes, folios 894, 993.

562 London Labour Party folios, ACC/2417/A/008/984.

563 ACC/2417/A/008 – London Labour Party folios – item 1024: Results of Boards of Guardians elections 5 April 1922.

564 Speech at Bromley, quoted in G. Lansbury, 1922, p. 383.

565 G.Lansbury, 1922, p. 385.

566 15 April 1922.

567 George Lansbury, 1922, p. 385.

568 Quoted in George Lansbury, 1922, p. 384.

569 Morgan, 1979:86, p. 226.

570 PBMA to Cooper, 12 April 1922, PBMA Correspondence file.

571 Cooper to Warren, 26 April 1922, PBMA Correspondence file.

572 The PBMA Correspondence file contains many letters arranging such meetings.

573 *Guilty And Proud Of It*, p. 19.

574 *London Labour Chronicle*, August 1922 p. 5.

575 Branson, 1979, p. 140.

576 Speaking at Labour Research Department conference, 23 September 1922.

577 1924, p. 12.

578 *Guilty And Proud Of It*, p. 1.

579 Postgate, 1951, p. 223.

580 *Guilty And Proud Of It*, p. 6.

581 *Guilty And Proud Of It*, p. 22.

582 *Guilty And Proud Of It*, p. 1.

583 *Guilty And Proud Of It*, p. 3.

584 *Daily Herald*, 16 June 1922.

585 LSE/LANSBURY/28/132-146.

586 Statutory Rules and Orders, 1922, no.649.

587 Examples, including Sheffield, Burnley and Preston, are quoted in Editors of the Poor Law Officers' Journal, 1924, p. 13.

588 House of Commons Hansard, 22 May 1922, reply from Sir Alfred Mond.

589 LSE/LANSBURY/28/147-154.

590 LSE/LANSBURY/28/127.

591 Johnson, 1990, p. 105, emphasis original.

592 LSE/LANSBURY/28/130.

593 PBMA to Mond, 7 September 1922, PBMA Correspondence file.

594 Report published 25 October 1922; included in Poplar Board of Guardians minutes, 28 February 1923, and in PBMA Correspondence file.

595 Poplar Board of Guardians minutes, 28 February 1923.

596 *London Labour Chronicle*, August 1922.

597 *London Labour Chronicle*, August 1922, p. 5.

598 *Daily Herald*, 31 August 1922.

599 G.Lansbury, 1928, p. 162.

600 Attlee, 'Labour and the Municipal Elections', *New Leader*, 13 October 1922.

601 Election pamphlet, held at Hackney Archive.

602 Hackney's five Labour aldermen, including Morrison, remained in office, having been appointed to serve until 1925.

603 Labour also lost all its council seats in Chelsea, Lambeth, Lewisham, Paddington and Stoke Newington.

604 3 November 1922, p. 8 'A Labour Rout'.

605 Donoghue & Jones, 1973, p. 47.

606 And also higher than the May 2006 London turnout of 35 per cent, and even a high point of 48 per cent during the rebellion against the Poll Tax in 1990.

607 John Scurr to PBMA, 1 November 1923, PBMA Correspondence file.

608 *London Labour Chronicle*, December 1922 & January 1923.

609 Scurr, 1923, p. 5.

610 Donoghue & Jones, 1973, p. 56.

611 G.Lansbury, 1925, p. 1-2.

612 G.Lansbury, 1925, p. 41.

613 Postgate, 1951, p. 221.

614 Bolitho, 1933, p. 232.

615 LSE/LANSBURY/28/157.

616 Laybourn, 2001, p. 83.

617 Morgan, 1987:92, p. 45.

618 The LRD published a report of the conference as a pamphlet, 'Poplar Finance and Poplar Policy'.

619 *East End News*, 31 January 1922.

620 Key, 1925, p. 44.

621 Taylor, 1965:92, p. 163.

622 Morrison, 1960, p. 89.

623 Campbell, 1928.

624 Joint Industrial council: negotiating body for local government workers' wages.

625 Quoted in Branson, 1979, p. 164.

626 Donoghue & Jones, 1973, p. 66.

627 Donoghue & Jones, 1973, p. 69.

628 Donoghue & Jones, 1973, p. 53.

629 *East London Advertiser*, 5 August 1922.

630 1906/7.

631 A future Liberal Parliamentary candidate.

632 *East London Advertiser*, 17 March 1923.

633 Arthur Robinson, First Secretary, Ministry of Health, to Arthur Griffith Boscawen, Minister of Health, 19 January 1923.

634 A post created by the 1834 Poor Law Amendment Act, to scrutinise authorities to prevent corruption.

635 Coombs, 1996, p. 50.

636 Section 62 of the Metropolis Management Act 1855.

637 Branson, 1979, p. 177.

638 The amalgamation took place at a special meeting on Wednesday 6 September 1922. It adopted the new name, Poplar, Bow and Bromley Ratepayers' Association (incorporating the Poplar Borough Municipal Alliance and the Poplar Ratepayers' Association), but continued to use the letterhead Poplar Borough Municipal Alliance, and this book will continue to refer to it by this title – letters from PBMA, 30 August and 13 September 1922, PBMA Correspondence file.

639 *The Times* law report, 22 November 1923.

640 Gillespie, 1984, p. 162.

641 FS12/135, Yearly Returns of the National Amalgamated Stevedores' and Dockers' Union to the Registrar of Friendly Societies, 1922 & 1923.

642 Gillespie, 1984, p. 170.

643 It would probably be unfair to label Petherick a scab. His Port of London Authority record card shows him striking in 1911, being sacked for striking in 1912, striking again in 1924, and taking part in the General Strike in 1926.

644 Richards, 1997, p. 55.

645 It had been legal – and established practice – until the 'Merthyr Tydfil Judgment', when the Powell Dyffryn Steam Coal Company took legal action against the Merthyr Tydfil guardians following a strike in 1898 – S.&B. Webb, 1929, p. 836-845.

646 *Daily Telegraph*, 4 October 1923.

647 *East London Observer*, 25 August 1923.

648 PO/BG/152/2 – Hunger Strike Marchers from Scotland 1922.

649 PBMA to Chamberlain, 9 August 1923, PBMA Correspondence file.

650 Harrison, 2003, p. 114.

651 Laybourn, 2001, p. 190.

652 The strike committee called off the action on 20 August 1923, and started a new union, the Amalgamated Stevedores' and Dockers' Union, but was not able to establish itself as a rival to the TGWU.

653 quoted in Branson, 1979, p. 202.

654 Letter, George Lansbury to Arthur Henderson, 15 January 1924, LSE/LANSBURY/28/162.

655 Postgate, 1951, p. 225.

656 Letter, George Lansbury to James Ramsay Macdonald, 18 January 1924, LSE/LANSBURY/28/163.

657 Macdonald, 1924, preface.

658 Edgar Lansbury in *New Leader*, February 1924.

659 Statutory Rules and Orders 1924, no.141 – The Relief Regulation (Poplar) Rescission Order, 1924, contained in MH 79/305.

660 *Daily Express*, 6 February 1924.

661 Article headline, *Morning Post*, 7 February 1924.

662 Memo, Wheatley to Cabinet, C.P. 114(24).

663 Speech to Indian students in London, reported in *Glasgow Herald*, 7 April 1924, p. 12, 'Socialists' Mistakes'.

664 'Poplar Explained – Spending Money to Save Life'.

665 *Westminster Gazette*, 15 February 1924.

666 Morrison, 1960, p. 100.

667 Morrison argued this line in the *London Labour Chronicle*, March 1924.

668 Extract from Cabinet conclusions no.14(24), contained in MH 79/305.

669 *Workers' Weekly*, 15 February 1924.

670 Letter, E.G. Allingham to George Lansbury, 7 June 1924, LSE/LANSBURY/8/185.

671 The Liberals proposed reprimanding the government; the Tories proposed a harsher amendment, which Labour and the Liberals voted down. Then the Liberals withdrew their censure proposal, saying they had sufficient reassurances from the government.

672 11 April 1925.

673 Richards, 1997, p. 69.

674 *East London Advertiser*, 6 June 1925.

675 John Kidd & co to Sir Alfred Warren, 11 August 1923, PBMA Correspondence file.

676 PBMA to members, 6 November 1923, PBMA Correspondence file.

677 PO/BG/152/3 – dock Strike Out-Relief, 1923.

678 Roberts vs Hopwood ([1925] A.C. 578).

679 Quoted in PBMA, 1925, p. 12.

680 *Lansbury's Labour Weekly*, open letter to the Law Lords, 11 April 1925.

681 Key 1925, p. 51-2.

682 Key 1925 p. 51-2. Key's comment proved prophetic, as in 1983, Conservative Bromley council took the Labour Greater London council (GLC) to court, seeking to have its 'Fare's Fair' policy of cheap transport fares ruled 'unreasonable' and therefore illegal. The court did so, quoting the 1925 Poplar case in its judgment. [1983] 1 A.C. 768

683 Branson, 1979, p. 223-4.

684 PBMA to Chamberlain, 22 October 1925, PBMA Correspondence file.

685 Poplar Borough Council, *The Work of Six Years 1919-1925*, 1925.

686 Poplar Borough Council, *The Work of Six Years 1919-1925*, 1925.

687 Poplar Borough Council, *The Work of Six Years 1919-1925*, 1925.

688 In *Lansbury's Labour Weekly*, 18 April 1925.

689 *East London Advertiser*, 6 June 1925.

690 PBMA to Chamberlain, 4 August 1925, PBMA Correspondence file, emphasis original.

691 Branson, 1979, p. 221.

692 Circular from p. Squire, PBMA President, 21 September 1925, PBMA Correspondence file.

693 Joseph Westwood & co to p. Squire, PBMA President, 4 May 1925, PBMA Correspondence file.

694 Self, 2006, p. 119.

695 Branson, 1979, p. 222.

696 PBMA, 1925, foreword.

697 PBMA, 1925, p. 13.

698 PBMA, 1925, p. 14.

699 Marriott, 1991, p. 151.

700 Letter to his sister, 20 June 1926, held in Birmingham University library, quoted in

Keith-Lucas and Richards, 1978, p. 87-88.

701 26 September 1925.

702 *Lansbury's Labour Weekly*, 11 July 1925.

703 Public meeting at Manchester's Free Trade Hall, Friday 2 July 1926, report contained in HO 144/5992.

704 Campbell, 1928.

705 Bolitho, 1933, p. 227.

706 It received Royal Assent on 15 July 1926.

707 PBMA resolution passed 30 September 1925, PBMA Correspondence file.

708 Marriott, 1991, p. 127.

709 *Stratford Express*, 30 October 1926.

710 Marriott, 1991, p. 159.

711 Dutton, 2001, p. 14, referring in particular to the 1929 Local Government Act.

712 Dutton, 2001, p. 193.

713 Self, 2006, p. 117.

714 *East London Observer*, 5 April 1930.

715 1934, p. 192.

716 Gillespie, 1989, p. 182.

717 Holman, 1990, p. 107.

718 Official Guide, 1927, part 1.

719 Shepherd, 2002, p. 349, based on a personal interview with Angela.

720 Gottfried, 1999, p. 32.

721 Gottfried, 1999, p. 18.

722 Rose, 1988, p. 64.

723 Gillespie, 1984, p. 178, citing *Daily Herald* 16 January 1924 and Annual Return to the Registrar of Friendly Societies 31 December 1926, PRO FS 12/135.

724 LSE/LANSBURY/9/31.

725 LSE/LANSBURY/9/32.

726 Rose, 1988, p. 64.

727 Wilson, 1976, p. 29.

728 Richards, 1997, p. 181.

729 Richards, 1997, p. 77.

730 Richards, 1997, p. 143, quoting Barbara Neid & John Saville, *Dictionary of Labour Biography* vol.4 p. 154-5.

731 So disgusting his trade union that it changed its rules in 1933 barring any N.U.R. General Secretary from sitting in Parliament.

732 White, 2004.

733 With Ben Turner, Chairman of the TUC General council.

734 Richman, 1974, p. 84.

735 Finch, 1996, p. 57.

736 photograph in Ramsey, 1997, p. 104.

737 Quoted in Cunningham, 1984.

738 Blake, 1972, p. 38.

739 Socialist academic and post-World War 2 Labour Party chair.

740 Laski, 1928, vix.

741 Quoted in Crowther, 1983, p. 106.

742 *East End News*, 1939, quoted in Richman, 1974, p. 135.

743 1987, p. 275.

744 Keith-Lucas and Richards 1978, part of the 'New Local Government' series.

745 Ackroyd, 2000, p. 680.

746 Rose, 1988.

747 Rose, 1988, p. 159.

748 Speaking at the opening of the Christian Socialist Movement's Archive, 26 April 2003, speech on website www.stephentimmsmp.org.uk.

749 Lax, 1927, p. 75.

750 Lax, 1927, p. 239.

751 Lax, 1927, p. 78.

752 Rose, 1989, p. 317.

753 Gillespie, 1984, p. ix.

754 Gillespie, 1984, p. x, footnote (9).

755 1984.

756 Gillespie, 1989, p. 169.

757 Gillespie, 1984, p. 370.

758 Gillespie, 1984, p. viii.

759 Morgan 1979:86, p. 216.

760 Gillespie, 1989, p. 168.

761 Gillespie, 1989, p. 172.

762 Gillespie, 1984, p. 373.

763 Gillespie, 1984, p. xiv.

764 S.&B. Webb, 1929, p. 862.

765 Gillespie, 1989, p. 164.

766 Morgan, 1979:86, p. 281.

767 Such as Lavalette, 2006.

768 *Daily Herald*, 14 October 1921.

769 Memo to Executive of London Labour Party, 7 April 1921, quoted in Donoghue & Jones, 1973, p. 76.

770 Gillespie, 1984, p. 396.

771 Gillespie, 1984, p. 368.

772 Gillespie, 1984, p. 368.

773 Rose, 1990.

774 Interviewed by Rose, 1988, p. 15.

775 Rowbotham, 1999, p. 127.

776 Nellie Cressall, Julia Scurr, Jennie MacKay and Jane March.

777 Bush, 1984, p. 232.

778 Susan Lawrence and Minnie Lansbury.

779 Shepherd, 2004, p. 353-4.

780 E.Lansbury, 1934, p. 140-1.

781 Sylvia opposed George's resignation, considering it 'precipitate'.

782 G.Lansbury, 1925, p. 77.

783 G.Lansbury, 1925, p. 84-5.

784 Qutoed in Richards, 1997, p. 25-6.

785 Johnson, 1990, p. 115.

786 *Workers' Weekly*, 15 February 1924.

787 E. Lansbury, 1934, p. 72.

788 Postgate, 1951, p. 217.

789 Gillespie, 1989, p. 163.

790 E. Lansbury in *Workers' Weekly*, 15 February 1924.

791 Gillespie, 1989, p. 182.

792 George Lansbury, quoted in Schneer, 1990, p. 123.

793 Gillespie, 1989, p. 174-5.

794 Gillespie, 1989, p. 175.

795 Gillespie, 1989, p. 180.

796 Historians' Group of the Communist Party 1953, preface.

797 1934, p. 73.

798 Statement from Sam March, LSE/LANSBURY/30.a.8.

799 5 September 1921.

800 *Daily Herald*, 30 July 1921.

801 G. Lansbury, 1928, p. 156.

802 *Workers' Dreadnought*, 20 September 1921.

803 Memo, Joynson-Hicks to Cabinet, 15 October 1923, contained in MH 79/305..

804 Baron Jessel of Westminster, Herbert Jessell, former Liberal Unionist and Conservative MP.

805 *Lansbury's Labour Weekly*, 31 October 1925.

806 Historians' Group of the Communist Party, 1953.

807 The same year, Clay Cross UDC was incorporated into the new North East Derbyshire District council.

808 For the full tale, read 'The Story of Clay Cross' by former councillor David Skinner and journalist Julia Langdon.

809 At a Socialist Campaign for a Labour Victory fringe meeting at 1979 Labour Party conference, reported in *Workers' Action*, 8 October 1979.

810 Benn, 1990:1991, p. 563-4.

811 Speech at opening of Christian Socialist Movement Archive, 26 April 2003, on website www.stephentimms.org.uk.

812 Finance Under-Secretary of the Association of Metropolitan Authorities.

813 There is a detailed account and analysis in Socialist Organiser's pamphlet *Illusions of Power*.

814 Militant's account is in their book 'Liverpool: A City That Dared To Fight'; a more critical assessment in Socialist Organiser's *Liverpool: What Went Wrong?*.

815 Thomas and O'Sullivan, *Illusions of Power*, p. 8.

816 18 February 1922.

817 Goss, 1988, p. 27.

818 *Building From The Bottom*, written jointly with Geoff Green.

819 At the Labour Research Department conference, 23 September 1922.

820 Crooks' death during the Rates Rebellion in 1921 was a painful loss for Lansbury.

821 Inwood, 1998, p. 633.

822 Postgate, 1951, p. 33.

823 Gillespie, 1984, p. 406.

824 Written under the name John Bryan, *The Call*, November 1919.

825 *The Socialist*, 6 May 1920.

826 Sylvia Pankhurst in *Workers' Dreadnought*, 6 October 1923.

827 Lenin, 1920:93, Chapter 9.

828 Lenin, 1920:93, p. 104.

829 Lenin, 1920:93, p. 120, emphasis original.

830 Lenin, 1920:93, p. 109.

831 *The Communist*, 28 October 1922.

832 *The Communist*, 28 October 1922.

833 Donoghue & Jones, 1973, p. 79.

834 Jones, 1973.

835 Quoted in O'Mahony, 1996, p. 14-5.

836 Lavalette, 2006, p. 6.

837 *The Communist*, 28 October 1922.

838 Marx and Engels, 1848.

839 Walker, 2002.

840 foreword to Key, 1925.

841 *Daily Herald*, 31 August 1921.

842 Gillespie, 1989, p. 175.

843 *Workers' Dreadnought*, 10 September 1921.

844 *War Against Poverty*, 1911.

845 1984.

846 Once antibiotics were developed in the 1950s, doctors could tackle TB much more effectively, and most people thought it had become a plague of the past. But disgracefully, in the 21 century this preventable, curable disease is making a comeback, with 400 people dying of TB each year in the UK and an 80 per cent increase in cases in London in the last decade - TB Alert website.

847 Shelter's 'Million Children campaign', June 2006.

848 Band D. Source: Department of Communities and Local Government.

849 1974, p. 124.

850 White, 2004.

851 Prescott vs. Birmingham Corporation [1955] Ch.210. Special legislation later overturned this ruling.

852 *Glasgow Herald*, 3 November 1922 p. 8, 'A Labour Rout'.

853 Castle Classic review.

854 Who had chaired the Commission which considered nationalising the coal industry.

855 Grandfather of Sir Richard!

856 Rates Dispute: Judgments – In the High Court of Justice, King's Bench Division, Divisional Court, 7 July 1921.

857 London County council minutes, 26 July 1921.

858 An English judge ranking immediately below the Lord Chief Justice, who presides over the Court of Appeal in the House of Lords.

859 Ellis & Ellis to Receiver of the Metropolitan Police, 4 August 1921, contained in MEPO 5/97, ref. 77.857/39.

860 The date of the bank holiday was changed to the last Monday in August on a trial basis in 1965 then confirmed by legislation in 1971, in order to shorten the gap

between the August holiday and Christmas.

861 1928, p. 156.
862 This and subsequent quoted descriptions of the court hearing are from the *East London Observer*, 15 October 1921.
863 *The Times*, law report, 22 November 1923.
864 Roberts vs Hopwood ([1925] A.C. 578).
865 Fennell, 1986.
866 LSE/LANSBURY/28/177
867 PBMA minutes, 2 June 1927.

Index

Page numbers in italics refer to illustrations